W9-BDM-343

Selected Letters of Horace Walpole

Horace Walpole, aged twenty-three, by Rosalba Carriera, Venice, 1741

SELECTED LETTERS OF

HORACE WALPOLE

Edited by W. S. Lewis,

Editor of the Yale Edition of
Horace Walpole's Correspondence

New Haven and London, Yale University Press, 1973

Copyright © 1973 by Yale University.
All rights reserved. This book may not be reproduced, in whole or in part, in any form (except by reviewers for the public press), without written permission from the publishers.
Library of Congress catalog card number: 72-91300
ISBN: 0-300-01643-3 (cloth), 0-300-01669-7 (paper)

Designed by John O. C. McCrillis
and set in Baskerville type.
Printed in the United States of America by
The Colonial Press Inc., Clinton, Massachusetts.

Published in Great Britain, Europe, and Africa by
Yale University Press, Ltd., London.
Distributed in Canada by McGill-Queen's University Press, Montreal; in Latin America by Kaiman & Polon, Inc., New York City; in Australasia and Southeast Asia by John Wiley & Sons Australasia Pty. Ltd., Sydney; in India by UBS Publishers' Distributors Pvt., Ltd., Delhi; in Japan by John Weatherhill, Inc., Tokyo.

To my colleagues, past and present, on the
Yale Edition of Horace Walpole's Correspondence

Illustrations

Preface

This book was proposed by Professor George B. Cooper of Trinity College, Hartford, and seconded by Professor Joseph W. Reed, Jr., of Wesleyan University, for use in their classrooms. It was suggested because there is no other paperback selection of Walpole's letters.

In selecting the letters I have had in mind readers who are encountering them for the first time rather than eighteenth-century scholars who go to them as a major historical source. Accordingly, the annotation has been kept to a minimum; readers who want further elucidation are referred to the Yale Edition of Horace Walpole's Correspondence and its hundreds of thousands of notes. The text is that of the Yale Walpole, in which Walpole's spelling and punctuation have been preserved. For the letters that have not yet appeared in it the Paget Toynbee edition has been used; the few passages that have been omitted are indicated by suspension points.

There have been several biographies of Walpole, including those by Austin Dobson and R. W. Ketton-Cremer. I have drawn on my *Horace Walpole*, the A. W. Mellon Lectures in the Fine Arts, 1960, Pantheon Books, 1961, in the following Introduction.

W.S.L.

Farmington, Connecticut
January 1973

Introduction

"The history of England throughout a very large segment of the eighteenth century," Leslie Stephen wrote, "is simply a synonym for the works of Horace Walpole." The "segment" begins in 1736 when at the age of eighteen Walpole wrote the first letter that appears here, and it ends with his death in 1797.

He was the youngest son of the great Prime Minister Sir Robert Walpole and so was born with every advantage of wealth and family influence. His father, according to the practice of the time, secured for him two lucrative government "places," which gave him a large income all his life and enabled him to indulge his taste for building and collecting. A few years before he died he succeeded his nephew as Earl of Orford, but did not take his seat in the House of Lords. He never married.

Following Eton and King's College, Cambridge, which he left for months at a time to be with his mother in her last long illness, he took his friend Thomas Gray, the poet, on the Grand Tour to Italy. After nearly two years of travel they parted company, as travelers often do, but were reconciled later, as travelers often are not. While he was still abroad, his father had him elected to Parliament where he sat for twenty-seven years. He was what today would be called a liberal, being one of the first to oppose the African slave trade and to deplore the infringement of liberty in America. His main political concern was advancing the career of his first cousin and closest friend, Henry Seymour Conway, who became a field marshal, a secretary of state, and leader of the House of Commons. Conway, Massachusetts, and Conway, New Hampshire, were named after him in gratitude for his part in repealing the Stamp Act. Walpole's *Memoirs*, which he wrote secretly from 1751 to 1791, are a primary source for the political history of the period. The public has yet to read them as they were written, because they were tinkered with by their first editors. When the projected unmutilated edition of them appears, readers will see at last what Walpole wrote.

He was a well-known author in his own day for his *Catalogue of the Royal and Noble Authors of England* (1758), *Anecdotes of Painting in England* (1762–71) in which appeared his "Essay on Modern Gardening," *The Castle of Otranto* (1765), and *Historic Doubts of the Life and Reign of Richard III* (1768). Each of these was a pioneer work and each is still remembered; *The Castle of Otranto* was the first of the Gothic novels, the *Historic Doubts*, which sought to exculpate Richard III of many of his crimes, is still discussed with emotion. He also wrote verse, essays, political tracts, a comedy, a tragedy, and two *catalogues raisonnés*—one of his house and its contents, and an earlier one of his father's great collection of pictures, the first catalogue of its kind in England.

His house, Strawberry Hill, was another pioneer achievement. It was at Twickenham, a village ten miles from London that was a forerunner of the modern fashionable suburb. Walpole bought a cottage there that he remodeled in the Gothic manner of his own devising. "Strawberry Hill Gothic" flowered into Victorian Gothic and spread throughout Britain and round the world to Italy, Germany, Sweden, and Russia, and from Maine to California. The house was a showplace in Walpole's day for its towers, crenellated roof, and collections of pictures, furniture, and "curiosities." In the preface to his *Description of Strawberry Hill* (1784), Walpole says that "it was built to please my own tastes, and in some degree, to realize my own visions." Although built of lath and plaster—it was said years before he died that "Mr. Walpole has already outlived three sets of his battlements"—its survival was one of his visions. He left it to the family of a favorite niece, but in 1842 the then owner sold its contents in one of the most famous of all English auctions. The house itself has survived against all probability, even a German fire bomb in 1941 did not destroy it, and it is no longer spoken of with amused condescension because its importance as the progenitor of the revived Gothic taste is now acknowledged. It was easy to laugh at it—late in his life Walpole himself confessed that he and his two friends, Chute and

Bentley, who helped him choose and adapt the Gothic details, had not "studied the science"—but it now has the antiquarian and architectural bloom that buildings acquire if they last long enough, for they are documents of their times. Visitors today make pilgrimages to Strawberry as a landmark of English taste and out of regard for its creator. They are welcomed by its hospitable owners, the principal and staff of St. Mary's College, who have preserved the house affectionately. Walpole's Chapel-Tribune, which he built because a medieval castle must have a chapel, is now consecrated. He would, I think, be pleased with the way things have turned out.

Strawberry Hill is also remembered for its printing press, the first in an English private house. Walpole set it up so that he could print what he pleased without having to deal with the booksellers, who were the publishers of the day; the Press was therefore another expression of his independence. He opened it in 1757 with two odes by Gray, "The Bard" and "The Progress of Poesy," and kept it going until 1789 when it expired with Hannah More's "Bishop Bonner's Ghost." The Press printed several books of lasting value—besides Gray's odes, there was a fine edition of Lucan's *Pharsalia*, Lord Herbert of Cherbury's autobiography, and Walpole's own *Royal and Noble Authors* and *Anecdotes of Painting*. There were thirty-four books in all and many ephemeral "detached pieces" of complimentary and occasional verses by Walpole and his friends. A few of the books were sold in London for the benefit of their authors, one for the poor of Twickenham, but Walpole gave most of them away. They were collected in his day and are collected in ours.

Walpole would have been remembered for his *Castle of Otranto*, *Historic Doubts*, *Anecdotes of Painting*, *Memoirs*, house, and Press, even if none of his letters, which rank with the best in our language, had survived. They began appearing in 1798, the year following his death, a selection of some 350 that he chose for the fifth volume of his *Works*, and additional letters have continued to appear ever since. How many more are lurking in their hiding places is of course unknown, but there will be over 4,000 from him in the completed Yale Edition of his correspondence. The first letter in the present selection was written in his nineteenth year, the last in his eightieth; they show that he mastered the now lost art of letter writing as a youth and practiced it smoothly and naturally as long as he lived. The chief subjects are politics, literature, "antiquities," and the life of the great world, but his letters must be consulted by all specialists on the eighteenth century no matter what their subjects are. I said this once in a talk and then paused to think of a fantastic exception, "Except writers on bee-keeping," I added, an unlucky instance, for the next "new" letter that turned up told how the Spanish farmers got their honey without destroying the bees as the British farmer wastefully and unfeelingly did. Whether or not a specialist finds something to his purpose in Walpole's letters, he will become more and more at home in the eighteenth century. The great events pass in review from the end of Sir Robert Walpole's long premiership to the rise of Bonaparte: surgical techniques improve; Sir William Herschel discovers a new planet; Dr. Benjamin Franklin experiments with electricity; balloonists float across the English Channel; John Howard begins prison reform; and the readers of Walpole's letters learn how the modern age dawned and how the rulers of it lived and what they thought.

Walpole's major correspondents, besides Conway and Conway's brother Lord Hertford, were Sir Horace Mann, the British Resident and Minister in Florence from 1739 to 1786; Walpole's Eton friends, Gray, George Montagu (an idle man who could write an amusing letter himself when he wanted to), and William Cole, the antiquary; the Countess of Upper Ossory; the Earl of Strafford; William Mason, the poet and biographer of Gray; Mme du Deffand in Paris; and at the end of his life Mary Berry, who became his literary executrix. In the back of his mind he was also writing to us, posterity. No one was ever more aware of unborn readers. "All we can do," he wrote Mason, "is to appeal to that undutiful urchin posterity." "Great posterity," he called us, "pert posterity." We would be his judges. He feared us, courted us, and tried to imagine the fabulous world we would live in and the discoveries and inventions we would make, especially in America: "I love to skip into futurity and imagine what will be done on the giant scale of a new hemisphere." "The next Augustan Age," he wrote in 1774, "will dawn on the other side of the Atlantic. There will perhaps be a Thucydides at Boston, a Xenophon at New York, and in time a Virgil at Mexico, and a Newton at Peru." He would have been pleased but not surprised to hear that Americans two hundred years later were reading his letters to learn about his time.

"Nothing," he wrote in middle life, "gives so just an idea of an age as genuine letters: nay, history waits for its last seal from them." "You desire I would burn your letters," he wrote Montagu four days before the earliest letter in this collection, "I desire you would keep mine," and Montagu, like most of Walpole's correspondents, did keep them. Walpole got back some thousand of them, which he annotated for his future editors. The first lot from Mann was returned in 1749. Walpole started transcribing the early letters himself, cutting out a few passages, notably his quarrel with Gray, but after a while he had his printer-secretary, Thomas Kirgate, do most of the copying while he merely numbered the letters and added an occasional note. His correspondence with Mann, upwards of eighteen hundred letters, extends from 1741 to Mann's death in 1786. Walpole had his side of it richly bound in eight volumes. On the title-page to the first volume he wrote an epigraph taken from a letter of Pliny the Younger to Tacitus that wondered whether posterity would have any concern about them, but Walpole didn't doubt posterity's interest in his letters to Mann. "Knowing how much pleasure not only himself, but many other persons have often found in a series of private and familiar letters," he wrote, he "thought it worth his while to preserve these, as they contain something of the customs, fashions, politics, diversions, and private history of several years; which if worthy of any existence, can be properly transmitted to posterity only in this manner." His letters would take us back to his time, as Mme de Sévigné's took him back to hers; and that is the way it has turned out. What surprised Henry Adams most in

Walpole was "that he is so extremely like ourselves. . . . I perpetually catch myself thinking of it all as of something I have myself known, until I trip over a sword, or discover there were no railways then." A hundred years after Adams wrote that, we have the same feeling of intimacy. It may come to us at any time, particularly when Walpole shows himself in a ludicrous situation, as in the letter to Lord Strafford when he tells how in helping a lady over a stile they both fell off and crashed to the ground in each other's arms just as a coach and six came thundering by and their friends in it wondered what was going on.

His correspondents were unwitting coadjutors in his grand design to transmit a full and dependable history of the time to us. Two of them, Gray and Mme du Deffand, were also first-class letter-writers in their own right, but Walpole wasn't critical of the less brilliant so long as they replied with news and did not make him self-conscious by praising his letters. Each correspondence has a predominant subject—antiquities for Cole, politics and foreign affairs for Mann, social gossip for Montagu and Lady Ossory—but he also sent his friends whatever news and reflections he thought would interest and entertain them. He wrote rapidly, "I have no patience," he said, "with people that don't write just as they would talk." Friends said that he talked as he wrote, a remark shown to be true when the gout forced him to dictate and he continued his letters with no change of tone or style. Letters, he said, ought to be "nothing but extempore conversations upon paper," yet notes on the backs of letters to him and scraps of paper show that these extempore conversations were planned with care, for his future life on earth depended upon them. Even when recording what he called "the follies of the day" he was very much in earnest.

He was quick to apologize when he thought he had been in the wrong and to smooth over occasional misunderstandings and ruffled feelings; for the most part, good nature prevails in his letters except when writing to Mason, who brought out the least amiable side of him. His bursts of self-revelation could have been tiresome if he had made them too often, but he was never a bore.

We who read his letters now can hardly imagine what it must have been like for their recipients to break the seals on them and read the latest news served up with his freshness, wit, and sentiment just for them, but we can survey, as his correspondents could not, the history of sixty-odd years. Saintsbury said that Walpole's letters are like a very long novel, vast, various, unfailing in interest, and with a "not too obviously intelligible life-panorama." Virginia Woolf concluded that "somehow he was not only the wittiest of men, but the most observant and not the least kindly. And among the writers of English prose he wears forever and with a peculiar grace a coronet of his own earning." She, like everyone else who has read and reread Walpole, speculated upon the "not too obviously intelligible life-panorama."

It is easy to see why he appears enigmatic and contradictory. A brilliant and sensitive man, he went his own way all his life, but needed the affection and good opinion of a cherished few. By the standards of his age he was quixotically honest in the conduct of his places at the Exchequer and Customs, although he loved what money can buy and went on sprees of collecting pictures, prints, coins, china, and "curiosities": "I would buy the Coliseum if I could," he said. Instead of having the sort of house that everybody else had he built a sham castle. The youthful dandy hated oppression and injustice; he called himself an infidel and supported the Established Church against atheists, Roman Catholics, and Methodists. As a young man his friends were amused by his taking equal pleasure in the card tables at White's Club and the tea tables of dowagers. When he was a child he heard his elders say "that child cannot possibly live," yet he reached his eightieth year. After he was charged with Chatterton's suicide, for which, as he wrote Lady Ossory, he was no more responsible than Julius Caesar, he stood up to the ordeal with coolness and dignity, although hypersensitive to ridicule and abuse. He lived by himself and became, one of his friends said, as much a curiosity to all foreigners as the tombs in Westminster Abbey and the lions in the Tower.

He was a controversial figure after his death. Wordsworth, Coleridge, Keats, and Hazlitt attacked him mistakenly for Chatterton's tragedy; Walter Scott and Byron praised him to the skies as a writer. His surviving friends received a jolt when the first of his *Memoirs* appeared in 1818. They recollected "good-natured Mr. Walpole," who was tireless in his attentions to his friends, who would sit up all night with a sick dog and open a window to let out a moth rather than kill it; yet his *Memoirs* are filled with portraits of his contemporaries that were written with the intention of destroying their characters. The *Memoirs* moved John Wilson Croker, who admired Walpole's letters, to conclude that Walpole had poisoned history at its source and that he was "as bad a man as ever lived," a very severe judgment indeed. Among Walpole's other detractors was Macaulay who followed Hazlitt's line that Walpole was "a heartless fribble." As a young man Macaulay wrote a review of the first installment of the letters to Mann with what Saintsbury called his "cocksure dexterity." Macaulay conceded that Walpole's letters are "incomparable" and that "no man who has written so much is so seldom tiresome," but decreed that Walpole was "a bundle of inconsistent whims and affectation," and that "his features were covered by mask upon mask," a caricature that still distorts Walpole's character.

Speaking up for him was the person best qualified to do so, Mary Berry, who with her father and sister had lived in a cottage at Strawberry Hill and who became, as I have said, Walpole's literary executrix. She stated in reply to Macaulay that his "hasty and general opinion" was "entirely and offensively unlike the original" and that "the warmth of Walpole's feelings and his capacity for sincere affection continued unenfeebled by age." As to Macaulay's much-quoted remark that Walpole "sneered at everybody," she pointed out that "sneering was not his way of showing dislike. He had very strong prejudices, sometimes adopted on very insufficient grounds, and he therefore made great mistakes in the appreciation of character; but when influenced by such impressions, he always expressed his opinions directly, and often too violently. The affections of his heart were bestowed on few," she also conceded, "but they were singularly warm, pure, and constant;

characterized not by the ardor of passion, but by the constant preoccupation of real affection." Macaulay's caricature is remembered, Miss Berry's portrait is forgotten, yet Walpole has not lacked still later friends. Thackeray was sentimental about him, Carlyle called him "a small steady light," "an irrefragable authority," and, as we have seen, Saintsbury, Leslie Stephen, and Virginia Woolf admired him.

As for the outward man, he was about average eighteenth-century height, perhaps five-feet-seven, excessively thin, his face and hands unnaturally pale, his eyes exceptionally bright. As a young man his gait was rapid and darting; in later life, halting and enfeebled by the gout. He dressed with elegance but not foppishly. His voice, said one lady, was "extremely pleasant and highly gentlemanly." A military neighbor spoke of his "cheerfulness, the sallies of his imagination, the liveliness of his manner, the unexpected impression on the ear of those who hear and listen to him. . . . I never met him but with pleasure," the general summed up, "and never left him but with regret."

When I am asked, "How do you feel about Horace Walpole after fifty years?" I answer that I think more highly of him all the time. Tens of thousands of notes in the Yale Edition of his correspondence prove the accuracy of his reporting: he did transmit to us the record of his time, and the more one studies the range of his contribution to posterity the more impressive it becomes. In answer to the question, "who were the three eighteenth-century English-speaking men who were most like the versatile men of the Renaissance?" I would nominate him for third place after Benjamin Franklin and Thomas Jefferson. Finally, I have come to like him more and more as a person.

This book introduces him to a new generation of the posterity he labored all his life to instruct and entertain. As one who has spent half a century trying to carry out his grand design, I naturally hope that his latest readers will value the legacy he left them.

To George Montagu, 6 May 1736

King's College, May 6, 1736.

Dear George,

I agree with you entirely in the pleasure you take in talking over old stories, but can't say but I meet every day with new circumstances, which will be still more pleasure to me to recollect. I think at our age 'tis excess of joy, to think, while we are running over past happinesses, that 'tis still in our power to enjoy as great. Narrations of the greatest actions of other people, are tedious in comparison of the serious trifles, that every man can call to mind of himself, while he was learning those histories: youthful passages of life, are the chippings of Pit's diamond,[1] set into little heart-rings with mottoes the stone itself more worth, the filings more genteel, and agreeable. Alexander at the head of the world never tasted the true pleasure, that boys of his own age have enjoyed at the head of a school. Little intrigues, little schemes, and policies, engage their thoughts, and at the same time that they are laying the foundation for their middle age of life, the mimic republic they live in furnishes materials of conversation for their latter age; and old men cannot be said to be children a second time with greater truth from any one cause, than their living over again their childhood in imagination. To reflect on the season when first they felt the titillation of love, the budding passions, and the first dear object of their wishes! how unexperienced they gave credit to all the tales of romantic loves! Dear George, were not the playing fields at Eton food for all manner of flights? No old maid's gown, though it had been tormented into all the fashions from King James to King George, ever underwent so many transformations, as those poor plains have in my idea. At first I was contented with tending a visionary flock, and sighing some pastoral name to the

1. The Pitt Diamond was bought for about £20,000 in India by Thomas Pitt (1653–1726), Governor of Madras and grandfather of the first Earl of Chatham. In 1717 it was purchased from him by the Regent Duc d'Orléans, on behalf of Louis XV, for &125,000. The fragments from it when cut were valued at several thousand pounds (Sir Cornelius Neale Dalton, *Life of Thomas Pitt* [Cambridge, 1915]).

echo of the cascade under the bridge: how happy should I have been to have had a kingdom, only for the pleasure of being driven from it, and living disguised in an humble vale. As I got farther into Virgil and *Clelia,*[1] I found myself transported from Arcadia, to the garden of Italy, and saw Windsor Castle in no other view than the *capitoli immobile saxum.* I wish a committee of the House of Commons may ever seem to be the senate; or a bill appear half so agreeable as a billet-doux. You see how deep you have carried me into old stories; I write of them with pleasure, but shall talk of them with more to you: I can't say I am sorry I was never quite a schoolboy; an expedition against bargemen, or a match at cricket may be very pretty things to recollect; but thank my stars, I can remember things that are very near as pretty. The beginning of my Roman history was spent in the Asylum, or conversing in Egeria's hallowed grove; not in thumping and pummelling King Amulius's herdsmen. I was sometimes troubled with a rough creature or two from the plow; one that one should have thought had worked with his head, as well as his hands, they were both so callous. One of the most agreeable circumstances I can recollect is the Triumvirate, composed of yourself, Charles,[2] and

Your sincere friend,

HOR. WALPOLE

TO RICHARD WEST, 21 April 1739, N.S.

Paris, April 21, N.S., 1739.

Dear West,

You figure us in a set of pleasures, which, believe me, we do not find: cards and eating are so universal, that they absorb all variation of pleasures. The operas indeed are much frequented three times a week; but to me they would be a greater penance than eating *maigre:* their music resembles a gooseberry tart as much as

1. *Clélie*, the romantic novel by Madeleine de Scudéry.
2. Charles Lyttelton (1714–68), Bishop of Carlisle.

it does harmony. We have not yet been at the Italian playhouse; scarce any one goes there. Their best amusement, and which in some parts beats ours, is the comedy; three or four of the actors excel any we have: but then to this nobody goes, if it is not one of the fashionable nights, and then they go, be the play good or bad —except on Molière's nights, whose pieces they are quite weary of. Gray and I have been at the *Avare* tonight: I cannot at all commend their performance of it. Last night I was in the Place de Louis le Grand (a regular octagon, uniform, and the houses handsome, though not so large as Golden Square), to see what they reckoned one of the finest burials that ever was in France. It was the Duke de Tresmes, Governor of Paris, and Marshal of France. It began on foot from his palace to his parish-church, and from thence in coaches to the opposite end of Paris, to be interred in the church of the Célestins, where is his family vault. About a week ago we happened to see the grave digging, as we went to see the church, which is old and small, but fuller of fine ancient monuments than any except St Denis, which we saw on the road, and excels Westminster; for the windows are all painted in mosaic, and the tombs as fresh and well-preserved as if they were of yesterday. In the Célestins' church is a votive column to Francis II which says, that it is one assurance of his being immortalized, to have had the martyr Mary Stuart for his wife. After this long digression I return to the burial, which was a most vile thing. A long procession of flambeaux and friars; no plumes, trophies, banners, led horses, scutcheons, or open chariots; nothing but

—friars,
White, black, and grey, with all their trumpery.

This goodly ceremony began at nine at night, and did not finish till three this morning; for, each church they passed, they stopped for a hymn and holy water. By the by, some of these choice monks, who watched the body while it lay in state, fell asleep one night, and let the tapers catch fire of the rich velvet mantle lined with ermine and powdered with gold flower-de-luces, which melted the lead coffin, and burned off the feet of the deceased before it wakened them. The French love show; but there is a meanness reigns through it all. At the house where I stood to see this procession, the room was hung with crimson damask and gold, and the windows were mended in ten or dozen places with paper. At dinner they give you three courses; but a third of the dishes is patched up with salads, butter, puff-paste, or some such miscarriage of a dish. None, but Germans, wear fine clothes; but their coaches are tawdry enough for the wedding of Cupid and Psyche. You would laugh extremely at their signs: some live at the *Y grec*, some at Venus's Toilette, and some at the Sucking Cat. You would not easily guess their notions of honour: I'll tell you one: it is very dishonourable for any gentleman not to be in the army, or in the King's service as they call it, and it is no dishonour to keep public gaming houses: there are at least an hundred and fifty people of the first quality in Paris who live by it. You may go into their houses at all hours of the night, and find hazard, pharaoh, etc. The men who keep the hazard-table at the Duke de Gesvres' pay him twelve guineas each night for the privilege. Even the princesses of the blood are dirty enough to have shares in the banks kept at their houses. We have seen two or three of them; but they are not young, nor remarkable but for wearing their red of a deeper dye than other women, though all use it extravagantly.

The weather is still so bad, that we have not made any excursions to see Versailles and the environs, not even walked in the Thuilleries; but we have seen almost everything else that is worth seeing in Paris, though that is very considerable. They beat us vastly in buildings, both in number and magnificence. The tombs of Richelieu and Mazarine at the Sorbonne and the Collège de Quatre Nations are wonderfully fine, especially the former. We have seen very little of the people themselves, who are not inclined to be propitious to strangers, especially if they do not play, and speak the language readily. There are many English here: Lord Holderness, Conway and Clinton, and Lord George Bentinck; Mr Brand, Offley, Frederic, Frampton, Bonfoy, etc. Sir John Cotton's son and a Mr Vernon of Cambridge passed through Paris last week. We shall stay here about a fortnight longer, and then go to Rheims with Mr Conway for two or three months. When you have nothing else to do, we shall be glad to hear from you; and any news. If we did not remember there was such a place as England, we should know nothing of it: the French never mention it, unless it happens to be in one of their proverbs. Adieu!

Yours ever,

H. W.

Tomorrow we go to the *Cid.* They have no farces, but *petites pièces* like our *Devil to Pay.*

To Richard West, 28 September 1739, N.S.

From a hamlet among the mountains of Savoy,
Sept. 28, 1739, N.S.

Precipices, mountains, torrents, wolves, rumblings, Salvator Rosa —the pomp of our park and the meekness of our palace! Here we are, the lonely lords of glorious desolate prospects. I have kept a sort of resolution which I made, of not writing to you as long as I stayed in France: I am now a quarter of an hour out of it, and write to you. Mind, 'tis three months since we heard from you. I begin this letter among the clouds; where I shall finish, my neighbour heaven probably knows: 'tis an odd wish in a mortal letter, to hope not to finish it on this side the atmosphere. You will have a billet tumble to you from the stars when you least think of it; and that I should write it too! Lord, how potent that sounds! But I am to undergo many transmigrations before I come to 'yours ever.' Yesterday I was a shepherd of Dauphiné; today an Alpine savage; tomorrow a Carthusian monk; and Friday a Swiss Calvinist. I have one quality which I find remains with me in all worlds and in all ethers; I brought it with me from your world, and am admired for it in this; 'tis my esteem for you: this is a common thought among you, and you will laugh at it, but it is new here; as new to remember one's friends in the world one has left, as for you to remember those you have lost.

Aix in Savoy, Sept. 30th.

We are this minute come in here, and here's an awkward abbé this minute come in to us. I asked him if he would sit down. *Oui, oui, oui.* He has ordered us a radish soup for supper, and has brought a chessboard to play with Mr Conway. I have left 'em in the act, and am set down to write to you. Did you ever see anything like the prospect we saw yesterday? I never did. We rode three leagues to see the Grande Chartreuse; expected bad roads, and the finest convent in the kingdom. We were disappointed pro and con. The building is large and plain, and has nothing remarkable but its primitive simplicity: They entertained us in the neatest manner, with eggs, pickled salmon, dried fish, conserves, cheese, butter, grapes and figs, and pressed us mightily to lie there. We tumbled into the hands of a lay-brother, who, unluckily having the charge of the meal and bran, showed us little besides. They desired us to set down our names in the list of strangers, where, among others, we found two mottoes of our countrymen for whose stupidity and brutality we blushed. . . . But the road, West, the road! winding round a prodigious mountain, and surrounded with others, all shagged with hanging woods, obscured with pines or lost in clouds! Below, a torrent breaking through cliffs, and tumbling through fragments of rocks! Sheets of cascades forcing their silver speed down channelled precipices, and hasting into the roughened river at the bottom! Now and then an old foot-bridge, with a broken rail, a leaning cross, a cottage, or the ruin of an hermitage! This sounds too bombast and too romantic to one that has not seen it, too cold for one that has. If I could send you my letter post between two lovely tempests that echoed each other's wrath, you might have some idea of this noble roaring scene, as you were reading it. Almost on the summit, upon a fine verdure, but without any prospect, stands the Chartreuse. We stayed there two hours, rode back through this charming picture, wished for a painter, wished to be poets! Need I tell you we wished for you?

Good night!

Geneva, Oct. 2.

BY beginning a new date, I should begin a new letter; but I have seen nothing yet, and the post is going out: 'tis a strange tumbled dab, and dirty too, I am sending you; but what can I do? There is no possibility of writing such a long history over again. I find there are many English in the town; Lord Brook, Lord Mansel, Lord Hervey's eldest son, and a son[1] of—of Mars and Venus, or of Antony and Cleopatra, or in short, of—. This is the boy in the bow of whose hat Mr Hedges pinned a pretty epigram: I don't know if you ever heard it: I'll suppose you never did, because it will fill up my letter:

> Give but Cupid's dart to me,
> Another Cupid I shall be;
> No more distinguished from the other,
> Than Venus would be from my mother.

Scandal says, Hedges thought the two last very like; and it says too, that she was not his enemy for thinking so.

Adieu! Gray and I return to Lyons in three days. Harry[2] stays here. Perhaps at our return we may find a letter from you: It ought to be very full of excuses, for you have been a lazy creature; I hope you have, for I would not owe your silence to any other reason.

Yours ever,

HOR. WALPOLE

1. Charles Churchill (ca. 1720–1812), of Chalfont Park, Bucks, later (1746) the husband of HW's half-sister, Lady Maria Walpole. He was the natural son of Lt. Gen. Charles Churchill (d. 1745) and Anne Oldfield (1683–1730), the actress. Mrs. Oldfield appeared as Cleopatra both in Dryden's *All for Love* (Drury Lane, 3 Dec. 1718) and in Cibber's *Cæsar in Egypt* (Drury Lane, 9–15 Dec. 1724).

2. Henry Seymour Conway.

To Richard West, 27 February 1740, N.S.

Florence, February 27, 1740, N.S.

Well, West, I have found a little unmasked moment to write to you; but for this week I have been so muffled up in my domino, that I have not had the command of my elbows. But what have you been doing all the mornings? Could you not write then? No, then I was masked too; I have done nothing but slip out of my domino into bed, and out of bed into my domino. The end of the Carnival is frantic, Bacchanalian; all the morn one makes parties in mask to the shops and coffee-houses, and all the evening to the operas and balls. *Then I have danced, good gods, how I have danced.* The Italians are fond to a degree of our country dances: *Cold and raw* they only know by the tune; *Blowzy-Bella* is almost Italian, and *Buttered Peas* is *Pizelli al buro.* There are but three days more; but the two last are to have balls all the morning at the fine unfinished palace of the Strozzi; and the Tuesday night a masquerade after supper: they sup first, to eat *gras*, and not encroach upon Ash Wednesday. What makes masquerading more agreeable here than in England, is the great deference that is showed to the disguised. Here they do not catch at those little dirty opportunities of saying any ill-natured thing they know of you, do not abuse you because they may, or talk gross bawdy to a woman of quality. I found the other day by a play of Etheridge's, that we have had a sort of Carnival ever since the Reformation; 'tis in *She Would if She Could*, they talk of going a-mumming in Shrove-tide.—After talking so much of diversions, I fear you will attribute to them the fondness I own I contract for Florence; but it has so many other charms, that I shall not want excuses for my taste. The freedom of the Carnival has given me opportunities to make several acquaintances; and if I have not found them refined, learned, polished, like some other cities, yet they are civil, good-natured, and fond of the English. Their little partiality for themselves, opposed to the violent vanity of the French, makes them very amiable in my eyes. I can give you a comical instance of their great prejudice about nobility; it happened yesterday. While we were at dinner at

Mr Mann's, word was brought by his secretary, that a cavalier demanded audience of him upon an affair of honour. Gray and I flew behind the curtain of the door. An elderly gentleman, whose attire was not certainly correspondent to the greatness of his birth, entered, and informed the British minister that one Martin an English painter had left a challenge for him at his house, for having said Martin was no gentleman. He would by no means have spoke of the duel before the transaction of it, but that his honour, his blood, his etc. would never permit him to fight with one who was no cavalier; which was what he came to inquire of His Excellency. We laughed loud laughs, but unheard: his fright or his nobility had closed his ears. But mark the sequel; the instant he was gone, my very English curiosity hurried me out of the gate St Gallo; 'twas the place and hour appointed. We had not been driving about above ten minutes, but out popped a little figure, pale but cross, with beard unshaved and hair uncombed, a slouched hat, and a considerable red cloak, in which was wrapped, under his arm, the fatal sword that was to revenge the highly injured Mr Martin, painter and defendant. I darted my head out of the coach, just ready to say 'Your servant, Mr Martin,' and talk about the architecture of the triumphal arch that was building there; but he would not know me, and walked off. We left him to wait for an hour, to grow very cold and very valiant the more it grew past the hour of appointment. We were figuring all the poor creature's huddle of thoughts, and confused hopes of victory, or fame, of his unfinished pictures, or his situation upon bouncing into the next world. You will think us strange creatures; but 'twas a pleasant sight, as we knew the poor painter was safe. I have thought of it since, and am inclined to believe that nothing but two English could have been capable of such a jaunt. I remember, 'twas reported in London that the plague was at a house in the city, and all the town went to see it.

I have this instant received your letter. Lord! I am glad I thought of those parallel passages, since it made you translate them. 'Tis excessively near the original; and yet, I don't know, 'tis very easy too.—It snows here a little tonight, but it never lies but on the mountains. Adieu!

Yours ever,

HOR. WALPOLE

PS. What is the history of the theatres this winter?

TO SIR HORACE MANN, 11 September 1741, O.S.

Calais, and Friday and here I
have been these two days. 1741.

Is the wind laid? Shall I never get aboard? I came here on Wednesday night, but found a tempest that has never ceased since. At Boulogne I left Lord Shrewsbury and his mother and brothers and sisters waiting too; Bulstrode passes his winter at the court of Boulogne, and then is to travel with two young Shrewsburys. I was overtaken by Amorevoli and Monticelli, who are here with me and the Viscontina and Barberina and Abate Vanneschi—what a coxcomb! I would have talked to him about the opera, but he preferred politics. I have wearied Amorevoli with questions about you: if he was not just come from you and could talk to me about you, I should hate him, for to flatter me, he told me that I talked Italian better than you: he did not know how little I think it a compliment to have anything preferred to you—besides you know the consistence of my Italian! They are all frightened out of their senses about going on the sea; and are not a little afraid of the English; they went aboard the *William and Mary* yacht yesterday which waits here for Lady Cardigan from Spa: the captain clapped the door, and swore in broad English that the Viscontina should not stir till she gave him a song, he did not care whether it was a catch or a moving ballad—but she would not submit—I wonder he did! When she came home and told me, I begged her not to judge of all the English from this specimen—but by the way she will find many sea-captains that grow on dry land.

Sittinburn, Sept. 13, O.S.

Saturday morning or yesterday we did set out, and after a good passage of four hours and a half landed at Dover. I begin to count my comforts, for I find their contraries thicken on my apprehension. I have at least done for a while with post-chaises. My trunks were a little opened at Calais, and they would have stopped my medals, but with much ado and much three louis's they let them pass. At Dover I found the benefit of the *Motion's* having miscarried last year, for they respected Sir Robert's son even in the person of his trunks. I came over in a yacht with East-India captains' widows, a Catholic girl coming from a convent to be married, with an Irish priest to guard her, who says he studied *medicines* for two years, and after that *he studied learning* for two years more. I have not brought over a word of French or Italian for common use; I have so taken pains to avoid affectation in this point, that I have failed only now and then in a *chi è là?* to the servants, who I can scarce persuade myself yet are English. The country I own (and you will believe me who, you know, am not prejudiced) delights me: the populousness, the ease, the gaiety, and well-dressed everybody amaze me. Canterbury which, on my setting out, I thought deplorable, is a paradise to Modena, Reggio, Parma etc. I had before discovered that there was nowhere but in England the distinction of *middling people;* I perceive now that there is peculiar to us, *middling houses:* how smug they are! I write tonight because I have time; tomorrow I get to London just as the post goes. Sir R[obert] is at Houghton.

I have nothing to tell you yet, but of a woman who was prayed for lately at Canterbury, on the point of marriage: She was devout and timorous, wanted a blessing on her design, which she thought hazardous; so the minister prayed for a gentlewoman *who was going to take a great affair in hand.*

Good night till another post—you are quite well I trust, but tell me so always. My loves to the Chutes and all the etc.s.

Oh! a story of Mr Pope and the Prince—'Mr Pope, you don't love Princes.' 'Sir, I beg your pardon.' 'Well, you don't love Kings then!' 'Sir, I own, I love the lion best before his claws are grown.'

—Was it possible to make a better answer to such simple questions?

Adieu! my dearest child!

Yours ten thousand times over.

PS. Patapan[1] does not seem yet to regret his own country.

To John Chute, 20 August 1743

Houghton, August 20, 1743.

Indeed, my dear Sir, you certainly did not use to be stupid, and till you give me more substantial proof that you are so, I shall not believe it. As for your temperate diet and milk bringing about such a metamorphosis, I hold it impossible. I have such lamentable proofs every day before my eyes of the stupefying qualities of beef, ale, and wine, that I have contracted a most religious veneration for your spiritual nouriture. Only imagine that I here every day see men, who are mountains of roast beef, and only seem just roughly hewn out into the outlines of human form, like the giant-rock at Pratolino! I shudder when I see them brandish their knives in act to carve, and look on them as savages that devour one another. I should not stare at all more than I do, if yonder Alderman at the lower end of the table was to stick his fork into his neighbour's jolly cheek, and cut a brave slice of brown and fat. Why, I'll swear I see no difference between a country gentleman and a sirloin; whenever the first laughs, or the latter is cut, there run out just the same streams of gravy! Indeed, the sirloin does not ask quite so many questions. I have an Aunt here, a family piece of goods, an old remnant of inquisitive hospitality and economy, who, to all intents and purposes, is as beefy as her neighbours. She wore me so down yesterday with interrogatories, that I dreamt all night she was at my ear with 'who's' and 'why's,' and 'when's' and 'where's,' till at last in my very sleep I cried out, 'For God in heaven's sake, Madam, ask me no more questions!'

1. Mr Walpole's dog. (HW's note)

Oh! my dear Sir, don't you find that nine parts in ten of the world are of no use but to make you wish yourself with that tenth part? I am so far from growing used to mankind by living amongst them, that my natural ferocity and wildness does but every day grow worse. They tire me, they fatigue me; I don't know what to do with them; I don't know what to say to them; I fling open the windows, and fancy I want air; and when I get by myself, I undress myself, and seem to have had people in my pockets, in my plaits, and on my shoulders! I indeed find this fatigue worse in the country than in town, because one can avoid it there and has more resources; but it is there too. I fear 'tis growing old; but I literally seem to have murdered a man whose name was Ennui, for his ghost is ever before me. They say there is no English word for *ennui;* I think you may translate it most literally by what is called 'entertaining people,' and 'doing the honours': that is, you sit an hour with somebody you don't know and don't care for, talk about the wind and the weather, and ask a thousand foolish questions, which all begin with 'I think you live a good deal in the country,' or, 'I think you don't love this thing or that.' Oh! 'tis dreadful!

I'll tell you what is delightful—the Dominichin! My dear Sir, if ever there was a Dominichin, if there was ever an original picture, this is one. I am quite happy; for my father is as much transported with it as I am. It is hung in the gallery, where are all his most capital pictures, and he himself thinks it beats all but the two Guidos. That of the Doctors and the Octagon—I don't know if you ever saw them? What a chain of thought this leads me into! but why should I not indulge it? I will flatter myself with your, some time or other, passing a few days here with me. Why must I never expect to see anything but Beefs in a gallery which would not yield even to the Colonna! If I do not most unlimitedly wish to see you and Mr Whithed in it this very moment, it is only because I would not take you from our dear *Miny*. Adieu! you charming people all. Is not Madam Bosville a Beef?

Yours most sincerely.

To Sir Horace Mann, 22 July 1744, O.S.

Arlington Street, July 22d, 1744.

I have not written to you, my dear child, a good while I know; but indeed it was from having nothing to tell you. You know I love you too well, for it to be necessary to be punctually proving it to you: so, when I have nothing worth your knowing, I repose myself upon the persuasion that you must have of my friendship. But I will never let that grow into any negligence, I should say idleness, which is always mighty ready to argue me out of everything I ought to do; and letter-writing is one of the first duties that the very best people let perish out of their rubric. Indeed I pride myself extremely in having been so good a correspondent, for besides that every day grows to make one hate writing more, it is difficult you must own to keep up a correspondence of this sort with any spirit, when long absence makes one entirely out of all the little circumstances of each other's society, and which are the soul of letters. We are forced to deal only in great events, like historians; and instead of being Horace Mann and Horace Walpole, seem to correspond as Guicciardin and Clarendon would:

> Discedo Alcæus puncto illius; ille meo quis?
> Quis nisi Callimachus?—

A propos to writing histories and Guicciardin; I wish to God, Boccalini was living! Never was such an opportunity for Apollo's playing off a set of fools, as there is now! The good City of London, who, from long dictating to the government, are now come to preside over taste and letters, have given one Carte, a Jacobite parson, fifty pounds a year for seven years, to write the history of England; and four aldermen and six Common Council men are to inspect his materials and the progress of the work. Surveyors of common sewers turned supervisors of literature! To be sure they think a history of England is no more than Stowe's survey of the parishes! Instead of having books published with the imprimatur of an university, they will be printed, as churches are whitewashed, John Smith and Thomas Johnson churchwardens.

But, brother historian, you will wonder I should have nothing to *communicate;* when all Europe is bursting with events, and every day *big with the fate of Cato and of Rome.*[1] But so it is; I know nothing: Prince Charles's great passage of the Rhine has hitherto produced nothing more: indeed the French armies are moving towards him from Flanders; and they tell us, ours is crossing the Schelde to attack the Count de Saxe, now that we are equal to him, from our reinforcements and his diminutions. In the meantime, as I am at least one of the principal heroes of my own politics, being secure of any invasion, I am going to leave all my *lares*, that is, all my antiquities, household gods and pagods, and take a journey into Siberia for six weeks, where my father's Grace of Courland has been for some time.

Lord Middlesex is going to be married to Miss Boyle, Lady Shannon's daughter; she has thirty thousand pounds, and may have as much more, if her mother, who is a plump widow, don't happen to *Nugentize*. The girl is low and ugly, but a vast scholar—*concumbet græce.*[2]

Young Churchill has got a daughter by the Frasi; Mr. Winnington calls it the *opéra comique;* the mother is an opera girl; the grandmother was Mrs Oldfield. I ruined myself t'other night upon the subject of operas; Mrs Phipps, who as all Herveys put on some character, is prude by profession, came in to my Lady Townshend's where I was; the latter said, 'My Lady Rich is breaking her heart on Monticelli's going.' I, who thought more of the style of the house where I was, than of the style of the visitor, replied, 'It will not hurt her much, for she has so often broken her heart about singers, that the *rent* must be very large by this time.' If I had pronounced the big words of all, the grave lady could not have been more shocked. Did I never tell you of the prints that my Lady Townshend gives about of herself? Behind mine I have written these two lines transposed from Rochester:

1. "The great, th'important day, big with the fate / Of Cato and of Rome" (Addison, *Cato* I.i.3–4).

2. "Concumbunt græce" (Juvenal, *Satires* VI.191): "their loves are conducted in Greek fashion."

This is the staple of the world's great trade;
On this soft bosom all mankind has laid.

Now I talk of prints, I must tell you of a very extraordinary one, which my Lady Burlington gives away, of her daughter Euston, with this inscription:

Lady Dorothy Boyle,
Once the pride, the joy, the comfort of her parents,
The Admiration of all that saw Her,
The Delight of all that knew Her.
Born May 14th 1724, married alas! Oct. 10th 1741, and delivered from extremest misery May 2d 1742.
This print was taken from a picture drawn by memory seven weeks after her death, by her most afflicted Mother
Dorothy Burlington.

I am forced to begin a new sheet, lest you should think my letter came from my Lady Burlington, as it ends so patly with her name. But is it not a most melancholy way of venting one's self? She has drawn numbers of these pictures: I don't approve her having them engraved; but sure the inscription is pretty.

I was accosted t'other night by a little pert *petit-maître*-figure, that claimed me for acquaintance. Do you remember to have seen at Florence an Abbé Durazzo of Genoa? Well, this was he: it is mighty dapper and French: however I will be civil to it: I never lose opportunities of paving myself an agreeable passage back to Florence. My dear Chutes, stay for me: I think the first gale of peace will carry me to you. Are you as fond of Florence as ever? Of me you are not, I am sure, for you never write me a line. You would be diverted with the grandeur of our old Florence beauty, Lady Carteret. She dresses more extravagantly, and grows more short-sighted every day: she can't walk a step without leaning on one of her ancient daughters-in-law. Lord Tweedale and Lord Bathurst are her constant gentlemen ushers. She has not quite digested her resentment to Lincoln yet. He was walking with her at Ranelagh t'other night, and a Spanish refugee Marquis, who is of the Carteret Court, but who not being quite perfect in the *carte du pays*, told my Lady that Lord Lincoln had promised him to make a very good husband to Miss Pelham. Lady Carteret with an accent of energy, replied, *'J'espère qu'il tiendra sa promesse!'* Here is a good epigram that has been made on her:

> Her beauty like the scripture feast,
> To which th'invited never came,
> Deprived of its intended guest,
> Was given to the old and lame.

Adieu! Here is company; I think I may be excused leaving off at the sixth side.

To Sir Horace Mann, 6 September 1745, O.S.

Arlington Street, Sept. 6, 1745.

It would have been inexcusable in me in our present circumstances, and after all I have promised you, not to have written to you for this last month, if I had been in London; but I have been at Mount Edgcumbe, and so constantly upon the road, that I neither received your letters, had time to write, or knew what to write. I came back last night, and found three packets from you, which I have no time to answer, and but just time to read. The confusion I have found, and the danger we are in, prevent my talking of anything else. The young Pretender, at the head of three thousand men, has got a march on General Cope, who is not eighteen hundred strong; and when the last accounts came away, was fifty miles nearer Edingburgh than Cope; and by this time is there. The clans will not rise for the government: the Dukes of Argyle and Athol are come post to town, not having been able to raise a man. The young Duke of Gordon sent for his uncle, and told him he must arm their clan. 'They are in arms.' 'They must march against the rebels.' 'They will wait on the Prince of Wales.' The Duke flew in a passion; his uncle pulled out a pistol, and told him it was in vain to dispute. Lord Loudon, Lord Fortrose and Lord Panmure have been very zealous and have raised some men

—but I look upon Scotland as gone! I think of what King William said to Duke Hamilton, when he was extolling Scotland; 'My Lord, I only wish it was an hundred thousand miles off, and that you was king of it.'

There are two manifestos published, signed Charles Prince, Regent for his father, King of Scotland, England, France and Ireland. By one, he promises to preserve everybody in their just rights; and orders all persons who have public moneys in their hands to bring it to him; and by the other dissolves the Union between England and Scotland.—But all this is not the worst! Notice came yesterday, that there are ten thousand men, thirty transports and ten men of war at Dunkirk. Against this force, we have—I don't know what—scarce fears! Three thousand Dutch we hope are by this time landed in Scotland; three more are coming hither: we have sent for ten regiments from Flanders, which may be here in a week, and we have fifteen men of war in the Downs. I am grieved to tell you all this; but when it is so, how can I avoid telling you? Your brother is just come in, who says he has written to you—I have not time to expatiate.

My Lady O[rford] is arrived; I hear she says, only to endeavour to get a certain allowance. Her mother has sent to offer her the use of her house—she is a poor weak woman.

I can say nothing to Marquis Riccardi, nor think of him; only tell him, that I will when I have time.

My sister[1] has married herself, that is, declared she will, to young Churchill. It is a foolish match;[2] but I have nothing to do with it.

Adieu! my dear Sir, excuse my haste, but you must imagine that one is not much at leisure to write long letters—hope if you can!

1. Lady Maria Walpole, daughter of Lord Orford, married Ch[arles] Churchill Esq. son of the General. (HW's note)

2. Because of the small fortunes of the bride and groom and the circumstance that Churchill, like Lady Mary, was illegitimate.

To Sir Horace Mann, 21 August 1746, O.S.

Windsor, Aug. 21, 1746.

You will perceive by my date that I am got into a new scene; and that I am retired hither like an old summer dowager; only that I have no toad-eater to take the air with me in the back part of my lozenge coach, and to be scolded. I have taken a small house here within the castle, and propose spending the greatest part of—every week here till the Parliament meets: but my jaunts to town will prevent my news from being quite provincial and marvellous. Then I promise you I will go to no races nor assemblies, nor make comments upon couples that come in chaises to the White Hart.

I came from town (for take notice, I put this place upon myself for the country) the day after the execution of the rebel lords: I was not at it, but had two persons come to me directly who were at the next house to the scaffold; and I saw another who was upon it, so that you may depend upon my accounts.

Just before they came out of the Tower, Lord Balmerino drank a bumper to King James's health. As the clock struck ten, they came forth on foot, Lord Kilmarnock all in black, his hair unpowdered in a bag, supported by Forster, the great Presbyterian, and by Mr Home, a young clergyman, his friend. Lord Balmerino followed alone, in a blue coat turned up with red, his rebellious regimentals, a flannel waistcoat, and his shroud beneath; their hearses following. They were conducted to a house near the scaffold; the room forwards had benches for spectators; in the second Lord Kilmarnock was put, and in the third backwards Lord Balmerino; all three chambers hung with black. Here they parted! Balmerino embraced the other, and said, 'My Lord, I wish I could suffer for both!' He had scarce left him, before he desired again to see him, and then asked him, 'My Lord Kilmarnock, do you know anything of the resolution taken in our army, the day before the Battle of Culloden, to put the English prisoners to death?' He replied, 'My Lord, I was not present, but since I came hither, I have had all the reason in the world to believe that there was such order taken; and I hear the Duke has the pocket book with the order.' Balmerino answered, 'It was a lie raised to excuse their barbarity to us.'—Take notice, that the Duke's charging this on Lord Kilmarnock (certainly on misinformation) decided this unhappy man's fate! The most now pretended, is, that it would have come to Lord Kilmarnock's turn to have given the word for the slaughter, as Lieutenant-General, with the patent for which he was immediately drawn into the rebellion, after having been staggered by his wife, her mother, his own poverty, and the defeat of Cope. He remained an hour and half in the house, and shed tears. At last he came to the scaffold, certainly much terrified, but with a resolution that prevented his behaving in the least meanly or unlike a gentleman. He took no notice of the crowd, only to desire that the bays might be lifted up from the rails, that the mob might see the spectacle. He stood and prayed some time with Forster, who wept over him, exhorted and encouraged him. He delivered a long speech to the sheriff, and with a noble manliness stuck to the recantation he had made at his trial; declaring he wished that all who embarked in the same cause might meet the same fate. He then took off his bag, coat and waistcoat with great composure, and after some trouble put on a napkin cap, and then several times tried the block, the executioner who was in white with a white apron, out of tenderness concealing the axe behind himself. At last the Earl knelt down, with a visible unwillingness to depart, and after five minutes dropped his handkerchief, the signal, and his head was cut off at once, only hanging by a bit of skin, and was received in a scarlet cloth by four of the undertaker's men kneeling, who wrapped it up and put it into the coffin with the body; orders having been given not to expose the heads, as used to be the custom. The scaffold was immediately new strowed with sawdust, the block new covered, the executioner new dressed, and a new axe brought. Then came old Balmerino, treading with the air of a general. As soon as he mounted the scaffold, he read the inscription on his coffin, as he did again afterwards: he then surveyed the spectators, who were in amazing numbers, even upon masts of ships in the river; and pulling out his spectacles read a treasonable speech which he delivered to the sheriff, and said, the young Pretender was so sweet a prince, that flesh and blood could not resist following him; and lying down to try the block, he said, 'If I had a thousand lives, I would lay them all down here in the same cause.' He said, if he had not taken the Sacrament the day before, he would have knocked down Williamson, the lieutenant of the Tower, for his ill usage of him. He took the axe and felt it, and asked the headsman, how many blows he had given Lord Kilmarnock; and gave him three guineas. Two clergymen, who attended him, coming up, he said, 'No, gentlemen, I believe you have already done me all the service you can.' Then he went to the corner of the scaffold, and called very loud for the warder, to give him his periwig, which he took off, and put on a nightcap of Scotch plaid, and then pulled off his coat and his waistcoat and laid down; but being told he was on the wrong side, vaulted round, and immediately gave the sign by tossing up his arm, as if he were giving the signal for battle. He received three blows, but the first certainly took away all sensation. He was not a quarter of an hour on the scaffold; Lord Kilmarnock above half an one. Balmerino certainly died with the intrepidity of a hero, but with the insensibility of one too. As he walked from his prison to execution, seeing every window and top of house filled with spectators, he cried out, 'Look, look! How they are all piled up like rotten oranges!' My Lady Townshend, who fell in love with Lord Kilmarnock at his trial, will go nowhere to dinner, for fear of meeting with a rebel pie; she says, everybody is so bloody minded, that they eat rebels! The Prince of Wales, whose intercession saved Lord Cromartie, says he did it in return for old Sir W. Gordon, Lady Cromartie's father, coming down out of his deathbed, to vote against my father in the Chippenham election. If his Royal Highness had not countenanced inveteracy, like that of Sir Gordon, he would have no occasion to exert his gratitude now in favour of rebels. His brother has plucked a very useful feather out of the cap of the ministry, by forbidding any application for posts in the army to be made to anybody but himself: a resolution I dare say he will keep as strictly and minutely, as he does the discipline and dress of the army. Adieu!

PS. I have just received yours of Aug. 9th. You had not then heard of the second great battle of Placentia, which has already occasioned new instructions, or in effect a recall being sent after Lord Sandwich.

To the Hon. Henry Seymour Conway, 8 June 1747

Twickenham, June 8, 1747.

You perceive by my date that I am got into a new camp, and have left my tub at Windsor. It is a little plaything-house that I got out of Mrs. Chenevix's shop,[1] and is the prettiest bauble you ever saw. It is set in enamelled meadows, with filigree hedges:

> A small Euphrates through the piece is roll'd,
> And little finches wave their wings in gold.[2]

Two delightful roads, that you would call dusty, supply me continually with coaches and chaises: barges as solemn as Barons of the Exchequer move under my window; Richmond Hill and Ham Walks bound my prospect; but, thank God! the Thames is between me and the Duchess of Queensberry. Dowagers as plenty as flounders inhabit all around, and Pope's ghost is just now skimming under the window by a most poetical moonlight. I have about land enough to keep such a farm as Noah's, when he set up in the ark with a pair of each kind; but my cottage is rather cleaner than I believe his was after they had been cooped up together forty days. The Chenevixes had tricked it out for themselves: up two pair of stairs is what they call Mr. Chenevix's library, furnished with three maps, one shelf, a bust of Sir Isaac Newton, and a lame telescope without any glasses. Lord John Sackville *predecessed* me here, and instituted certain games called *cricketalia*, which have been celebrated this very evening in honour of him in a neighbouring meadow.

You will think I have removed my philosophy from Windsor

1. A famous toy-shop. (HW's note)
2. A parody of a couplet in Pope's *Epistle to Addison*.

with my tea-things hither; for I am writing to you in all this tranquillity, while a Parliament is bursting about my ears. You know it is going to be dissolved: I am told, you are taken care of, though I don't know where, nor whether anybody that chooses you will quarrel with me because he does choose you, as that little bug the Marquis of Rockingham did; one of the calamities of my life which I have bore as abominably well as I do most about which I don't care. They say the Prince has taken up two hundred thousand pounds, to carry elections which he won't carry:—he had much better have saved it to buy the Parliament after it is chosen. A new set of peers are in embryo, to add more dignity to the silence of the House of Lords.

I make no remarks on your campaign,[1] because, as you say, you do nothing at all; which, though very proper nutriment for a thinking head, does not do quite so well to write upon. If any one of you can but contrive to be shot upon your post, it is all we desire, shall look upon it as a great curiosity, and will take care to set up a monument to the person so slain; as we are doing by vote to Captain Cornewall, who was killed at the beginning of the action in the Mediterranean four years ago. In the present dearth of glory, he is canonized; though, poor man! he had been tried twice the year before for cowardice.

I could tell you much election news, none else; though not being thoroughly attentive to so important a subject, as to be sure one ought to be, I might now and then mistake and give you a candidate for Durham in place of one for Southampton, or name the returning officer instead of the candidate. In general, I believe, it is much as usual—those sold in detail that afterwards will be sold in the representation—the ministers bribing Jacobites to choose friends of their own—the name of well-wishers to the present establishment, and Patriots, outbidding ministers that they may make the better market of their own patriotism:—in short, all England, under some name or other, is just now to be

1. Mr. Conway was in Flanders with William, Duke of Cumberland. (HW's note)

bought and sold; though, whenever we become posterity and forefathers, we shall be in high repute for wisdom and virtue. My great-great-grandchildren will figure me with a white beard down to my girdle; and Mr. Pitt's will believe him unspotted enough to have walked over nine hundred hot ploughshares, without hurting the sole of his foot. How merry my ghost will be, and shake its ears to hear itself quoted as a person of consummate prudence! Adieu, dear Harry!

Yours ever,

HOR. WALPOLE.

TO THE HON. HENRY SEYMOUR CONWAY, 29 August 1748

Strawberry Hill, Aug. 29, 1748.

Dear Harry,—Whatever you may think, a campaign at Twickenham furnishes as little matter for a letter as an abortive one in Flanders. I can't say indeed that my generals wear black wigs, but they have long full-bottomed hoods which cover as little entertainment to the full.

There's General my Lady Castlecomer, and General my lady Dowager Ferrers! Why, do you think I can extract more out of them than you can out of Hawley or Honeywood? Your old women dress, go to the Duke's levee, see that the soldiers cock their hats right, sleep after dinner, and soak with their led-captains till bed-time, and tell a thousand lies of what they never did in their youth. Change hats for head-clothes, the rounds for visits, and led-captains for toad-eaters, and the life is the very same. In short, these are the people I live in the midst of, though not with; and it is for want of more important histories that I have wrote to you so seldom; not, I give you my word, from the least negligence. My present and sole occupation is planting, in which I have made great progress, and talk very learnedly with the nurserymen, except that now and then a lettuce run to seed overturns all my botany, as I have more than once taken it for a curious West Indian flowering shrub. Then the deliberation with which trees grow, is extremely inconvenient to my natural impatience, I lament living in so barbarous an age, when we are come to so little perfection in gardening I am persuaded that a hundred and fifty years hence it will be as common to remove oaks a hundred and fifty years old, as it is now to transplant tulip-roots. I have even begun a treatise or panegyric on the great discoveries made by posterity in all arts and sciences, wherein I shall particularly descant on the great and cheap convenience of making trout-rivers—one of the improvements which Mrs. Kerwood wondered Mr. Hedges would not make at his country-house, but which was not then quite so common as it will be. I shall talk of a secret for roasting a wild boar and a whole pack of hounds alive, without hurting them, so that the whole chase may be brought up to table; and for this secret, the Duke of Newcastle's grandson, if he can ever get a son, is to give a hundred thousand pounds. Then the delightfulness of having whole groves of humming-birds, tame tigers taught to fetch and carry, pocket spying-glasses to see all that is doing in China, with a thousand other toys, which we now look upon as impracticable, and which pert posterity would laugh in one's face for staring at, while they are offering rewards for perfecting discoveries, of the principles of which we have not the least conception! If ever this book should come forth, I must expect to have all the learned in arms against me, who measure all knowledge backward: some of them have discovered symptoms of all arts in Homer; and Pineda had so much faith in the accomplishments of his ancestors, that he believed Adam understood all sciences but politics. But as these great champions for our forefathers are dead, and Boileau not alive to hitch me into a verse with Perrault, I am determined to admire the learning of posterity, especially being convinced that half our present knowledge sprung from discovering the errors of what had formerly been called so. I don't think I shall ever make any great discoveries myself, and therefore shall be content to propose them to my descendants, like my Lord Bacon, who, as Dr. Shaw says very prettily in his preface to Boyle, 'had the art of inventing arts': or rather like a Marquis of Worcester, of whom I have seen a little book which he calls *A Century of Inventions*, where he has set down a hundred machines to do impossibilities with, and not a single direction how to make the machines themselves.

If I happen to be less punctual in my correspondence than I intend to be, you must conclude I am writing my book, which being designed for a panegyric, will cost me a great deal of trouble. The dedication, with your leave, shall be addressed to your son that is coming, or, with my Lady Ailesbury's[1] leave, to your ninth son, who will be unborn nearer to the time I am writing of; always provided that she does not bring three at once, like my Lady Berkeley.

Well! I have here set you the example of writing nonsense when one has nothing to say, and shall take it ill if you don't keep up the correspondence on the same foot. Adieu!

Yours ever,

HOR. WALPOLE.

TO SIR HORACE MANN, 3 May 1749, O.S.

Strawberry Hill, May 3d, 1749.

I am come hither for a few days to repose myself after a torrent of diversions, and am writing to you in my charming bow-window, with a tranquillity and satisfaction, which, I fear, I am grown old enough to prefer to the hurry of amusements, in which the whole world has lived for this last week. We have at last celebrated the peace, and that as much in extremes as we generally do everything, whether we have reason to be glad or sorry, pleased or angry. Last Tuesday it was proclaimed; the King did not go to St Paul's, but at night the whole town was illuminated. The next day was what was called 'a jubilee masquerade in the Venetian manner' at Ranelagh: it had nothing Venetian in it, but was by far

1. Conway's wife. She was the only daughter of the fourth Duke of Argyll, and married as her first husband the third Earl of Ailesbury. He died in 1746, and she married Conway the following year. She died in 1803.

the best understood, and the prettiest spectacle I ever saw: nothing in a fairy tale ever surpassed it. One of the proprietors, who is a German and belongs to Court, had got my Lady Yarmouth to persuade the King to order it. It began at three o'clock, and about five, people of fashion began to go. When you entered, you found the whole garden filled with masks, and spread with tents, which remained all night *very commodely*. In one quarter was a Maypole dressed with garlands, and people dancing round it to a tabor and pipe and rustic music, all masked, as were all the various bands of music, that were disposed in different parts of the garden, some like huntsmen with French horns, some like peasants, and a troop of harlequins and scaramouches, in the little open temple on the mount. On the canal was a sort of gondola, adorned with flags and streamers, and filled with music, rowing about. All round the outside of the amphitheatre were shops filled with Dresden china, japan, etc., and all the shopkeepers in mask. The amphitheatre was illuminated, and in the middle was a circular bower, composed of all kinds of firs in tubs, from twenty to thirty feet high: under them orange trees, with small lamps in each orange, and below them all sorts of the finest auriculas in pots; and festoons of natural flowers hanging from tree to tree. Between the arches too were firs, and smaller ones in the balconies above. There were booths for tea and wine, gaming tables and dancing, and about two thousand persons. In short it pleased me more than anything I ever saw. It is to be once more, and probably finer as to dresses, as there has since been a subscription masquerade, and people will go in their rich habits. The next day were the fireworks, which by no means answered the expense, the length of preparation, and the expectation that had been raised: indeed for a week before, the town was like a country fair, the streets filled from morning to night, scaffolds building wherever you could or could not see; and coaches arriving from every corner of the kingdom. This hurry and lively scene, with the sight of the immense crowds in the park and on every house, the guards and the machine itself which was very beautiful, was all that was worth seeing. The rockets and whatever was thrown up into the air succeeded mighty well, but the wheels and all that was to compose the principal part, were pitiful and ill-conducted, with no changes of coloured fires and shapes: the illumination was mean, and lighted so slowly that scarce anybody had patience to wait the finishing; and then what contributed to the awkwardness of the whole, was the right pavilion catching fire, and being burned down in the middle of the show. The King, the Duke and Princess Emily saw it from the library, with their courts: the Prince and Princess with their children from Lady Middlesex's, no place being provided for them, nor any invitation given to the library. The Lords and Commons had galleries built for them and the chief citizens along the rails of the Mall: the Lords had four tickets apiece, and each commoner, at first but two, till the Speaker bounced and obtained a third. Very little mischief was done, and but two persons killed: at Paris there were forty killed, and near three hundred wounded, by a dispute between the French and Italians in the management, who quarrelling for precedence in lighting the fires, both lighted at once and blew up the whole. Our mob was extremely tranquil, and very unlike those I remember in my father's time, when it was a measure in the Opposition to work up everything to mischief, the Excise and the French players, the Convention and the Gin Act. We are as much now in the opposite extreme, and in general so pleased with the peace, that I could not help being struck with a passage I read lately in Pasquier, an old French author, who says, 'that in the time of Francis I, the French used to call their creditors, *Des Anglais*, from the facility with which the English gave credit to them in all treaties, though they had broken so many.' On Saturday we had a *serenata* at the opera house, called, *Peace in Europe,* but it was a wretched performance. On Monday there was a subscription-masquerade, much fuller than that of last year, but not so agreeable or so various in dresses. The King was well disguised in an old-fashioned English habit, and much pleased with somebody who desired him to hold their cup as they were drinking tea. The Duke had a dress of the same kind, but was so immensely corpulent, that he looked like Cacofogo, the drunken captain in *Rule a Wife and have a Wife*. The Duchess of

Richmond was a lady mayoress in the time of James I, and Lord Delawar, Queen Elizabeth's porter, from a picture in the guard chamber at Kensington: they were admirable masks. Lady Rochford, Miss Evelyn, Miss Bishop, Lady Strafford, and Mrs Pitt were in vast beauty, particularly the last, who had a red veil, which made her look gloriously handsome. I forgot Lady Kildare. Mr Conway was the Duke in Don Quixote and the finest figure I ever saw. Miss Chudleigh was Iphigenia, but so naked that you would have taken her for Andromeda: and Lady Betty Smithson had such a pyramid of baubles upon her head, that she was exactly the Princess of Babylon in Grammont. You will conclude that after all these diversions, people begin to think of going out of town—no such matter: the Parliament continues sitting, and will till the middle of June; Lord Egmont told us we should sit till Michaelmas. There are many private bills, no public ones of any fame. We were to have had some chastisement for Oxford, where, besides the late riots, the famous Dr King, the Pretender's great agent, made a most violent speech at the opening of the Ratcliffe Library. The ministry denounced judgment; but, in their old style, have grown frightened, and dropped it. However this menace gave occasion to a meeting and union between the Prince's party and the Jacobites, which Lord Egmont has been labouring all the winter. They met at the St Alban's tavern near Pallmall last Monday morning, an hundred and twelve Lords and Commoners. The Duke of Beaufort opened the assembly with a panegyric on the stand that had been made this winter against so corrupt an administration, and hoped it would continue; and desired harmony. Lord Egmont seconded this strongly, and begged they would come up to Parliament early next winter. Lord Oxford spoke next; and then Potter with great humour, and to the great abashment of the Jacobites, said, he was very glad to see this union, and from thence hoped that if another attack like the last rebellion should be made on the royal family, they would all stand by them. No reply was made to this. Then Sir Watkyn Williams spoke, Sir Francis Dashwood, and Tom Pitt, and the meeting broke up. I don't know what this coalition may produce; it will require time with no better heads than compose it at present, though the great Mr Doddington had carried to the conference the assistance of his. In France a very favourable event has happened for us, the disgrace of Maurepas, one of our bitterest enemies, and the greatest promoter of their marine. Just at the beginning of the war in a very critical period, he had obtained a very large sum for that service, but which one of the other factions, lest he should gain glory and credit by it, got to be suddenly given away to the King of Prussia.

Sir Charles Williams is appointed envoy to this last King: here is an epigram which he has just sent over on Lord Egmont's opposition to the Mutiny Bill:

> Why has Lord Egmont 'gainst this bill
> So much declamatory skill
> So tediously exerted?
> The reason's plain: but t'other day
> He mutinied himself for pay,
> And he has twice deserted.

I must tell you a bon mot that was made t'other night at the *serenata* of *Peace in Europe* by Wall, who is much in fashion, and a kind of Gondomar. Grossatesta, the Modenese minister, a very low fellow, with all the jack-puddinghood of an Italian, asked, *'Mais qui est-ce qui représente mon maître?'* Wall replied, *'Mais, mon Dieu! L'abbé, ne savez-vous pas que ce n'est pas un opera bouffon?'* And here is another bon mot of my Lady Townshend: we were talking of the Methodists; somebody said, 'Pray, Madam, is it true that Whitfield has *recanted?*' 'No, Sir, he has only *canted.*'

If you ever think of returning to England, as I hope it will be long first, you must prepare yourself with Methodism; I really believe that by that time it will be necessary: this sect increases as fast as almost ever any religious nonsense did. Lady Fanny Shirley has chosen this way of bestowing the dregs of her beauty upon Jesus Christ; and Mr Lyttelton is very near making the same sacrifice of the dregs of all those various characters that he has worn. The Methodists love your big sinners, as proper subjects to work upon—and indeed they have a plentiful harvest—I think what you call flagrancy was never more in fashion. Drinking is at the highest wine-mark; and gaming joined with it so violent, that at the last Newmarket meeting, in the rapidity of both, a bank bill was thrown down, and nobody immediately claiming it, they agreed to give it to a man that was standing by—mind, I now break off all connection, to tell you that my Lady [Pomfret] is setting out for Constantinople, trailing along with her—not my Lord, but a Miss [Shelley] whom Winnington used to call *filial piety,* for imitating her father, in bearing affection to her own sex. I don't know how, still to be sure without connection, but I must tell you of Stosch's letter, which he had the impertinence to give you without telling the contents. It was to solicit the arrears of his pension, which I beg you will tell him I have no manner of interest to procure; and to tell me of a Galla Placidia, a gold medal lately found. It is not for myself, but I wish you would ask him the price for a friend of mine who would like to buy it.

Adieu! my dear child; I have been long in arrears to you, but I trust you will take this huge letter as an acquittal. You see my villa makes me a good correspondent: how happy I should be to show it you, if I could with no mixture of disagreeable circumstances to you. I have made a vast plantation! Lord Leicester told me t'other day that he heard I would not buy some old china, because I was laying out all my money in trees: 'Yes,' said I, 'my Lord, I used to love blue trees, but now I like green ones.'

To Sir Horace Mann, 2 April 1750, O.S.

Arlington Street, April 2d, 1750.

You will not wonder so much at our earthquakes, as at the effects they have had. All the women in town have taken them up upon the foot of *judgments;*[1] and the clergy, who have had no windfalls of

1. By *judgments* here is not meant anything that is the effect of *judiciousness,* but a kind of punishment, invented by divines, by which, on any great calamity, God is supposed to chastise a general people or posterity, for the crimes of particulars, or for the sins of their ancestors. (HW's note)

a long season, have driven horse and foot into this opinion. There has been a shower of sermons and exhortations: Secker, the Jesuitical Bishop of Oxford, began the mode; he heard the women were all going out of town to avoid the next shock; and so for fear of losing his Easter offerings, he set himself to advise them to await God's good pleasure in fear and trembling. But what is more astonishing, Sherlock, who has much better sense, and much less of the popish confessor, has been running a race with him for the old ladies, and has written a pastoral letter, of which ten thousand were sold in two days; and fifty thousand have been subscribed for, since the two first editions. You never read so impudent, so absurd a piece! This earthquake, which has done no hurt, in a country where no earthquake ever did any, is sent, according to the Bishop, to punish bawdy prints, bawdy books[1] (in one of which a Mrs Pilkington drew his Lordship's picture) gaming, drinking—(no, I think, drinking and avarice, those orthodox vices are omitted) and all other sins, natural or not; particularly heretical books, which he makes a principal ingredient in the composition of an earthquake, because not having been able to answer a late piece, which Middleton has writ against him, he has turned the Doctor over to God for punishment, even in this world. Here is an epigram, which this subject put into my head:

When Whitfield preaches, and when Whiston writes,
All cry, that madness dictates either's flights.
When Sherlock writes, or canting Secker preaches,
All think good sense inspires what either teaches.
Why, when all four for the same Gospel fight,
Should two be crazy, two be in the right?
Plain is the reason—ev'ry son of Eve
Thinks the two madmen, what they teach, believe.

I told you the women talked of going out of town: several fami-

1. "Have not the histories or romances of the vilest prostitutes been published" (Thomas Sherlock, *A Letter . . . to the Clergy and People of London and Westminster on Occasion of the Late Earthquakes*, 1750). On 16 March O.S., the *Memoirs of Fanny Hill* had been suppressed (*Daily Advertiser*, 19 March O.S.).

lies are literally gone, and many more going today and tomorrow; for what adds to the absurdity, is, that the second shock having happened exactly a month after the former, it prevails that there will be a third on Thursday next, another month, which is to swallow up London. I am almost ready to burn my letter now I have begun it, lest you should think I am laughing at you: but it is so true, that Arthur of White's told me last night that he should put off the last ridotto, which was to be on Thursday, because he hears nobody would come to it. I have advised several who are going to keep their next earthquake in the country, to take the bark for it, as it is so periodic. Dick Leveson and Mr Rigby, who had supped and stayed late at Bedford House t'other night, knocked at several doors, and in a watchman's voice cried, 'Past four o'clock and a dreadful earthquake!'—but I have done with this ridiculous panic: two pages were too much to talk of it!

We have had nothing in Parliament but trade bills, on one of which the Speaker humbled the arrogance of Sir John Barnard, who had reflected upon the proceedings of the House. It is to break up on Thursday sennight, and the King goes this day fortnight. He has made Lord Vere Beauclerc a baron, at the solicitation of the Pelhams, as this Lord had resigned upon a pique with Lord Sandwich. Lord Anson, who is treading in the same path, and leaving the Bedfords to follow his father-in-law the Chancellor, is made a privy councillor with Sir Thomas Robinson and Lord Hyndford. Lord Conway is to be an earl, and Sir John Rawdon (whose follies you remember, and whose boasted loyalty of having been kicked down stairs for not drinking the Pretender's health, though even that was false, is at last rewarded) and a Sir John Veezy are to be Irish lords; and a Sir William Beauchamp Proctor, and a Mr Loyd, Knights of the Bath.

I was entertained t'other night at the house of much such a creature as Sir John Rawdon, and one whom you remember too, Naylor. He has a wife who keeps the most indecent house of all those that are called decent: every *Sunday* she has a contraband assembly: I had had a card for *Monday* a fortnight before. As the day was new, I expected a great assembly, but found scarce six persons. I asked where the company was—I was answered—'Oh! they are not come yet; they will be here presently; they all supped here last night, stayed till morning, and I suppose are not up yet.' In the bedchamber I found two beds, which is too cruel to poor Naylor, to tell the whole town that he is the only man in it who does not lie with his wife!

My Lord Bolinbroke has lost his wife. When she was dying, he acted grief, flung himself upon her bed and asked her if she could forgive him. I never saw her, but have heard her wit and parts excessively commended. Dr Middleton told me a compliment she made him two years ago, which I thought pretty. She said she was persuaded that he was a very great writer, for she understood his works better than any other English book, and that she had observed that the best writers were always the most intelligible.

Wednesday.

I had not time to finish my letter on Monday—I return to the earthquake, which I had mistaken; it is to be today. This frantic terror prevails so much, that within these three days 730 coaches have been counted passing Hyde Park Corner, with whole parties removing into the country; here is a good advertisement which I cut out of the papers today;

On Monday next will be published (price 6*d*.) A true and exact list of all the nobility and gentry who have left or shall leave this place through fear of another earthquake.

Several women have made earthquake gowns—that is, warm gowns to sit out of doors all tonight. These are of the more courageous. One woman still more heroic is come to town on purpose: she says, all her friends are in London, and she will not survive them. But what will you think of Lady Catherine Pelham, Lady Frances Arundel, and Lord and Lady Galway, who go this evening to an inn ten miles out of town, where they are to play at brag till five in the morning, and then come back—I suppose, to look for the bones of their husbands and families under the rubbish! The prophet of all this (next to the Bishop of London, whom

Mr Chute and I have agreed not to believe till he has been three days in a whale's belly) is a trooper of Lord Delawar's, who was yesterday sent to Bedlam. His *colonel* sent to the man's wife, and asked her if her husband had ever been disordered before—She cried, 'Oh! dear my Lord, he is not mad now; if your *Lordship* would but get any *sensible* man to examine him, you would find he is quite in his right mind.'

I shall now tell you something more serious: Lord Dalkeith is dead of the smallpox in three days. It is so dreadfully fatal in his family, that besides several uncles and aunts, his eldest boy died of it last year; and his only brother, who was ill but two days, putrified so fast, that his limbs fell off, as they lifted the body into the coffin. Lady Dalkeith is five months gone with child; she was hurrying to him, but was stopped on the road by the physician who told her it was a military fever. They were remarkably happy.

The King goes on Monday sennight; it is looked upon as a great event that the Duke of Newcastle has prevailed on him to speak to Mr Pitt, who has detached himself from the Bedfords. The Monarch, who had kept up his Hanoverian resentments, though he had made him paymaster, is now beat out of the dignity of his silence: he was to pretend not to know Pitt, and was to be directed to him by the lord-in-waiting. Pitt's jealousy is of Lord Sandwich, who knows his own interest and unpopularity so well, that he will prevent any breach, and thereby what you fear, which yet I think you would have no reason to fear. I could not say enough of my anger to your father, but I shall take care to say nothing, as I have not forgot how my zeal for you made me provoke him once before.

Your genealogical affair is in great train, and will be quite finished in a week or two. Mr Chute has laboured it indefatigably: General Guise has been attesting the authenticity of it today before a justice of peace. You will find yourself mixed with every drop of blood in England that is worth bottling up: the Duchess of Norfolk and you grow on the same bough of the tree. I must tell you a very curious anecdote that [the] Strawberry King-at-Arms has discovered by the way as he was fumbling over the mighty dead in the herald's office. You have heard me speak of the great injustice that the Protector Somerset did to the children of his first wife, in favour of those by his second; so much that he not only had the dukedom settled on the younger brood, but to deprive the eldest of the title of Lord Beauchamp, which he wore by inheritance, he caused himself to be anew created *Viscount* Beauchamp. Well, in Vincent's *Baronage*, a book of great authority, speaking of the Protector's wives are these remarkable words: *'Katherina, filia et una coh. Gul: Fillol de Fillol's hall in Essex, uxor prima; repudiata, quia pater ejus post nuptias eam cognovit.'* The Speaker has since referred me to our journals, where are some notes of a trial in the reign of James I, between Edward, the second son of Katherine the *dutyful*, and the Earl of Hertford, son of Anne Stanhope, which in some measure confirms our MS for it says, the Earl of Hertford objected, that John, the eldest son of all, was begotten while the Duke was in France. This title, which now comes back at last to Sir Edward Seymour, is disputed: my Lord Chancellor has refused him the writ, but referred his case to the Attorney-General, the present great opinion of England, who, they say, is clear for Sir Edward's succession.

I shall now go and show you Mr Chute in a different light from heraldry, and in one in which I believe you never saw him. He will shine as usual; but as a little more severely than his good nature is accustomed to, I must tell you that he was provoked by the most impertinent usage. It is a parcel of epigrams on Lady C[aroline] P[etersham] whose present fame is coupled with young Harry Vane.

What makes Clodio, who always was fond of new faces,
So notoriously constant to Fulvia's embraces?
Ask Fulvia the cause—She can tell you the true one,
Who makes her old face ev'ry morning a new one.

The next is on her and her friend Miss A[she].

Fulvia the tall wears Nana on her arm,
Both vain, both varnish'd, wanton both and warm:

Twin sisters both in ev'ry thing but this;
Nana leaps up and Fulvia stoops to kiss.

Of the next I must tell you the history: I told Lady C[aroline] that I had great curiosity to know if the earthquake had happened at any *critical* time to any married couple— She replied with her usual frankness, 'No, indeed, not to me; my Lord was just come home cross from losing at White's: I waked him and told him there was an earthquake; he answered, "pho! it was only you gave a great flounce!" ' You will find the story a little transposed:

Cried Sir John t'other night, 'Don't you feel the bed shake?'
'Lord! no,' said my Lady! 'ah! why did I wake?
'How could you disturb one for nothing at all?
'An earthquake! a fiddle! I dreamt of a ball.
'Before I believe it, I'll feel it again:
'—But alas! both your fears and my wishes are *Vain.*'

Who is This?

Her face has beauty we must all confess,
But beauty on the brink of ugliness:
Her mouth's a rabbit feeding on a rose;
With eyes—ten times too good for such a nose!

Her blooming cheeks—what paint could ever draw 'em?
That paint, for which no mortal ever saw 'em.
Air without shape—of royal race divine—
'Tis Emily—oh! fie!—'tis Caroline.

Do but think of my beginning a third sheet! But as the Parliament is rising, and I shall probably not write you a tolerably long letter again these eight months, I will lay in a stock of merit with you to last me so long. Mr Chute has set me too upon making epigrams, but as I have not his art, mine is almost a copy of verses: the story he told me, and is literally true of an old Lady Bingley:

Celia now had completed some thirty campaigns,
And for new generations was hammering chains;
When whetting those terrible weapons, her eyes,
To Jenny, her handmaid, in anger she cries;
'Careless creature! did mortal e'er see such a glass!

'Who that saw me in this, could e'er guess what I was!
'Much you mind what I say! pray how oft have I bid you
'Provide me a new one? How oft have I chid you?'—
'Lord! Madam,' cried Jane, 'you're so hard to be pleased!
'I am sure ev'ry glassman in town I have teased:
'I have hunted each shop from Pallmall to Cheapside:
'Both Miss Carpenter's man and Miss Banks's I've tried'—
'Don't tell me of those girls!—all I know to my cost
'Is, the looking-glass art must be certainly lost!
'One used to have mirrors so smooth and so bright,
'They did one's eyes justice, they heightened one's white,
'And fresh roses diffused o'er one's bloom—but alas!
'In the glasses made now, one detests one's own face:
'They pucker one's cheeks up, and furrow one's brow,
'And one's skin looks as yellow as that of Miss Howe!'

After an epigram that seems to have found out the longitude, I shall tell you but one more, and that wondrous short— It is said to be made by a cow: you must not wonder; we tell as many strange stories as Baker and Livy:

A warm winter, a dry spring,
A hot summer, a new King.

Though the sting is very epigrammatic, the whole of the distich has more of the truth that becomes prophecy; that is, it is false; for the spring is wet and cold.

There is come from France a Madame Bocage, who has translated Milton: my Lord Chesterfield prefers the copy to the original; but that is not uncommon for him to do, who is the patron of bad authors and bad actors. She has written a play too which was damned—and worthy my Lord's approbation. You would be more diverted with a Mrs Holman, whose passion is keeping an assembly, and inviting literally everybody to it. She goes to the Drawing-Room to watch for sneezes; whips out a curtsy, and then sends next morning to know how your cold does, and to desire your company next Thursday.

Mr Whithed has taken my Lord Pembroke's house at Whitehall; a glorious situation, but as madly built as my Lord himself was. He has bought some delightful pictures too of Claud, Gaspar and good masters, to the amount of £400.

Good night! I have nothing more to tell you, but that I have lately seen a Sir William Boothby, who saw you about a year ago, and adores you, as all the English you receive ought to do. He is much in my favour.

To George Montagu, 23 June 1750

Arlington Street, June 23d, 1750.

As I am not Vannecked,[1] I have been in no hurry to thank you for your congratulation, and to assure you that I never knew what solid happiness was till I was married. Your Trevors and Rices[2] dined with me last week at Strawberry Hill, and would have had me answer you upon the matrimonial tone, but I thought I should imitate cheerfulness in that style as ill as if I really were married. I have had another of your friends with me there some time, whom I adore, Mr Bentley;[3] he has more sense, judgment and wit, more taste and more misfortunes than sure ever met in any man. I have heard that Dr Bentley[4] regretting his wanting taste for all such learning as his, which is the very want of taste, used to sigh and say, 'Tully had his Marcus!' If the sons resembled as much as the fathers did, at least in vanity, I would be the modest agreeable Marcus. Mr Bentley tells me that you press him much to visit you at Hawkhurst; I advise him, and assure him he will make his fortune under you there, that you are agent from the Board of Trade to the smugglers, and wallow in contraband wine, tea and silk handkerchiefs. I found an old newspaper t'other day with a list of outlawed smugglers; there were John Price alias Miss Marjoram, Bob Plunder, Bricklayer Tom, and Robin Cursemother, all of Hawkhurst in Kent: when Miss Harriot[5] is thoroughly hardened

1. HW's first cousin of the same name had married a Miss van Neck.
2. Montagu's cousins.
3. Richard Bentley (1708–82), HW's correspondent.
4. Richard Bentley (1662–1742), the great classical scholar, his father.
5. Montagu's sister.

at Buxton, as I hear she is by lying in a public room with the whole Wells, from drinking waters I conclude she will come to sip nothing but run brandy.

As jolly and abominable a life as she may have been leading, I defy all her enormities to equal a party of pleasure that I had t'other night. I shall relate it to you to show you the manners of the age, which are always as entertaining to a person fifty miles off, as to one born an hundred and fifty years after the time. I had a card from Lady Caroline Petersham to go with her to Vauxhall. I went accordingly to her house at half an hour after seven, and found her and little Ashe, or the pollard Ashe, as they call her; they had just finished their last layer of red, and looked as handsome as crimson could make them. On the cabinet stood a pair of Dresden candlesticks, a present from the virgin hands of Sir John Bland; the branches of each formed a little bower over a cock and hen treading, yes literally! We issued into the Mall to assemble our company, which was all the town if we could get it, for just so many had been summoned, except Harry Vane, whom we met by *chance.* We mustered the Duke of Kingston whom Lady Caroline says she has been trying for these seven years, but alas! his beauty is at the fall of the leaf, Lord March, Mr Whithed, a pretty Miss Beauclerc and a very foolish Miss Sparre. These two damsels were trusted by their mothers for the first time of their lives to the matronly conduct of Lady Caroline. As we sailed up the Mall with all our colours flying, Lord Petersham with his nose and legs twisted to every point of crossness, strode by us on the outside, and repassed again on the return. At the end of the Mall, she called to him, he would not answer; she gave a familiar spring, and between laugh and confusion ran up to him, 'My Lord, my Lord, why you don't see us!' We advanced at a little distance, not a little awkward in expectation how all this would end, for my Lord never stirred his hat or took the least notice of anybody; she said, 'Do you go with us, or are you going anywhere else'—'I don't go with you, I am going somewhere else,' and away he stalked as sulky as a ghost that nobody will speak to first. We got into the best order we could and marched to our barge, with a boat of

French horns attending and little Ashe singing. We paraded some time up the river and at last debarked at Vauxhall. There if we had so pleased we might have had the vivacity of our party increased by a quarrel, for a Mrs Loyd, who is supposed to be married to Lord Haddington, seeing the two girls following Lady C. and Miss Ashe said aloud, 'Poor girls, I am sorry to see them in such bad company.' Miss Sparre who desired nothing so much as the fun of seeing a duel, a thing which, though she is fifteen, she has never been so lucky to see, took due pains to make Lord March resent this, but he, who is very lively and agreeable, laughed her out of this charming frolic with a great deal of humour. Here we picked up Lord Granby, arrived very drunk from Jenny's Whim where, instead of going to old Strafford's catacombs to make honourable love, he had dined, with Lady Fitzroy, and left her and eight other women and four other men playing at brag. He would fain have made over his honourable love upon any terms to poor Miss Beauclerc, who is very modest, and did not know at all what to do with his whispers or his hands. He then addressed himself to the Sparre, who was very well disposed to receive both, but the tide of champagne turned, he hiccupped at the reflection of his marriage, of which he is wondrous sick, and only proposed to the girl to shut themselves up and rail at the world for three weeks. If all the adventures don't conclude as you expect at the beginning of a paragraph, you must not wonder, for I am not making a history, but relating one strictly as it happened, and I think with full entertainment enough to content you. At last we assembled in our booth, Lady Caroline in the front with the vizor of her hat erect, and looking gloriously jolly and handsome. She had fetched my brother Orford from the next box where he was enjoying himself with his Norsa and his *petite partie*, to help us mince chickens: we minced seven chickens into a china dish, which Lady C. stewed over a lamp with three pats of butter and a flagon of water, stirring, and rattling and laughing, and we every minute expecting to have the dish fly about our ears. She had brought Betty the fruit girl with hampers of strawberries and cherries from Rogers's, and made her wait upon us, and then made her sup by us at a little table. The conversation was no less lively than the whole transaction—There is a Mr Obrien arrived from Ireland who would get the Duchess of Manchester from Mr Hussey, if she were still at liberty. I took up the biggest hautboy in the dish, and said to Lady Car., 'Madam, Miss Ashe desires you will eat this Obrien-strawberry'; she replied immediately, 'I won't, you Hussey!'—You may imagine the laugh this reply occasioned—after the tempest was a little calmed, the Pollard said, 'Now how anybody would spoil this story that was to repeat it, and say, I won't you jade!'—In short the whole air of our party was sufficient as you will easily imagine to take up the whole attention of the garden, so much so, that from eleven o'clock till half an hour after one, we had the whole concourse round our booth; at last they came into the little gardens of each booth on the sides of ours, till Harry Vane took up a bumper and drank their healths, and was proceeding to treat them with still greater freedom. It was three o'clock before we got home—I think I have told you the chief passages. Lord Granby's temper had been a little ruffled the night before, the Prince had invited him and Dick Lyttelton to Kew, where he won eleven hundred pound of the latter and eight of the former, then cut, and told them he would play with them no longer, for he saw they played so idly, that they were capable of *losing more than they would like!*

Adieu! I expect in return for this long tale, that you tell me some of your frolics with Robin Cursemother, and some of Miss Marjoram's bon mots.

Yours ever,

H. W.

PS. Dr Middleton[1] called on me yesterday; he is come to town to consult his physician for a jaundice and swelled legs, symptoms which the doctor tells him and which he believes can be easily cured: I think him visibly broke and near his end. He lately ad-

1. Conyers Middleton (1683–1750), librarian of Cambridge University and a major influence on HW there.

vised me to marry, on the sense of his own happiness, but if anybody had advised him to the contrary at his time of life, I believe he would not have broke so fast.

To Sir Horace Mann, 12 June 1753

Strawberry Hill, June 12th, 1753.

I could not rest any longer with the thought of your having no idea of a place of which you hear so much, and therefore desired Mr Bentley to draw you as much idea of it, as the post would be persuaded to carry from Twickenham to Florence. The enclosed enchanted little landscape then is Strawberry Hill; and I will try to explain so much of it to you as will help to let you know whereabouts we are, when we are talking to you, for it is uncomfortable in so intimate a correspondence as ours, not to be exactly master of every spot where one another is writing or reading or sauntering. This view of the castle is what I have just finished, and is the only side that will be at all regular. Directly before it is an open grove, through which you see a field which is bounded by a serpentine wood of all kind of trees and flowering shrubs and flowers. The lawn before the house is situated on the top of a small hill, from whence to the left you see the town and church of Twickenham encircling a turn of the river, that looks exactly like a seaport in miniature. The opposite shore is a most delicious meadow, bounded by Richmond Hill which loses itself in the noble woods of the park to the end of the prospect on the right, where is another turn of the river and the suburbs of Kingston as luckily placed as Twickenham is on the left; and a natural terrace on the brow of my hill, with meadows of my own down to the river, commands both extremities. Is not this a tolerable prospect? You must figure that all this is perpetually enlivened by a navigation of boats and barges, and by a road below my terrace, with coaches, post-chaises, wagons and horsemen constantly in motion, and the fields speckled with cows, horses and sheep. Now you shall walk into the house. The bow-window below leads into a little parlour hung with a stone-colour Gothic paper and Jackson's Venetian prints, which I could never endure while they pretended, infamous as they are, to be after Titian etc. but when I gave them this air of barbarous bas-reliefs, they succeeded to a miracle: it is impossible at first sight not to conclude that they contain the history of Attila or Tottila, done about the very era. From hence under two gloomy arches, you come to the hall and staircase, which it is impossible to describe to you, as it is the most particular and chief beauty of the castle. Imagine the walls covered with (I call it paper, but it is really paper painted in perspective to represent) Gothic fretwork: the lightest Gothic balustrade to the staircase, adorned with antelopes (our supporters) bearing shields; lean windows fattened with rich saints in painted glass, and a vestibule open with three arches on the landing place, and niches full of trophies of old coats of mail, Indian shields made of rhinoceros's hides, broadswords, quivers, long bows, arrows and spears—all *supposed* to be taken by Sir Terry Robsart in the holy wars. But as none of this regards the enclosed drawing, I will pass to that. The room on the ground floor nearest to you is a bedchamber, hung with yellow paper and prints, framed in a new manner invented by Lord Cardigan, that is, with black and white borders printed. Over this is Mr Chute's bedchamber, hung with red in the same manner. The bow-window room one pair of stairs is not yet finished; but in the tower beyond it is the charming closet where I am now writing to you. It is hung with green paper and water-colour pictures; has two windows; the one in the drawing looks to the garden, the other to the beautiful prospect; and the top of each glutted with the richest painted glass of the arms of England, crimson roses, and twenty other pieces of green, purple, and historic bits. I must tell you by the way, that the castle, when finished, will have two and thirty windows enriched with painted glass. In this closet, which is Mr Chute's college of arms, are two presses with books of heraldry and antiquities, Madame Sévigné's letters, and any French books that relate to her and her acquaintance. Out of this closet is the room where we always live, hung with a blue and white paper in stripes adorned with festoons, and a thousand plump chairs, couches and luxurious settees covered with linen of the same pattern, and with a bow-window commanding the prospect, and gloomed with limes that shade half each window, already darkened with painted glass in chiaroscuro, set in deep blue glass. Under this room is a cool little hall where we generally dine, hung with paper to imitate Dutch tiles.

I have described so much, that you will begin to think that all the accounts I used to give you of the diminutiveness of our habitation were fabulous; but it is really incredible how small most of the rooms are. The only two good chambers I shall have, are not yet built; they will be an eating-room and a library, each 20 by 30, and the latter 15 feet high. For the rest of the house, I could send it you in this letter as easily as the drawing, only that I should have nowhere to live till the return of the post. The Chinese summer house which you may distinguish in the distant landscape, belongs to my Lord Radnor. We pique ourselves upon nothing but simplicity, and have no carvings, gildings, paintings, inlayings or tawdry businesses.

You will not be sorry I believe by this time to have done with Strawberry Hill, and to hear a little news. The end of a very dreaming session has been extremely enlivened by an accidental bill which has opened great quarrels, and those not unlikely to be attended with interesting circumstances. A bill to prevent clandestine marriages, so drawn by the judges as to clog all matrimony in general, was inadvertently espoused by the Chancellor, and having been strongly attacked in the House of Commons by Nugent, the Speaker, Mr Fox and others, the last went very great lengths of severity on the whole body of the law, and on its chieftain in particular, which however at the last reading, he softened and explained off extremely. This did not appease; but on the return of the bill to the House of Lords, where our amendments were to be read, the Chancellor in the most personal terms harangued against Fox, and concluded with saying that 'he despised his scurrility as much as his adulation and recantation.' As Christian charity is not one of the oaths taken by privy councillors, and as it is not the most eminent virtue in either of the champions, this quarrel is not likely to be soon reconciled. There are natures whose disposition it is to patch up political breaches, but whether they will succeed, or try to succeed in healing this, can I tell you?

The match for Lord Granville which I announced to you, is not concluded: his rampant flames are cooled in that quarter as well as in others.

I begin a new sheet to you, which does not match with the other, for I have no more of the same paper here. Dr Cameron is executed,[1] and died with the greatest firmness. His parting with his wife the night before, was heroic, and tender: he let her stay till the last moment, when being aware that the gates of the Tower would be locked, he told her so; she fell at his feet in agonies: he said, 'Madam, this was not what you promised me' and embracing her, forced her to retire: then with the same coolness, looked at the window till her coach was out of sight; after which he turned about and wept. His only concern seemed to be at the ignominy of Tyburn: he was not disturbed at the dresser for his body, or at the fire to burn his bowels. The crowd was so great, that a friend who attended him, could not get away, but was forced to stay and behold the execution—but what will you say to the minister or priest who accompanied him? The wretch, after taking leave, went into a landau, where not content with seeing the Doctor hanged, he let down the top of the landau for the better convenience of seeing him embowelled! I cannot tell you positively that what I hinted of this Cameron being commissioned from Prussia was true; but so it is believed. Adieu! my dear child; I think this is a very tolerable letter for summer!

To Richard Bentley, September 1753

Arlington Street, September, 1753.

My Dear Sir,

I am going to send you another volume of my travels; I don't know whether I shall not, at last, write a new *Camden's Britannia;*

1. Dr. Archibald Cameron (1707–53), Jacobite.

but lest you should be afraid of my itinerary, I will at least promise you that it shall not be quite so dry as most surveys, which contain nothing but lists of impropriations and glebes, and carucates, and transcripts out of Domesday, and tell one nothing that is entertaining, describe no houses nor parks, mention no curious pictures, but are fully satisfied if they inform you that they believe that some nameless old tomb belonged to a knight-templar, or one of the crusado, because he lies crossed-legged. Another promise I will make you is, that my love of abbeys shall not make me hate the Reformation till that makes me grow a Jacobite, like the rest of my antiquarian predessors; of whom, Dart in particular wrote Billingsgate against Cromwell and the regicides; and Sir Robert Atkins concludes his summary of the Stuarts with saying, *that it is no reason, because they have been so, that this family should always continue unfortunate.*

I have made my visit at Hagley, as I intended. On my way I dined at Park Place, and lay at Oxford. As I was quite alone, I did not care to see anything; but as soon as it was dark, I ventured out, and the moon rose as I was wandering among the colleges, and gave me a charming venerable Gothic scene, which was not lessened by the monkish appearance of the old fellows stealing to their pleasures. Birmingham is large, and swarms with people and trade, but did not answer my expectation from any beauty in it: yet, new as it is, I perceived how far I was got back from the London hegira; for every ale-house is here written *mug-house,* a name one has not heard of since the riots in the late King's time.

As I got into Worcestershire, I opened upon a landscape of country which I prefer even to Kent, which I had reckoned the most beautiful county in England: but this, with all the richness of Kent, is bounded with mountains. Sir George Lyttelton's house is immeasurably bad and old: one room at the top of the house, which was reckoned a *conceit* in those days, projects a vast way into the air. There are two or three curious pictures, and some of them extremely agreeable to me for their relation to Grammont: there is *le sérieux Lyttelton,* but too old for the date of that book; Mademoiselle Stuart, Lord Brouncker, and Lady Southesk; besides, a portrait of Lord Clifford the treasurer, with his staff, but drawn in armour (though no soldier) out of flattery to Charles II, as he said the most glorious part of his life was attending the King at the battle of Worcester. He might have said, that it was as *glorious* as any part of his Majesty's life. You might draw, but I can't describe, the enchanting scenes of the park: it is a hill of three miles, but broke into all manner of beauty; such lawns, such wood, rills, cascades, and a thickness of verdure quite to the summit of the hill, and commanding such a vale of towns, and meadows, and woods extending quite to the Black Mountain in Wales, that I quite forgot my favourite Thames! Indeed, I prefer nothing to Hagley but Mount Edgecumbe. There is extreme taste in the park: the seats are not the best, but there is not one absurdity. There is a ruined castle, built by Miller, that would get him his freedom even of Strawberry: it has the true rust of the Barons' Wars. Then there is a scene of a small lake, with cascades falling down such a Parnassus! with a circular temple on the distant eminence; and there is such a fairy dale, with more cascades gushing out of rocks! and there is a hermitage, so exactly like those in Sadeler's prints, on the brow of a shady mountain, stealing peeps into the glorious world below! and there is such a pretty well under a wood, like the Samaritan woman's in a picture of Nicolò Poussin! and there is such a wood without the park, enjoying such a prospect! and there is such a mountain on t'other side of the park commanding all prospects, that I wore out my eyes with gazing, my feet with climbing, and my tongue and my vocabulary with commending! The best notion I can give you of the satisfaction I showed, was, that Sir George proposed to carry me to dine with my Lord Foley; and when I showed reluctance, he said, 'Why, I thought you did not mind any strangers, if you were to see anything!' Think of my not minding strangers! I mind them so much, that I missed seeing Hartlebury Castle, and the Bishops of Worcester's chapel of painted glass there, because it was his public day when I passed by his park.—Miller has built a Gothic house in the village at Hagley for a relation of Sir George: but there he is not more than Miller; in his castle he is almost Bentley. There is a genteel tomb in the church to Sir George's first wife, with a Cupid and a pretty urn in the Roman style.

You will be diverted with my distresses at Worcester. I set out boldly to walk down the High Street to the cathedral: I found it much more peopled than I intended, and, when I was quite embarked, discovered myself up to the ears in a contested election. A new candidate had arrived the night before, and turned all their heads. Nothing comforted me, but that the opposition is to Mr. Trevis; and I purchased my passage very willingly with crying, 'No Trevis! No Jews!' However, the inn where I lay was Jerusalem itself, the very headquarters where Trevis the Pharisee was expected; and I had scarce got into my room, before the victorious mob of his enemy, who had routed his advanced guard, broke open the gates of our inn, and almost murdered the ostler—and then carried him off to prison for being murdered.

The cathedral is pretty, and has several tombs, and clusters of light pillars of Derbyshire marble, lately cleaned. Gothicism and the restoration of that architecture, and not of the bastard breed, spreads extremely in this part of the world. Prince Arthur's tomb, from whence we took the paper for the hall and staircase, to my great surprise, is on a less scale than the paper, and is not of brass but stone, and that wretchedly whitewashed. The niches are very small, and the long slips in the middle are divided every now and then with the trefoil. There is a fine tomb for Bishop Hough, in the Westminster Abbey style; but the obelisk at the back is not loaded with a globe and a human figure, like Mr. Kent's design for Sir Isaac Newton: an absurdity which nothing but himself could surpass, when he placed three busts at the foot of an altar—and, not content with that, placed them at the very angles—where they have as little to do as they have with Shakespeare.

From Worcester I went to see Malvern Abbey. It is situated halfway up an immense mountain of that name: the mountain is very long, in shape like the prints of a whale's back: towards the larger end lies the town. Nothing remains but a beautiful gateway and a church, which is very large: every window has been glutted with painted glass, of which much remains, but it did not answer:

blue and red there is in abundance, and good faces; but the portraits are so high, I could not distinguish them. Besides, the woman who showed me the church would pester me with Christ and King David, when I was hunting for John of Gaunt and King Edward. The greatest curiosity, at least what I had never seen before, was, the whole floor and far up the sides of the church has been, if I may call it so, wainscoted with red and yellow tiles, extremely polished, and diversified with coats of arms, and inscriptions, and mosaic. I have since found the same at Gloucester, and have even been so fortunate as to purchase from the sexton about a dozen, which think what an acquisition for Strawberry! They are made of the natural earth of the country, which is a rich red clay that produces everything. All the lanes are full of all kind of trees, and enriched with large old apple-trees, that hang over from one hedge to another. Worcester city is large and pretty. Gloucester city is still better situated, but worse built, and not near so large. About a mile from Worcester you break upon a sweet view of the Severn. A little farther on the banks is Mr. Lechmere's house; but he has given strict charge to a troop of willows never to let him see the river: to his right hand extends the fairest meadow covered with cattle that ever you saw: at the end of it is the town of Upton, with a church half ruined, and a bridge of six arches, which I believe, with little trouble, he might see from his garden.

The vale increases in riches to Gloucester. I stayed two days at George Selwyn's house, called Matson, which lies on Robin Hood's Hill: it is lofty enough for an Alp, yet is a mountain of turf to the very top, has wood scattered all over it, springs that long to be cascades in twenty places of it; and from the summit it beats even Sir George Lyttelton's views, by having the city of Gloucester at its foot, and the Severn widening to the horizon. His house is small, but neat. King Charles lay here at the siege; and the Duke of York, with typical fury, hacked and hewed the window-shutters of his chamber, as a memorandum of his being there. Here is a good picture of Dudley Earl of Leicester in his later age, which he gave to Sir Francis Walsingham, at whose house in Kent it remained till removed hither; and what makes it very curious, is his age marked on it, fifty-four in 1572. I had never been able to discover before in what year he was born. And here is the very flower-pot and counterfeit association, for which Bishop Sprat was taken up, and the Duke of Marlborough sent to the Tower. The reservoirs on the hill supply the city. The late Mr. Selwyn governed the borough by them—and I believe by some wine too. The Bishop's house is pretty, and restored to the Gothic by the last Bishop. Price has painted a large chapel window for him, which is scarce inferior for colours, and is a much better picture than any of the old glass. The eating-room is handsome. As I am a Protestant Goth, I was glad to worship Bishop Hooper's room, from whence he was led to the stake: but I could almost have been a Hun, and set fire to the front of the house, which is a small pert portico, like the conveniences at the end of a London garden. The outside of the cathedral is beautifully light; the pillars in the nave outrageously plump and heavy. There is a tomb of one Abraham Blackleach, a great curiosity; for, though the figures of him and his wife are cumbent, they are very graceful, designed by Vandyck, and well executed. Kent designed the screen; but knew no more there than he did anywhere else how to enter into the true Gothic taste. Sir Christopher Wren, who built the tower of the great gateway at Christ Church, has catched the graces of it as happily as you could do: there is particularly a niche between two compartments of a window, that is a masterpiece.

But here is a *modernity,* which beats all antiquities for curiosity: just by the high altar is a small pew hung with green damask, with curtains of the same; a small corner cupboard, painted, carved, and gilt, for books in one corner, and two troughs of a bird-cage, with seeds and water. If any mayoress on earth was small enough to enclose herself in this tabernacle, or abstemious enough to feed on rape and canary, I should have swòrn that it was the shrine of the queen of the alderman. It belongs to a Mrs. Cotton, who, having lost a favourite daughter, is convinced her soul is transmigrated into a robin-red-breast; for which reason she passes her life in making an aviary of the cathedral of Gloucester.

The chapter indulge this whim, as she contributes abundantly to glaze, whitewash, and ornament the church.

King Edward the Second's tomb is very light and in good repair. The old wooden figure of Robert, the Conqueror's unfortunate eldest son, is extremely genteel, and, though it may not be so ancient as his death, is in a taste very superior to anything of much later ages. Our Lady's Chapel has a bold kind of portal, and several ceilings of chapels, and tribunes in a beautiful taste: but of all delight, is what they call the abbot's cloister. It is the very thing that you would build, when you had extracted all the quintessence of trefoils, arches, and lightness. In the church is a star-window of eight points, that is prettier than our rose-windows.

A little way from the town are the ruins of Lantony Priory: there remains a pretty old gateway, which G. Selwyn has begged, to erect on the top of his mountain, and it will have a charming effect.

At Burford I saw the house of Mr. Lenthal, the descendant of the Speaker. The front is good; and a chapel connected by two or three arches, which let the garden appear through, has a pretty effect; but the inside of the mansion is bad and ill-furnished. Except a famous picture of Sir Thomas More's family, the portraits are rubbish, though celebrated. I am told that the Speaker, who really had a fine collection, made his peace by presenting them to Cornbury, where they were well known, till the Duke of Marlborough bought that seat.

I can't go and describe so known a place as Oxford, which I saw pretty well on my return. The whole air of the town charms me; and what remains of the true Gothic *un-Gibbs'd*, and the profusion of painted glass, were entertainment enough to me. In the Picture Gallery are quantities of portraits; but in general they are not only not so much as copies, but *proxies*—so totally unlike they are to the persons they pretend to represent. All I will tell you more of Oxford is, that Fashion has so far prevailed over her collegiate sister, Custom, that they have altered the hour of dinner from twelve to one. Does not it put one in mind of reformations in religion? One don't abolish Mahommedism; one only brings it back to where the impostor himself left it.—I think it is at the South Sea House, where they have been forced to alter the hours of payment, instead of from ten to twelve, to from twelve to two; so much do even moneyed citizens sail with the current of idleness!

Was not I talking of religious sects? Methodism is quite decayed in Oxford, its cradle. In its stead, there prevails a delightful fantastic system, called the sect of the Hutchinsonians, of whom one seldom hears anything in town. After much inquiry, all I can discover is, that their religion consists in driving Hebrew to its fountain head, till they find some word or other in every text of the Old Testament, which may seem figurative of something in the New, or at least of something that may happen God knows when, in consequence of the New. As their doctrine is novel, and requires much study, or at least much invention, one should think that they could not have settled half the canon of what they are to believe—and yet they go on zealously, trying to make and succeeding in making converts.—I could not help smiling at the thoughts of *etymological salvation;* and I am sure you will smile when I tell you, that according to their gravest doctors, 'Soap is an excellent type of Jesus Christ, and the York Buildings waterworks of the Trinity.' I don't know whether this is not as entertaining as the passion of the Moravians for the 'little side-hole'! Adieu, my dear sir!

Yours ever,

HOR. WALPOLE.

TO SIR HORACE MANN, 28 January 1754

Arlington Street, Jan. 28, 1754.

'Her Serene Highness the Great Duchess Bianca Capello[1] is ar-

1. The portrait of Bianca Cappello (1548–87), Grand Duchess of Tuscany, a present to HW from Horace Mann, was by Vasari.

rived safe at a palace lately taken for her in Arlington Street: she has been much visited by the quality and gentry, and pleases universally by the graces of her person and comeliness of her deportment'— My dear child, this is the least that the newspapers would say of the charming Bianca: I who feel all the agreeableness of your manner, must say a great deal more, or should say a great deal more, but I can only commend the picture enough, not you. The head is painted equal to Titian, and though done, I suppose, after the clock had struck five and thirty, yet she retains a great share of beauty. I have bespoken a frame for her, with the grand ducal coronet at top, her story on a label at bottom, which Gray is to compose in Latin as short and expressive as Tacitus (one is lucky when one can bespeak and have executed such an inscription!) the Medici arms on one side, and the Capello's on the other. I must tell you a critical discovery of mine *à propos:* in an old book of Venetian arms, there are two coats of Capello, who from their *name* bear a *hat,* on one of them is added a flower-de-luce on a blue ball, which I am persuaded was given to the family by the Great Duke, in consideration of this alliance; the Medicis you know bore such a badge at the top of their own arms; this discovery I made by a talisman, which Mr Chute calls the *sortes Walpolianæ*, by which I find everything I want *à point nommé* wherever I dip for it. This discovery indeed is almost of that kind which I call *serendipity,* a very expressive word, which as I have nothing better to tell you, I shall endeavour to explain to you: you will understand it better by the derivation than by the definition. I once read a silly fairy tale, called *The Three Princes of Serendip*: as their highnesses travelled, they were always making discoveries, by accidents and sagacity, of things which they were not in quest of: for instance, one of them discovered that a mule blind of the right eye had travelled the same road lately, because the grass was eaten only on the left side, where it was worse than on the right—now do you understand *serendipity?* One of the most remarkable instances of this *accidental sagacity* (for you must observe that *no* discovery of a thing you *are* looking for, comes under this description) was of my Lord Shaftsbury, who happening to dine at Lord Chancellor Clarendon's, found out the marriage of the Duke of York and Mrs Hyde, by the respect with which her mother treated her at table. I will send you the inscription in my next letter; you see I endeavour to grace your present as it deserves.

Your brother would have me say something of my opinion about your idea of taking the name of *Guise;* but he has written so fully, that I can only assure you in addition, that I am stronger even than he is against it, and cannot allow of your reasoning on families, because however families may be prejudiced about them, and however foreigners (I mean *great foreigners*) here may have those prejudices too, yet they never operate here, where there is any one reason to counterbalance them. A minister who has the least disposition to promote a creature of his, and to set aside a Talbot or a Nevil, will at one breath puff away a genealogy that would reach from hence to Herenhausen. I know a *great foreigner* who always says that my Lord Denbigh is the best gentleman in England, because he is descended from the old Counts of Hapsburg; and yet my Lord Denbigh (and though he is descended from what one should think of much more consequence here, the old Counts of Denbigh) has for many years wanted a place or a pension, as much as if he were only what I think the first Count of Hapsburg was, the Emperor's butler. Your instance of the Venetians refusing to receive Valenti, can have no weight; Venice might bully a Duke of Mantua; but what would all her heralds signify against a British envoy? in short, what weight do you think family has here, when the very last minister whom we have dispatched is Sir James Gray—nay, and who has already been in a public character at Venice? his father was first a box-keeper, and then footman to James II—and this is the man exchanged against the Prince de San Severino! One of my father's maxims was, *quieta non movere;* and he was a wise man in that his day. My dear child, if you will suffer me to conclude with a pun, content yourself with your *Manhood* and Tuscany: it would be thought injustice to remove you from thence for anybody else:

bespeak & have executed such an Inscription!) the Medici-arms on one side, & the Capello's on the other. I must tell you a critical discovery of mine apropos: in an old book of Venetian arms, there are two coats of Capello, who from their name bear a hat, on one of them is added a flowerdeluce on a blue ball, which I am persuaded was given to the family by the Great Duke, in consideration of this alliance; the Medicis you know bore such a badge at the top of their own arms; This discovery I made by a talisman, which Mr Chute calls the sortes Walpolianae, by which I find every thing I want à pointe nommée where ever I dip for it. This discovery indeed is almost of that kind which I call Serendipity, a very expressive word, which as I have nothing better to tell you, I shall endeavour to explain to you: you will understand it better by the derivation than by the definition. I once read a silly fairy tale, called the three Princes of Serendip: as their Highnesses travelled, they were always making discoveries, by accidents & sagacity, of things which they were not in quest of: for instance, one of them discovered that a Mule blind of the right eye had travelled the same road lately, because the grass was eaten only on the left side, where it was worse than on the right — now do you understand Serendipity? one of the most remarkable instances of this accidental sagacity (for you must observe that no discovery of a thing you are looking for, comes under this description) was of mylord Shaftsbury, who happening to dine at Lord Chancellor Claren=don's, found out the marriage of the Duke of York & Mrs Hyde, by the res=pect with which her Mother treated her at table. I will send you the inscription in my next letter; you see I endeavour to grace your present as it deserves.

Your Brother woud have me say something of my opinion about your idea of taking the name of Guise; but he has written so fully, that I can only assure you in addition, that I am stronger even than he is against it, & cannot allow of your reasoning on families, because however families may be prejudiced ~~about~~ them, & however Foreigners (I mean Great Foreigners) here may have those prejudices too, yet they never operate here, where there is any one reason to counterbalance them. A Minister who has the least disposition to promote a creature of his, & to set aside a Talbot or a Nevil, will at one breath puff away a genealogy that woud reach from hence to Herenhausen. I know a great Foreigner who always says that mylord Denbigh is the best gentleman in England, because he is descended from the old Counts

Walpole's copy of his letter to Mann, 28 January 1754

when once you shift about, you lose the benefit of prescription, and subject yourself to a thousand accidents. I speak very seriously; I know the *carte du pays*. . . .

To Richard Bentley, 3 November 1754

Strawberry Hill, November 3, 1754.

I have finished all my parties, and am drawing towards a conclusion here: the Parliament meets in ten days: the House, I hear, will be extremely full—curiosity drawing as many to town as party used to do. The minister[1] in the House of Lords is a new sight in these days.

Mr. Chute and I have been at Mr. Barrett's at Belhouse; I never saw a place for which one did not wish, so totally void of faults. What he has done is in Gothic, and very true, though not up to the perfection of the Committee.[2] The hall is pretty: the great dining-room hung with good family pictures; among which is his ancestor, the Lord Dacre who was hanged. I remember when Barrett was first initiated to the College of Arms by the present Dean of Exeter at Cambridge, he was overjoyed at the first ancestor he put up, who was one of the murderers of Thomas Becket. The chimney-pieces, except one little miscarriage into total Ionic (he could not resist statuary and Siena marble) are all of a good King James the First Gothic. I saw the heronry so fatal to Po Yang, and told him that I was persuaded they were descended from Becket's assassin, and I hoped from my Lord Dacre too. He carried us to see the famous plantations and buildings of the last Lord Petre. They are the Brobdingnag of bad taste. The unfinished house is execrable, massive, and split through and through: it stands on the brow of a hill, rather to see *for* a prospect than to see one, and turns its back upon an outrageous avenue, which is closed with a screen of tall trees, because he would not be

1. The Duke of Newcastle. (HW's note)

2. The Committee of Taste, formed by Walpole to remodel Strawberry Hill. Its members were Bentley, Chute, and Walpole himself.

at the expense of beautifying the back front of his house. The clumps are gigantic, and very ill placed.

George Montagu and the Colonel have at last been here, and have screamed with approbation through the whole *Cu*-gamut.[1] Indeed, the library is delightful. They went to the Vine, and approved as much. Do you think we wished for you? I carried down incense and mass-books, and we had most Catholic enjoyment of the chapel. In the evenings, indeed, we did *touch a card*[2] a little to please George—so much, that truly I have scarce an idea left that is not spotted with clubs, hearts, spades, and diamonds. There is a vote of the Strawberry Committee for great embellishments to the chapel, of which it will not be long before you hear something. It will not be longer than the spring, I trust, before you see something of it. In the mean time, to rest your impatience, I have enclosed a scratch of mine, which you are to draw out better, and try if you can give yourself a perfect idea of the place. All I can say is, that my sketch is at least more intelligible than Gray's was of Stoke,[3] from which you made so like a picture.

Thank you much for the box of Guernsey lilies, which I have received. I have been packing up a few seeds, which have little merit but the merit they will have with you, that they come from the Vine and Strawberry. My chief employ in this part of the world, except surveying my library, which has scarce anything but the painting to finish, is planting at Mrs. Clive's,[4] whither I remove all my superabundancies. I have lately planted the green lane, that leads from her garden to the common: 'Well,' said she, 'when it is done, what shall we call it?' 'Why,' said I, 'what would you call it but Drury Lane?' I mentioned desiring some samples of your Swiss's[5] abilities: Mr. Chute and I even propose, if he should

1. Mr. George Montagu, who used many odd expressions, called his own family, the Montagu's, the *Cu's.* (HW's note)

2. An expression of Mr. Montagu's. (HW's note)

3. A sketch of Stoke Manor House, from which Bentley made his design in illustration of *The Long Story*, Gray's poem.

4. Catherine Raftor Clive, the actress, who lived in Little Strawberry Hill.

5. Mr. Müntz, a Swiss painter. (HW's note)

be tolerable, and would continue reasonable, to tempt him over hither, and make him work upon your designs—upon which, you know, it is not easy to make you work. If he improves upon our hands, do you think we shall purchase the fee-simple of him for so many years, as Mr. Smith did of Canaletti? We will sell to the English. Can he paint perspectives, and cathedral-aisles, and holy glooms? I am sure you could make him paint delightful insides of the chapel at the Vine and of the library here. I never come up the stairs without reflecting how different it is from its primitive state, when my Lady Townshend, all the way she came up the stairs, cried out, 'Lord God! Jesus! what a house! It is much such a house as a parson's, where the children lie at the feet of the bed!' I can't say that to-day it puts me much in mind of another speech of my lady's, 'That it would be a very pleasant place, if Mrs. Clive's face did not rise upon it and make it so hot!' The sun and Mrs. Clive seem gone for the winter.

The West Indian war has thrown me into a new study: I read nothing but American voyages, and histories of plantations and settlements. Among all the Indian nations, I have contracted a particular intimacy with the Ontaouanoucs, a people with whom I beg you will be acquainted: they pique themselves upon speaking the purest dialect. How one should delight in the grammar and dictionary of their Crusca! My only fear is, that if any of them are taken prisoners, General Braddock is not a kind of man to have proper attentions to so polite a people; I am even apprehensive that he would damn them, and order them to be scalped, in the very worst plantation-accent. I don't know whether you know that none of the people of that immense continent have any labials: they tell you *que c'est ridicule* to shut the lips in order to speak. Indeed, I was as barbarous as any polite nation in the world, in supposing that there was nothing worth knowing among these charming savages. They are in particular great orators, with this little variation from British eloquence, that at the end of every important paragraph, they make a present; whereas we expect to receive one. They begin all their answers with recapitulating what has been said to them; and their method for this is, the respondent gives a little stick to each of the bystanders, who is, for his share, to remember such a paragraph of the speech that is to be answered. You will wonder that I should have given the preference to the Ontaouanoucs, when there is a much more extraordinary nation to the north of Canada, who have but one leg, and p—— from behind their ear; but I own I had rather converse for any time with people who speak like Mr. Pitt, than with a nation of jugglers, who are only fit to go about the country, under the direction of Taafe and Montagu. Their existence I do not doubt; they are recorded by Père Charlevoix, in his much-admired history of New France, in which there are such outrageous legends of miracles for the propagation of the Gospel, that his fables in natural history seem strict veracity.

Adieu! You write to me as seldom as if you were in an island where the Duke of Newcastle was sole minister, parties at an end, and where everything had done happening.

Yours ever,
HOR. WALPOLE.

P.S. I have just seen in the advertisements that there are arrived two new volumes of Madame de Sévigné's *Letters.* Adieu, my American studies;—adieu, even my favorite Ontaouanoucs!

To Richard Bentley, 23 February 1755

Arlington Street, Feb. 23, 1755.

My dear Sir—Your *Argosie* is arrived safe; thank you for shells, trees, cones; but above all, thank you for the landscape. As it is your first attempt in oils, and has succeeded so much beyond my expectation (and being against my advice too, you may believe the sincerity of my praises) I must indulge my Vasarihood, and write a dissertation upon it. You have united and mellowed your colours, in a manner to make it look like an old picture; yet there is something in the tone of it that is not quite right. Mr. Chute thinks that you should have exerted more of your force in tipping with light the edges on which the sun breaks; my own opinion is, that the result of the whole is not natural, by your having joined a Claude Lorrain summer sky to a wintry sea, which you have drawn from the life. The water breaks finely, but the distant hills are too strong, and the outlines much too hard. The greatest fault is the trees (not apt to be your stumbling-block): they are not of a natural green, have no particular resemblance, and are out of all proportion too large for the figures. Mend these errors, and work away in oil. I am impatient to see some Gothic ruins of your painting. This leads me naturally to thank you for the sweet little *cul-de-lampe* to the *Entail:* it is equal to anything you have done in perspective and for taste; but the boy is too large.

For the block of granite I shall certainly think a louis well bestowed—provided I do but get the block, and that you are sure it will be equal to the sample you sent me. My room remains in want of a table; and as it will take so much time to polish it, I do wish you would be a little expeditious in sending it.

I have but frippery news to tell you; no politics; for the rudiments of a war, that is not to be a war, are not worth detailing. In short, we have acted with spirit, have got ready thirty ships of the line, and conclude that the French will not care to examine whether they are well manned or not. The House of Commons *bears* nothing but elections; the Oxfordshire till seven at night three times a week: we have passed ten evenings on the Colchester election, and last Monday sat upon it till near two in the morning. Whoever stands a contested election, and pays for his seat, and attends the first session, surely buys the other six very dear!

The great event is the catastrophe of Sir John Bland, who has *flirted* away his whole fortune at hazard. He t'other night exceeded what was lost by the late Duke of Bedford, having at one period of the night (though he recovered the greatest part of it) lost two-and-thirty thousand pounds. The citizens put on their double-channeled pumps and trudge to St. James's Street, in expectation of seeing judgements executed on White's—angels with flaming swords, and devils flying away with dice-boxes, like the prints in Sadeler's Hermits. Sir John lost this immense sum to a Captain Scott, who at present has nothing but a few debts and his commission.

Garrick has produced a detestable English opera, which is crowded by all true lovers of their country. To mark the opposition to Italian operas, it is sung by some cast singers, two Italians and a French girl, and the chapel boys; and to regale us with sense, it is Shakespeare's *Midsummer Night's Dream*, which is forty times more nonsensical than the worst translation of any Italian opera-books.—But such sense and such harmony are irresistible!

I am at present confined with a cold, which I caught by going to a fire in the middle of the night, and in the middle of the snow, two days ago. About five in the morning Harry waked me with a candle in his hand, and cried, 'Pray, your honour, don't be frightened!'—'No, Harry, I am not: but what is it that I am not to be frightened at?'—'There is a great fire here in St. James's Street.'—I rose, and indeed thought all St. James's Street was on fire, but it proved in Bury Street. However, you know I can't resist going to a fire; for it is certainly the only horrid sight that is fine. I slipped on my slippers, and an embroidered suit that hung on the chair, and ran to Bury Street, and stepped into a pipe that was broken up for water.—It would have made a picture—the horror of the flames, the snow, the day breaking with difficulty through so foul a night, and my figure, party per *pale*, mud and gold. It put me in mind of Lady Margaret Herbert's providence, who asked somebody for a *pretty* pattern for a nightcap. 'Lord!' said they, 'what signifies the pattern of a nightcap?'—'Oh! child,' said she, 'but you know, in case of fire.' There were two houses burnt, and a poor maid; an officer jumped out of window, and is much hurt, and two young beauties were conveyed out the same way in their shifts. There have been two more great fires. Alderman Belchier's house at Epsom, that belonged to the Prince, is burnt, and Beckford's fine house in the country, with pictures and furniture to a great value. He says, 'Oh! I have an odd fifty thousand pounds in a drawer: I will build it up again: it won't be above a thousand pounds apiece difference to my thirty children.' Adieu!

Yours ever,

HOR. WALPOLE.

To Richard Bentley, 15 August 1755

Strawberry Hill, August 15, 1755.

My dear Sir,—Though I wrote to you so lately, and have certainly nothing new to tell you, I can't help scribbling a line to you to-night, as I am going to Mr. Rigby's for a week or ten days, and must thank you first for the three pictures. One of them charms me, the Mount Orgueil, which is absolutely fine; the sea, and shadows upon it, are masterly. The other two I don't, at least won't, take for finished. If you please, Elizabeth Castle shall be Mr. Muntz's performance: indeed I see nothing of you in it. I do reconnoitre you in the Hercules and Nessus; but in both, your colours are dirty, carelessly dirty: in your distant hills you are improved, and not hard. The figures are too large—I don't mean in the Elizabeth Castle, for there they are neat; but the centaur, though he dies as well as Garrick can, is outrageous. Hercules and Deianira are by no means so: he is sentimental, and she most improperly sorrowful. However, I am pleased enough to beg you would continue. As soon as Mr. Muntz returns from the Vine, you shall have a supply of colours. In the mean time why give up the good old trade of drawing? Have you no Indian ink, no soot-water, no snuff, no coat of onion, no juice of anything? If you love me draw: you would if you knew the real pleasure you can give me. I have been studying all your drawings; and next to architecture and trees, I determine that you succeed in nothing better than animals. Now (as the newspapers say) the late ingenious Mr. Seymour is dead, I would recommend horses and greyhounds to you. I should think you capable of a landscape or two with delicious bits of architecture. I have known you execute the light of a torch or lanthorn so well, that if it was called Schalken, a house-keeper at Hampton Court or Windsor, or a Catherine at Strawberry Hill, would show it, and say it cost ten thousand pounds. Nay, if I could believe that you would ever execute any more designs I proposed to you, I would give you a hint for a picture that struck me t'other day in Péréfixe's *Life of Henry IV.* He says, the king was often seen lying upon a common straw-bed among the soldiers with a piece of brown bread in one hand, and a bit of charcoal in t'other, to draw an encampment, or town that he was besieging. If this is not character and a picture, I don't know what is.

I dined to-day at Garrick's: there were the Duke of Grafton, Lord and Lady Rochford, Lady Holdernesse, the crooked Mostyn, and Dabreu the Spanish minister; two regents, of which one is Lord Chamberlain, the other Groom of the Stole; and the wife of a Secretary of State. This is being *sur un assez bon ton* for a player! Don't you want to ask me how I like him? Do want, and I will tell you.—I like her exceedingly; her behaviour is all sense, and all sweetness too. I don't know how, he does not improve so fast upon me: but there is a great deal too of mimicry and burlesque. I am very ungrateful, for he flatters me abundantly; but unluckily I know it. I was accustomed to it enough when my father was first minister: on his fall I lost it all at once: and since that I have lived with Mr. Chute, who is all vehemence; with Mr. Fox, who is all disputation; with Sir Charles Williamson who has no time from flattering himself; with Gray, who does not hate to find fault with me; with Mr. Conway, who is all sincerity; and with you and Mr. Rigby, who have always laughed at me in a good-natured way. I don't know how, but I think I like all this as well—I beg his pardon, Mr. Raftor[1] does flatter me; but I should be a cormorant for praise, if I could swallow it whole as he gives it me.

Sir William Yonge, who has been extinct so long, is at last dead; and the war, which began with such a flirt of vivacity, is I think gone to sleep. General Braddock has not yet sent over to claim the surname of Americanus. But why should I take pains to show you in how many ways, I know nothing?—Why; I can tell it you in one word—why Mr. Cambridge knows nothing!—I wish you good night!

Yours ever,

HOR. WALPOLE.

1. Mrs. Clive's brother who lived with her at Little Strawberry Hill.

To Richard Bentley, 16 November 1755

Arlington Street, Nov. 16, 1755.

Never was poor invulnerable immortality so soon brought to shame! Alack! I have had the gout! I would fain have persuaded myself that it was a sprain; and, then, that it was only the gout come to look for Mr. Chute at Strawberry Hill: but none of my evasions will do! I was, certainly, lame for two days; and though I repelled it—first, by getting wet-shod, and then by spirits of camphire; and though I have since tamed it more rationally by leaving off the little wine I drank, I still know where to look for it whenever I have an occasion for a political illness.—Come, my constitution is not very much broken, when, in four days after such a mortifying attack, I could sit in the House of Commons, full as possible, from two at noon till past five in the morning, as we did but last Thursday. The new opposition attacked the Address.—Who are the new opposition?—Why, the old opposition: Pitt and the Grenvilles; indeed, with Legge instead of Sir George Lyttelton. Judge how entertaining it was to me to hear Lyttelton answer Grenville, and Pitt Lyttelton! The debate, long and uninterrupted as it was, was a great deal of it extremely fine: the numbers did not answer to the merit: the new friends, the Duke of Newcastle and Mr. Fox, had 311 to 105. The *bon mot* in fashion is, that the staff was very good, but they wanted private men. Pitt surpassed himself, and then I need not tell you that he surpassed Cicero and Demosthenes. What a figure would they, with their formal, laboured, cabinet orations, make *vis-a-vis* his manly vivacity and dashing eloquence at one o'clock in the morning, after sitting in that heat for eleven hours! He spoke above an hour and a half, with scarce a bad sentence: the most admired part was a comparison he drew of the two parts of the new administration, to the conflux of the Rhône and the Saône; 'the latter a gentle, feeble, languid stream, languid but not deep; the other a boisterous and overbearing torrent; but they join at last; and long may they continue united, to the comfort of each other, and to the glory, honour, and happiness of this nation!' I hope you are not mean-spirited enough to dread an invasion, when the senatorial contests are reviving in the temple of Concord.—*But will it make a party?* Yes, truly; I never saw so promising a prospect. Would not it be cruel, at such a period to be laid up?

I have only had a note from you to promise me a letter; but it is not arrived:—but the partridges are, and well; and I thank you.

England seems *returning:* for those who are not in Parliament, there are nightly riots at Drury Lane, where there is an anti-Gallican party against some French dancers. The young men of quality have protected them till last night, when, being Opera night, the galleries were victorious.

Montagu writes me many kind things for you: he is in Cheshire, but comes to town this winter. Adieu! I have so much to say, that I have time to say but very little.

Yours ever,

HOR. WALPOLE.

P.S. George Selwyn hearing much talk of a sea-war or a continent, said, 'I am for a sea-war and a *continent* admiral.'

TO THE EARL OF STRAFFORD, 6 June 1756

Strawberry Hill, June 6, 1756.

My dear Lord,

I am not sorry to be paving my way to Wentworth Castle by a letter, where I suppose you are by this time, and for which I waited: it is not that I stayed so long before I executed my embassy *auprès de milord* Tylney. He has but one pair of gold pheasants at present, but promises my Lady Strafford the first fruits of their loves. He gave me hopes of some pied peacocks sooner, for which I asked directly, as one must wait for the lying-in of the pheasants. If I go on *negotiating* so successfully, I may hope to arrive at a peerage a little sooner than my uncle has.

As your Lordship, I know, is so good as to interest yourself in the calamities of your friends, I will, as shortly as I can, describe and grieve your heart with a catastrophe that has happened to two of them. My Lady A[ilesbury], Mr Conway, and Miss Rich passed two days last week at Strawberry Hill. We were returning from Mrs Clive's through the long field, and had got over the high stile that comes into the road, that is, three of us. It had rained, and the stile was wet. I could not let Miss Rich straddle across so damp a palfrey; but took her in my arms to lift her over. At that instant I saw a coach and six come thundering down the hill from my house; and hurrying to set down my charge, and stepping backwards, I missed the first step, came down headlong with the nymph in my arms: but turning quite round as we rushed to the ground, the first thing that touched the earth was Miss Rich's head. You must guess in how improper a situation we fell; and you must not tell my Lady Strafford before anybody, that every petticoat, etc. in the world were canted—high enough indeed! The coach came on, and never stopped. The apprehension that it would run over my Chloe, made me lie where I was, holding out my arm to keep off the horses, which narrowly missed trampling us to death. The ladies, who were Lady Holderness, Miss Pelham, and your sister Lady M[ary] C[oke], stared with astonishment at the theatre which they thought I had chosen to celebrate our loves; the footmen laughed; and you may imagine the astonishment of Mr Conway and Lady A[ilesbury], who did not see the fall, but turned and saw our attitude. It was these spectators that amazed Miss Pelham, who described the adventure to Mrs Pitt, and said, 'What was most amazing, there was Mr. Conway and Lady A[ilesbury] looking on!' I shall be vexed to have told you this long story, if Lady Mary has writ it already; only tell me honestly if she had described it as decently as I have.

If you have not got the new letters and mémoires of Madame Maintenon, I beg I may recommend them for your summer reading. As far as I have got, which is but into the fifth volume of the letters, I think you will find them very curious, and some very entertaining. The fourth volume has persuaded me of the sincerity of her devotion; and two or three letters at the beginning of my present tome have made me even a little jealous for my adored Madame de Sévigné. I am quite glad to find that they do *not* continue equally agreeable.—The extreme misery to which France was reduced at the end of Queen Anne's war, is more striking than one could conceive. I hope it is a debt that they are not going to pay, though the news that arrived on Wednesday have but a black aspect.—The consternation on the behaviour of Byng, and on the amazing council of war at Gibraltar, is extreme: many think both next to impossibilities. In the meantime we fear the loss of Minorca! I could not help smiling t'other day at two passages in Madame Maintenon's letters relating to the Duc de Richelieu, when he first came into the world: 'Jamais homme n'a mieux réussi à la cour, la première fois qu'il y a paru: c'est réellement une très jolie créature!' Again:—'C'est la plus aimable poupée qu'on puisse voir.' How mortifying, that this *jolie poupée* should be the avenger of the Valoises!

Adieu, my Lord!—I don't believe that a daughter of the Duke of Argyle will think that the present I have announced in the first part of my letter balances the inglorious article in the end. I wish you would both renew the breed of heroes, which seems scarcer than that of gold pheasants!

Your most faithful servant,

Hor. Walpole

To the Hon. Henry Seymour Conway, 12 February 1756

Arlington Street, Feb. 12, 1756.

I will not write to my Lady Ailesbury to-night, nor pretend to answer the prettiest letter in the world, when I am out of spirits. I am very unhappy about poor Mr. Mann,[1] who I fear is in a deep

1. Galfridus Mann, brother of Horace. He died shortly after this.

consumption: the doctors do not give him over, and the symptoms are certainly a little mended this week; but you know how fallacious that distemper is, and how unwise it would be to trust to it! As he is at Richmond, I pass a great deal of my time out of town to be near him, and so may have missed some news; but I will tell you all I know.

The House of Commons is dwindled into a very dialogue between Pitt and Fox—one even begins to want Admiral Vernon again for variety. Sometimes it is a little *piquant;* in which though Pitt has attacked, Fox has generally had the better. These three or four last days we have been solely upon the Pennsylvanian regiment, bickering, and but once dividing, 165 to 57. We are got but past the first reading yet. We want the French to put a little vivacity into us. The Duke of Newcastle has expected them every hour: he was terribly alarmed t'other night; on his table he found a mysterious card with only these words, *Charles is very well, and is expected in England every day*. It was plainly some friend that advertised him of the Pretender's approaching arrival. He called up all the servants, ransacked the whole house, to know who had been in his dressing-room:—at last it came out to be an answer from the Duchess of Queensberry to the Duchess of Newcastle about Lord Charles Douglas. Don't it put you in mind of my Lord Treasurer Portland in Clarendon, *Remember Cesar!*

The French have promised letters of *noblesse* to whoever fits out even a little privateer. I could not help a melancholy smile when my Lady Ailesbury talked of coming over soon. I fear major-general *you* will scarce be permitted to return to your plough at Park Place, when we grudge every man that is left at the plough. Between the French and the earthquakes,[1] you have no notion how good we are grown; nobody makes a suit of clothes now but of sackcloth turned up with ashes. The fast was kept so devoutly, that Dick Edgecumbe, finding a very lean hazard at White's, said with a sigh, 'Lord, how the times are degenerated! Formerly a fast

1. The dreadful earthquake which had taken place at Lisbon towards the end of the preceding year. (HW's note)

would have brought everybody hither; now it keeps everybody away!' A few nights before, two men walking up the Strand, one said to t'other, 'Look how red the sky is! Well, thank God! there is to be no masquerade!' . . .

The Duchess of Norfolk opened her new house: all the earth was there last Tuesday. You would have thought there had been a comet, everybody was gaping in the air and treading on one another's toes. In short, you never saw such a scene of magnificence and taste. The tapestry, the embroidered bed, the illumination, the glasses, the lightness and novelty of the ornaments, and the ceilings, are delightful. She gives three Tuesdays, would you could be at one! Somebody asked my Lord Rockingham afterwards at White's what was there? He said, 'Oh! there was all the company afraid of the Duchess, and the Duke afraid of all the company.'—It was not a bad picture. . . .

You would laugh if you saw in the midst of what trumpery I am writing. Two porters have just brought home my purchases from Mrs. Kennon the mid-wife's sale: Brobdingnag combs, old broken pots, pans, and pipkins, a lantern of scraped oyster-shells, scimitars, Turkish pipes, Chinese baskets, etc., etc. My servants think my head is turned: I hope not: it is all to be called the personal estate and movables of my great-great-grandmother, and to be deposited at Strawberry. I believe you think my letter as strange a miscellany as my purchases.

Yours ever,

HOR. WALPOLE.

P.S. I forgot that I was outbid for Oliver Cromwell's nightcap.

TO GEORGE MONTAGU, 14 October 1756

Strawberry Hill, Oct. 14, 1756.

I shall certainly not bid for the chariot for you; do you estimate an old Dowager's new machine but at ten pound? You could scarce have valued herself at less! It is appraised here at fifty.

There are no family pictures but such as you might buy at any perpe[tu]al sale, that is, there are three portraits without names. If you had offered ten pounds for a set of *Pelhams,* perhaps I should not have thought you had underprized them.

You bid me give you some account of myself; I can in very few words: I am quite alone; in the morning I view a new pond I am making for goldfish, and stick in a few shrubs or trees wherever I can find a space, which is very rare: in the evening I scribble a little;[1] all this mixed with reading, that is, I can't say I read much, but I pick up a good deal of reading. The only thing I have done that can compose a paragraph, and which I think you are Whig enough to forgive me, is, that on each side of my bed I have hung the *Magna Charta*, and the warrant for King Charles's execution, on which I have written *Major Charta*, as I believe without the latter the former by this time would be of very little importance. You will ask where Mr Bentley is; confined with five sick Infantas, who live in spite of the epidemic distemper and as if they were Infantas, and in bed himself with a fever and the same sore throat, though he sends me word he mends.

The King of Prussia has sent us over a victory; which is very kind, as we are not likely to get any of our own—not even by the secret expedition which you apprehend, and which I believe still less than I did the invasion—perhaps indeed there may be another port on the coast of France, which we hope to discover as we did one in the last war. By degrees and somehow or other I believe we shall be fully acquainted with France. I saw the German letter you mention, think it very mischievous and very well written for the purpose.

You talk of being better than you have been for many months; pray, which months were they, and what was the matter with you? Don't send me your fancies; I shall neither pity nor comfort you. You are perfectly well, and always was, ever since I knew you, which is now—I won't say how long; but within this century. Thank God you have good health, and don't call it names.

John and I are just going to Garrick's with a grove of cypresses

1. On his *Memoirs of George II*.

in our hands, like the Kentish men at the conquest. He has built a temple to his master Shakespear, and I am going to adorn the outside, since his modesty would not let me decorate it within, as I proposed, with these mottoes;

Quod spiro et placeo, si placeo, tuum est.

That I spirit have and nature,
That sense breathes in ev'ry feature,
That I please, if please I do,
Shakespear, all I owe to you.

Adieu!

Yours ever

H. W.

To John Chute, 12 July 1757

Strawberry Hill, July 12, 1757.

It would be very easy to persuade me to a *Vine-voyage,*[1] without your being so indebted to me, if it were possible. I shall represent my impediments, and then you shall judge. I say nothing of the heat of this magnificent weather, with the glass yesterday up to three-quarters of sultry. In all English probability this will not be a hindrance long: though at present, so far from travelling, I have made the tour of my own garden but once these three days before eight at night, and then I thought I should have died of it. For how many years we shall have to talk of the summer of fifty-seven!—But hear: my Lady Ailesbury and Miss Rich come hither on Thursday for two or three days: and on Monday next the Officina Arbuteana[2] opens in form. The Stationers' Company, that is, Mr. Dodsley, Mr. Tonson,[3] &c. are summoned to meet here on Sunday night. And with what do you think we open? *Ce-*

1. To visiting Mr. Chute at the Vine, his seat in Hampshire. (HW's note)
2. The Strawberry Hill Press.
3. James Dodsley and James Tonson, booksellers and publishers.

dite, Romani Impressores—with nothing under *Graii Carmina.*[1] I found him in town last week: he had brought his two Odes to be printed. I snatched them out of Dodsley's hands, and they are to be the first-fruits of my press. An edition of Hentznerus,[2] with a version by Mr. Bentley and a little preface of mine, were prepared, but are to wait.—Now, my dear Sir, can I stir?

Not ev'n thy virtues, tyrant, shall avail! [3]

Is not it the plainest thing in the world that I cannot go to you yet, but that you must come to me?

I tell you no news, for I know none, think of none. Elzevir, Aldus, and Stephens are the freshest personages in my memory. Unless I was appointed printer of the *Gazette*, I think nothing could at present make me read an article in it. Seriously, you must come to us and shall be witness that the first holidays we have I will return with you. Adieu!

Yours ever,

HOR. WALPOLE.

TO SIR HORACE MANN, 4 August 1757

Strawberry Hill, Aug. 4, 1757.

Mr Phelps (who is Mr Phelps?) has brought me the packet[4] safe, for which I thank you. I would fain have persuaded him to stay and dine, that I might ask him more questions about you. He told me how low your ministerial spirits are: I fear the news that came last night will not exalt them. The French attacked the Duke for three days together, and at last defeated him. I find it is called at Kensington an encounter of fourteen squadrons; but any defeat

1. Gray's odes, "The Progress of Poesy" and "The Bard," published under the title *Odes by Mr Gray*.

2. The *Journey into England* of Paul Hentzner (1558–1623), of which 220 copies were printed at the Strawberry Hill Press in 1757.

3. Line 6 of "The Bard."

4. HW's letters to Mann, returned at HW's request.

must be fatal to Hanover. I know few particulars, and those only by a messenger dispatched to me by Mr Conway on the first tidings: the Duke exposed himself extremely, but is unhurt, as they say all his small family are. In what a situation is our Prussian hero, surrounded by Austrians, French and Muscovites—even impertinent Sweden is stealing in to pull a feather out of his tail—What devout plunderers will every little Catholic prince of the Empire become! The only good I hope to extract out of this mischief is, that it will stifle our secret expedition and preserve Mr Conway from going on it: I have so ill an opinion of our secret expeditions, that I hope they will forever remain so. What a melancholy picture is there of an old monarch at Kensington, who has lived to see such inglorious and fatal days! Admiral Boscawen is disgraced— I know not the cause exactly, as ten miles out of town are a thousand out of politics—He is said to have refused to serve under Sir Edward Hawke in this armament. Shall I tell you what, more than distance, has thrown me out of attention to news? A little packet which I shall give your brother for you, will explain it. In short, I am turned printer, and have converted a little cottage here into a printing-office— My abbey is a perfect college or academy— I keep a painter[1] in the house and a printer—not to mention Mr Bentley who is an academy himself. I send you two copies (one for Dr Cocchi) of a very honourable opening of my press—two amazing odes of Mr Gray—they are Greek, they are Pindaric, they are sublime—consequently I fear a little obscure—the second particularly by the confinement of the measure and the nature of prophetic vision is mysterious; I could not persuade him to add more notes; he says whatever wants to be explained, don't deserve to be: I shall venture to place some in Dr Cocchi's copy, who need not be supposed to understand Greek and English together, though he is so much master of both separately. To divert you in the mean time I send you the following copy of a letter written by my printer[2] to a friend in Ireland. I should tell you that

1. J. H. Müntz.

2. Will Robinson, first printer to the press at Strawberry Hill (HW's note). He remained as HW's printer until he ran away in 1759 (*post* 22 June 1759).

he has the most sensible look in the world; Garrick said he would give any money for four actors with such eyes—they are more Richard III's than Garrick's own—but whatever his eyes are, his head is Irish. Looking for something I wanted in a drawer, I perceived a parcel of strange romantic words in a large hand beginning a letter—he saw me see it, yet left it, which convinces me it was left on purpose: it is the grossest flattery to me couched in most ridiculous scraps of poetry which he has retained from things he has printed—but it will best describe itself.

'Sir

I date this from shady bowers, nodding groves and amaranthine shades—close by old Father Thames's silver side— Fair Twickenham's luxurious shades—Richmond's near neighbour, where great George the King resides—you'll wonder at my prolixity—in my last I informed you that I was going into the country to transact business for a private gentleman— This gentleman is the Honourable Horatio Walpole, son to the late great Sir Robert Walpole, who is very studious, and an admirer of all the liberal arts and sciences, amongst the rest he admires printing. He has fitted out a complete printing-house at this his country seat, and has done me the favour to make me sole manager and operator (there being no one but myself) all men of genius resorts his house, courts his company and admires his understanding—what with his own and their writings, I believe I shall be pretty well employed—I have pleased him and I hope to continue so to do. Nothing can be more warm than the weather has been here, this time past, they have in London by the help of glasses, roasted in the artillery-ground fowls and quarters of lamb—the coolest day that I have felt since May last are equal to, nay far exceed the warmest I ever felt in Ireland—the place I am in now, is all my comfort, from the heat—the situation of it is close to the Thames (and is Richmond gardens, if you were ever in them) in miniature, surrounded by bowers, groves, cascades and ponds, and on a rising ground, not very common in this part of the country—the building elegant, and the furniture of a peculiar taste, magnificent and superb— He is a bachelor, and spends his time in the studious rural taste—not like his father tossed in the weather-beaten vessel of state—many people censured, but his conduct was far better, than our late pilots at the helm, and more to the interest of England—they follow his advice now, and court the assistance of Spain, instead of provoking a war, for that was ever against England's interest——'

I laughed for an hour at this picture of myself, which is much more like to the studious magician in the enchanted opera of *Rinaldo*—not but Twickenham has a romantic genteelness that would figure in a more luxurious climate— It was but yesterday that we had a new kind of auction—it was of the orange trees and plants of your old acquaintance Admiral Martin— It was one of the warm days of this jubilee summer, which appears only once in fifty years—the plants were disposed in little clumps about the lawn; the company walked to bid from one to t'other, and the auctioneer knocked down the lots on the orange tubs— Within three doors was an auction of china—you did not imagine that we were such a metropolis! Adieu!

To George Montagu, 25 August 1757

Strawberry Hill, Aug. 25th, 1757.

I did not know that you expected the pleasure of seeing the Colonel so soon: it is plain that *I* did *not* solicit leave of absence for him. Make him my many compliments. I should have been happy to have seen you and Mr John, but must not regret it as you was so agreeably prevented. You are very particular I can tell you in liking Gray's *Odes*—but you must remember that the age likes Akinside, and did like Thomson! Can the same people like both? Milton was forced to wait till the world had done admiring Quarles. Cambridge told me t'other night that my Lord Chesterfield had heard Stanley read them as his own, but that must have been a mistake of my Lord's deafness. Cambridge said, 'Perhaps they are Stanley's, and not caring to own them, he gave them to Gray.' I think this would hurt Gray's dignity ten times more than his poetry not succeeding. My humble share as his printer has been more favourably received. We proceed soberly. I must give you some account of *les amusements des eaux de Straberri.* T'other day my Lady Rochford, Lady Townshend, Miss Bland and the new Knight of the Garter dined here, and were carried into the printing-office, and were to see the man print. There were some lines ready placed, which he took off; I gave them to my Lady Townshend; here they are;

The Press speaks;
From me wits and poets their glory obtain;
Without me their wit and their verses were vain.
Stop, Townshend, and let me but *print* what you say;
You, the fame I on others bestow, will repay.

They then asked, as I foresaw, to see the man compose; I gave him four lines out of *The Fair Penitent*, which he set, but while he went to place them in the press, I made them look at something else; without their observing, and in an instant he whipped away what he had just set, and to their great surprise when they expected to see *Were ye, ye Fair*, he presented to my Lady Rochford the following lines;

The Press speaks;
In vain from your properest name you have flown,
And exchanged lovely Cupid's for Hymen's dull throne;
By my art shall your beauties be constantly sung,
And in spite of yourself you shall ever be Young.[1]

You may imagine, whatever the poetry was, that the gallantry of it succeeded.

Poor Mr Bentley has been at the extremity with a fever and inflamation in his bowels; but is so well recovered that Mr Müntz is gone to fetch him hither today.

I don't guess what sight I have to come in Hampshire, unless it is Abbotstone. I am pretty sure I have none to come at the Vine,

1. Lady Rochford's maiden name.

where I have done advising, as I see Mr Chute will never execute anything. The very altar-piece that I sent for to Italy is not placed yet. But when he could refrain from making the little Gothic columbarium for his family which I proposed and Mr Bentley had drawn so divinely, it is not probable he should do anything else.

Adieu! Yours ever

H. Walpole

To George Montagu, 2 June 1759

[Strawberry Hill] June 2d, 1759.

Strawberry Hill is grown a perfect Paphos, it is the land of beauties. On Wednesday the Duchesses of Hamilton and Richmond, and Lady Ailesbury dined there, the two latter stayed all night. There never was so pretty a sight as to see them all three sitting in the shell;[1] a thousand years hence, when I begin to grow old, if that can ever be, I shall talk of that event and tell young people how much handsomer the women of my time were than they will be then; I shall say, 'Women alter now. I remember Lady Ailesbury looking handsomer than her daughter the pretty Duchess of Richmond, as they were sitting on the shell on my terrace with the Duchess of Hamilton, one of the famous Gunnings'—Yesterday the t'other, more famous, Gunning dined there—she has made a friendship with my charming niece,[2] to disguise her jealousy of the new Countess's beauty. There were they two, their lords, Lord Buckingham and Charlotte[3]—you will think that I do not choose men for my parties so well as women—I don't include Lord Waldegrave in this bad election.

Loo is mounted to its zenith; the parties last till one and two in the morning: We played at Lady Hertford's last week, the last night of her lying-in, till deep into Sunday morning, after she and

1. The shell bench in the garden designed by Bentley.
2. Maria Walpole, recently married to Lord Waldegrave.
3. Walpole.

her lord were retired. It is now adjourned to Mrs Fitzroy's, whose child the town calls *Pam*-ela. I proposed that instead of receiving cards for assemblies, one should send in a morning to Dr Hunter's, the man-midwife, to know where there is loo that evening.

I find poor Charles Montagu is dead—is it true, as the papers say, that his son comes into Parliament?

The invasion is not half so much in fashion as loo; and the King's demanding the assistance of the militia, does not add much dignity to it. The great Pam of Parliament,[1] who made the motion, entered into a wonderful definition of the several sorts of fear; *from fear that comes from pusillanimity,* up to *fear from magnanimity*. It put me in mind of that wise Pythian my Lady Londonderry, who when her sister Lady Donegal was dying, pronounced, that if it was a *fever from a fever* she would live, but if it was a *fever from death* she would die.

Mr Mason[2] has published another drama, called *Caractacus;* there are some incantations poetical enough, and odes so Greek as to have very little meaning. But the whole is laboured, uninteresting, and no more resembling the manners of Britons than of Japanese. It is introduced by a piping elegy; for Mason, in imitation of Gray, *will cry and roar all night* without the least provocation.

Adieu! I shall be glad to hear that your Strawberry tide is fixed.

Yours ever

H. W.

To Sir Horace Mann, 13 December 1759

Arlington Street, Dec. 13, 1759.

That ever you should pitch upon me for a mechanic or geometric commission! How my own ignorance has laughed at me since I read your letter! I say, *your* letter, for as to Dr Perelli's, I know no

1. Pitt.

2. Rev. William Mason (1725–97), poet and biographer of Gray; later one of HW's major correspondents.

more of a Latin term in mathematics, than Mrs Goldsworthy[1] had an idea of verbs. I will tell you an early anecdote in my own life, and you shall judge. When I first went to Cambridge, I was to learn mathematics of the famous blind Professor Sanderson. I had not frequented him a fortnight, before he said to me, 'Young man, it is cheating you, to take your money: believe me, you never can learn these things; you have no capacity for them.'— I can smile now, but I cried then, with mortification. The next step, in order to comfort myself, was not to believe him: I could not conceive that I had not talents for anything in the world. I took, at my own expense, a private instructor, who came to me once a day for a year. Nay, I took infinite pains, but had so little capacity, and so little attention, (as I have always had to anything that did not immediately strike my inclinations) that after mastering any proposition, when the man came the next day, it was as new to me as if I had never heard of it; in short, even to common figures, I am the dullest dunce alive. I have often said it of myself, and it is true, that nothing that has not a proper name of a man or a woman to it, affixes any idea upon my mind. I could remember who was King Ethelbald's great-aunt, and not be sure whether she lived in the year 500, or 1500. I don't know whether I ever told you, that when you sent me the seven gallons of drams, and they were carried to Mr Fox by mistake for Florence wine, I pressed him to keep as much as he liked, for, said I, I have seen the bill of lading, and there is a vast quantity. He asked how much? I answered 70 gallons; so little idea I have of quantity. I will tell you one more story of myself, and you will comprehend what sort of a head I have! Mrs Leneve[2] said to me one day, 'There is a vast waste of

1. Wife of the English consul at Leghorn, where when she was learning Italian by grammar, she said, "Oh! give me a language in which there are no verbs!" concluding, as she had not learnt her own language by grammar, that there were no verbs in English. (HW's note)

2. Mrs Isabella Leneve, a gentlewoman of a very ancient family in Norfolk, who had been brought up by Lady Anne Walpole, aunt of Sir Robert Walpole, with his sister Lady Townshend, and afterwards had the care of Sir Robert's daughter Lady Maria, after whose marriage with Mr Churchill, she lived with Mr Walpole

coals in your house; you should make the servants take off the fires at night.' I recollected this as I was going to bed;—and out of *economy* put my fire out with a bottle of Bristol Water!— However, as I certainly will neglect nothing to oblige you, I went to Sisson and gave him the letter. He has undertaken both the engine and the drawing, and has promised the utmost care in both. The latter, he says, must be very large, and that it will take some time to have it performed very accurately. He has promised me both in six or seven weeks. But another time, don't imagine because I can bespeak an enamelled bauble, that I am fit to be entrusted with the direction of the machine at Marli.[1] It is not to save myself trouble, for I think nothing so for you, but I would have you have credit, and I should be afraid of dishonouring you.

There! there is the King of Prussia has turned all our war and peace topsy-turvy! If Mr Pitt will conquer Germany too, he must go and do it himself. Fourteen thousand soldiers and nine generals taken, as it were, in a partridge-net! and what is worse, I have not heard yet that the monarch owns his rashness. As often as he does indeed, he is apt to repair it. You know I have always dreaded Daun—one cannot make a blunder, but he profits of it—and this just at the moment that we heard of nothing but new bankruptcy in France—I want to know what a kingdom is to do, when it is forced to run away?

14th—Oh! I interrupt my reflections—here is another bit of victory! Prince Henry, who has already succeeded to his brother's crown, as king of the fashion, has beaten a parcel of Wirtembergers and taken four battalions—Daun is gone into Bohemia, and Dresden is still to be ours. The French are gone into winter quarters—thank God! What weather is here to be lying on the ground! Men should be statues or will be so, if they go through it. Hawke is enjoying himself in Quiberon Bay, but I believe has done no more execution. Dr Hay says, it will soon be as shameful to beat a

to her death. She had an excellent understanding and a great deal of wit. (HW's note)

1. Which conveyed the water from Marly to Versailles.

Frenchman, as to beat a woman. Indeed one is forced to ask every morning, what victory there is? for fear of missing one. We talk of a congress at Breda, and some think Lord Temple will go thither: if *he* does, I shall really believe it will be peace; and a good one, as it will then be of Mr Pitt's making.

I was much pleased that the watch succeeded so triumphantly, and *beat the French* watches, though they were two to one. For the *Fugitive Pieces;* the inscription for the column was written when I was with you at Florence, though I don't wonder that you have forgotten it after so many years. I would not have it talked of, for I find some grave personages are offended with the liberties I have taken with so imperial a head. What could provoke them to give a column christian burial? Adieu!

To George Montagu, 28 January 1760

Arlington Street, Jan. 28th, 1760.

I shall almost frighten you from coming to London, for whether you have the constitution of a horse or a man, you will be equally in danger. All the horses in town are laid up with sore throats and colds, and are so hoarse you cannot hear them speak. I with all my immortality have been half killed; that violent bitter weather was too much for me; I have had a nervous fever these six or seven weeks every night, and have taken bark enough to have made a rind for Daphne: nay, have even stayed at home two days; but I think my eternity begins to bud again. I am quite of Dr Garth's mind, who, when anybody commended a hard frost to him, used to reply, 'Yes, Sir, 'fore Gad, very fine weather, Sir, very wholesome weather; kills trees, Sir, very good for a man, Sir.' There has been cruel havoc among the ladies; my Lady Granby is dead, and the famous Polly Duchess of Bolton, and my Lady Besborough. I have no great reason to lament the last, and yet the circumstances of her death, and the horror of it to her family make one shudder. It was the same sore throat and fever that carried off four of their children a very few years ago. My Lord now fell ill of it, very ill, and the eldest daughter slightly. My Lady caught it, attending her husband, and concealed it as long as she could. When at last the physician insisted on her keeping her bed, she said as she went into her room, 'Then, Lord have mercy upon me, I shall never come out of it again,' and died in three days. Lord Besborough grew outrageously impatient at not seeing her, and would have forced into her room when she had been dead about four days—they were obliged to tell him the truth—never was an answer that expressed so much horror! He said, 'And how many children have I left?'—not knowing how far his calamity might have reached. Poor Lady Coventry is near completing this black list. You have heard I suppose a horrid story of another kind, of Lord Ferrers murdering his steward in the most barbarous and deliberate manner. He sent away all his servants but one, and like that heroic murderess Queen Christina, carried the poor man, through a gallery and several rooms, locking them after him, and then bid the man kneel down for he was determined to kill him. The poor creature flung himself at his feet but in vain, was shot and lived twelve hours. Mad as this action was, from the consequences, there was no frenzy in his behaviour. He got drunk, and at intervals talked of it coolly: but did not attempt to escape till the colliers beset his house and were determined to take him alive or dead. He is now in the jail at Leicester, and will soon be removed to the Tower, then to Westminster Hall, and I suppose to Tower-Hill; unless as Lord Talbot prophesied in the House of Lords, 'Not being thought mad enough to be shut up till he had killed somebody, he will then be thought too mad to be executed.' But that madman, Lord Talbot, was no more honoured in his vocation, than other prophets are in their own country.

As you seem amused with my entertainments, I will tell you how I passed yesterday. A party was made to go to the Magdalen-House.[1] We met at Northumberland House at five, and set out in four coaches; Prince Edward, Colonel Brudenel his groom, Lady Northumberland, Lady Mary Coke, Lady Carlisle, Miss Pelham,

1. Recently opened for reformed prostitutes.

Lady Hertford, Lord Beauchamp, Lord Huntingdon, old Bowman, and I. This new convent is beyond Goodman's Fields, and I assure you would content any Catholic alive. We were received by—oh! first, a vast mob, for princes are not so common at that end of the town as at this. Lord Hertford at the head of the Governors with their white staves met us at the door, and led the Prince directly into the chapel, where before the altar was an armchair for him, with a blue damask cushion, a prie-dieu, and a footstool of black cloth with gold nails. We sat on forms near him. There were Lord and Lady Dartmouth, in the odour of devotion, and many City ladies. The chapel is small and low, but neat, hung with Gothic paper and tablets of benefactions. At the west end were inclosed the sisterhood, above an hundred and thirty, all in greyish brown stuffs, broad handkerchiefs, and flat straw hats with a blue ribband, pulled quite over their faces. As soon as we entered the chapel, the organ played, and the Magdalens sung a hymn in parts; you cannot imagine how well. The chapel was dressed with orange and myrtle, and there wanted nothing but a little incense, to drive away the devil—or to invite him. Prayers then began, psalms, and a sermon; the latter by a young clergyman, one Dodd;[1] who contributed to the Popish idea one had imbibed, by haranguing entirely in the French style, and very eloquently and touchingly. He apostrophized the lost sheep, who sobbed and cried from their souls—so did my Lady Hertford and Fanny Pelham, till I believe the City dames took them both for Jane Shores.[2] The confessor then turned to the audience, and addressed himself to the Royal Highness, whom he called, most illustrious Prince, beseeching his protection. In short, it was a very pleasing performance, and I got *the most illustrious* to desire it might be printed. We had another hymn, and then were conducted to the *parloir,* where the Governors kissed the Prince's hand, and then

1. The celebrated forger who was later executed.

2. Jane Shore (d. 1527?), mistress of Edward IV and of Thomas Grey, 1st M. of Dorset; forced to do penance by Richard III, according to historical tradition (see, however, HW's *Historic Doubts of . . . Richard III, Works,* ii. 174). She was familiar to the eighteenth century as the heroine of a tragedy by Nicholas Rowe.

the lady abbess or matron brought us tea. From thence we went to the refectory, where all the nuns, without their hats, were ranged at long tables ready for supper. A few were handsome, many who seemed to have no title to their profession, and two or three of twelve years old: but all recovered, and looking healthy. I was struck and pleased with the modesty of two of them, who swooned away with the confusion of being stared at—one of these is a niece of Sir Clement Cotterel. We were showed their work, which is, making linen, and bead-work; they earn ten pounds a week. One circumstance diverted me, but amidst all this decorum I kept it to myself. The wands of the governors are white, but twisted at top with black and white, which put me in mind of Jacob's rods that he placed before the cattle to make them breed. My Lord Hertford would never have forgiven me if I had joked on this; so I kept my countenance very demurely, nor even inquired whether among the pensioners there were any *novices* from Mrs Naylor's.

The court-martial on Lord George Sackville is appointed; General *Onslow* is to be *Speaker* of it. Adieu! till I see you; I am glad it will be so soon.

Yours ever

H. W.

To George Montagu, 13 November 1760

Arlington Street, Nov. 13th, 1760.

Even the honeymoon of a new reign don't produce events every day. There is nothing but the common toying of addresses and kissing hands. The chief difficulty is settled; Lord Gower yields the Mastership of the Horse to Lord Huntingdon, and removes to the Great Wardrobe, from whence Sir Thomas Robinson was to have gone into Ellis's place, but he is saved, and Sir Thomas remains as lumber, not yet disposed of. The City however have a mind to be out of humour; a paper has been fixed on the Royal Exchange with these words, 'No petticoat government, no Scotch minister, no Lord George Sackville.' Two hints totally unfounded, and the other scarce true. No petticoat ever governed less; it is left at Leicester-house; Lord George's breeches are as little concerned; and except Lady Susan Stuart, and Sir Harry Erskine, nothing has yet been done for any Scots. For the King himself he seems all good-nature, and wishing to satisfy everybody. All his speeches are obliging. I saw him again yesterday, and was surprised to find the levee room had lost so entirely the air of the lion's den. This young man don't stand in one spot, with his eyes fixed royally on the ground, and dropping bits of German news. He walks about and speaks to everybody. I saw him afterwards on the throne, where he is graceful and genteel, sits with dignity, and reads his answers to addresses well. It was the Cambridge address, carried by the Duke of Newcastle in his Doctor's gown, and looking like the *médecin malgré lui.* He had been vehemently solicitous for attendance, for fear my Lord Westmoreland, who vouchsafes himself to bring the address from Oxford, should outnumber him. Lord Litchfield and several other Jacobites have kissed hands; George Selwyn says they go to St James's, because now there are so many *Stuarts* there.

Do you know I had the curiosity to go to the burying t'other night; I had never seen a royal funeral. Nay, I walked as a rag of quality,[1] which I found would be, and so it was, the easiest way of seeing it. It is absolutely a noble sight. The Prince's Chamber hung with purple and a quantity of silver lamps, the coffin under a canopy of purple velvet, and six vast chandeliers of silver on high stands had a very good effect: the ambassador from Tripoli and his son were carried to see that chamber. The procession through a line of foot-guards, every seventh man bearing a torch, the horse-guards lining the outside, their officers with drawn sabres and crape sashes, on horseback, the drums muffled, the fifes, bells tolling and minute guns, all this was very solemn. But the charm was the entrance of the Abbey, where we were received by the Dean and chapter in rich copes, the choir and almsmen all bearing torches; the whole Abbey so illuminated, that one saw it

1. That is, as an earl's younger son.

to greater advantage than by day; the tombs, long aisles, and fretted roof all appearing distinctly, and with the happiest chiaroscuro. There wanted nothing but incense, and little chapels here and there with priests saying mass for the repose of the defunct—yet one could not complain of its not being Catholic enough. I had been in dread of being coupled with some boy of ten years old—but the heralds were not very accurate, and I walked with George Grenville, taller and older enough to keep me in countenance. When we came to the chapel of Henry VII all solemnity and decorum ceased—no order was observed, people sat or stood where they could or would, the yeomen of the guard were crying out for help, oppressed by the immense weight of the coffin, the Bishop read sadly, and blundered in the prayers, the fine chapter, *Man that is born of a woman,* was chanted not read, and the anthem, besides being unmeasurably tedious, would have served as well for a nuptial. The real serious part was the figure of the Duke of Cumberland, heightened by a thousand melancholy circumstances. He had a dark brown adonis, and a cloak of black cloth with a train of five yards. Attending the funeral of a father, how little reason soever he had to love him, could not be pleasant. His leg extremely bad, yet forced to stand upon it near two hours, his face bloated and distorted with his late paralytic stroke, which has affected too one of his eyes, and placed over the mouth of the vault, into which in all probability he must himself so soon descend—think how unpleasant a situation! He bore it all with a firm and unaffected countenance. This grave scene was fully contrasted by the burlesque Duke of Newcastle—he fell into a fit of crying the moment he came into the chapel and flung himself back in a stall, the Archbishop hovering over him with a smelling bottle—but in two minutes his curiosity got the better of his hypocrisy and he ran about the chapel with his glass to spy who was or was not there, spying with one hand and mopping his eyes with t'other. Then returned the fear of catching cold, and the Duke of Cumberland, who was sinking with heat, felt himself weighed down, and turning round, found it was the Duke of Newcastle standing upon his train to avoid the chill of the marble. It was very theatric to look down into the vault, where the coffin lay, attended by mourners with lights. Clavering, the Groom of the Bedchamber, refused to sit up with the body, and was dismissed by the King's order.

I have nothing more to tell you but a trifle, a very trifle—the King of Prussia has totally defeated Marshal Daun. This which would have been prodigious news a month ago, is nothing today; it only takes its turn among the questions, 'Who is to be Groom of the Bedchamber?' 'What is Sir T. Robinson to have?' I have been at Leicester Fields today; the crowd was immoderate; I don't believe it will continue so. Good night.

Yours ever

H. W.

To Lady Mary Coke, 12 February 1761

Newmarket, Feb. 12th, 1761

You would be puzzled to guess, Madam, the reflections into which solitude and an inn have thrown me. Perhaps you will imagine that I am regretting not being at loo at Princess Emily's,[1] or that I am detesting the corporation of Lynn[2] for dragging me from the amusements of London; perhaps that I am meditating what I shall say to a set of people I never saw; or—which would be more like me, determining to be out of humour the whole time I am there, and show how little I care whether they elect me again or not. If your absolute sovereignty over me did not exclude all jealousy, you might possibly suspect that the Duchess of Grafton[3] has at least as much share in my chagrin as Pam[4] himself.

1. Princess Amelia Sophia Eleanora (1711–86), daughter of George II.

2. HW had been M.P. for King's Lynn, Norfolk, since February 1757, but he had never visited his constituency. He was now on his way to show himself to the electors before the elections of March 1761.

3. Hon. Anne Liddell (ca. 1738–1804); m. 1 (1756) Augustus Henry Fitzroy, 3d D. of Grafton (divorced, 1769); m. 2 (1769) John Fitzpatrick, 2d E. of Upper Ossory; HW's correspondent.

4. "The knave of clubs, esp. in the game of five card loo, in which this card is the highest trump" (*OED*).

Come nearer to the point, Madam, and conclude I am thinking of Lady Mary Coke—but in a style much more becoming so sentimental a lover than if I was merely concerned for your absence. In short, Madam, I am pitying you, actually pitying you! how debasing a thought for your dignity! but hear me. I am lamenting your fate; that you, with all your charms and all your merit, are not yet immortal! Is not it provoking that, with so many admirers and so many pretensions, you are likely to be adored only so long as you live? Charming, in an age when Britain is victorious in every quarter of the globe, you are not yet enrolled in the annals of its fame! Shall Wolfe[1] and Boscawen[2] and Amherst[3] be the talk of future ages, and the name of Mary Coke not be known? 'Tis the height of disgrace! When was there a nation that excelled the rest of the world whose beauties were not as celebrated as its heroes and its orators? Thais, Aspasia, Livia, Octavia—I beg pardon for mentioning any but the last when I am alluding to you—are as familiar to us as Alexander, Pericles, or Augustus; and, except the Spartan ladies, who were always locked up in the two pair of stairs making child-bed linen and round-eared caps, there never were any women of fashion in a gloriously-civilized country, but who had cards sent to invite them to the Table of Fame in common with those drudges, the men, who had done the dirty work of honour. I say nothing of Spain, where they had so true a notion of gallantry, that they never ventured having their brains knocked out, but with a view to the glory of their mistress. If her name was but renowned from Segovia to Saragossa they thought all the world knew it and were content. Nay, Madam, if you had but been lucky enough to be born in France a thousand years ago, that is fifty or sixty, you would have gone down to eternity hand in hand with Louis Quatorze; and the sun would never have

1. Maj. Gen. James Wolfe (1727–59), commander of British forces at Quebec, 1759.

2. Adm. Edward Boscawen (1711–61). He had won a decisive victory over part of the French fleet at Lagos Bay in 1759.

3. Gen. Sir Jeffrey Amherst (1717–97), K.B., Lord Amherst, commander-in-chief of British forces in North America, 1758–64.

shined on him, as it did purely for seventy years, but a ray of it would have fallen to your share. You would have helped him to pass the Rhine and been coupled with him at least in a *bout rimé.*

And what are we thinking of? Shall we suffer posterity to imagine that we have shed all this blood to engross the pitiful continent of America? Did General Clive drop from heaven only to get half as much as Wortley Montagu? yet this they must suppose, unless we immediately set about to inform them in authentic verse that your eyes and half a dozen other pair lighted up all this blaze of glory. I will take my death your Ladyship was one of the first admirers of Mr Pitt, and all the world knows that his eloquence gave this spirit to our arms. But, unluckily, my deposition can only be given in prose. I am neither a hero nor a poet, and, though I am as much in love as if I had cut a thousand throats or made ten thousand verses, posterity will never know anything of my passion. Poets alone are permitted to tell the real truth. Though an historian should, with as many asseverations as Bishop Burnet, inform mankind that the lustre of the British arms under George II was singly and entirely owing to the charms of Lady Mary Coke, it would not be believed—the slightest hint of it in a stanza of Gray would carry conviction to the end of time.

Thus, Madam, I have laid your case before you. You may, as you have done, inspire Mr Pitt with nobler orations than were uttered in the House of Commons of Greece or Rome; you may set all the world together by the ears; you may send for all the cannon from Cherbourg, all the scalps from Quebec, and for every Nabob's head in the Indies; posterity will not be a jot the wiser, unless you give the word of command from Berkeley Square in an ode, or you and I meet in the groves of Sudbrook in the midst of an epic poem. 'Tis a vexatious thought, but your Ladyship and this age of triumphs will be forgotten unless somebody writes verses worthy of you both.

I am your Ladyship's most devoted slave,

HOR. WALPOLE

To George Montagu, 25 March 1761

Houghton, March 25th, 1761.

Here I am, at Houghton! and alone! in this spot, where (except two hours last month) I have not been in sixteen years! Think, what a crowd of reflections!—No, Gray and forty churchyards could not furnish so many. Nay, I know one must feel them with greater indifference than I possess, to have patience to put them into verse. Here I am, probably for the last time of my life, though not for the last time—every clock that strikes tells me I am an hour nearer to yonder church—that church,[1] into which I have not yet had courage to enter, where lies that mother on whom I doted, and who doted on me! There are the two rival mistresses of Houghton,[2] neither of whom ever wished to enjoy it! There too lies he who founded its greatness, to contribute to whose fall Europe was embroiled—there he sleeps in quiet and dignity, while his friend and his foe, rather his false ally and real enemy, Newcastle and Bath, are exhausting the dregs of their pitiful lives in squabbles and pamphlets!

The surprise the pictures gave me is again renewed—accustomed for many years to see nothing but wretched daubs and varnished copies at auctions, I look at these as enchantment. My own description[3] of them seems poor—but shall I tell you truly—the majesty of Italian ideas almost sinks before the warm nature of Flemish colouring! Alas! Don't I grow old? My young imagination was fired with Guido's ideas—must they be plump and prominent as Abishag to warm me now? Does great youth feel with poetic limbs, as well as see with poetic eyes? In one respect I am very young; I cannot satiate myself with looking—an incident contributed to make me feel this more strongly. A party arrived, just as I did, to see the house, a man and three women in riding-dresses, and they rode post through the apartments—I could not hurry

1. HW is buried in its crypt.

2. Sir Robert m. 1 (1700) Catharine Shorter (ca. 1682–1737), HW's mother; m. 2 (1738) Maria Skerret (ca. 1702–38), formerly his mistress.

3. The *Ædes Walpolianæ*.

before them fast enough—they were not so long in *seeing* for the first time, as I could have been in one room to examine what I knew by heart. I remember formerly being often diverted with this kind of *seers*—they come, ask what such a room is called, in which Sir Robert lay, write it down, admire a lobster or a cabbage in a market-piece, dispute whether the last room was green or purple, and then hurry to the inn for fear the fish should be over-dressed—how different my sensations! Not a picture here, but recalls a history; not one, but I remember in Downing Street or Chelsea, where queens and crowds admired them, though *seeing* them as little as these travellers!

When I had drunk tea, I strolled into the garden—they told me, it was now called *the pleasure ground*—what a dissonant idea of pleasure—those groves, those *allées,* where I have passed so many charming moments, are now stripped up, or overgrown; many fond paths I could not unravel, though with a very exact clue in my memory—I met two gamekeepers, and a thousand hares! In the days when all my soul was tuned to pleasure and vivacity (and you will think perhaps it is far from being out of tune yet) I hated Houghton and its solitude—yet I loved this garden; as now, with many regrets, I love Houghton—Houghton, I know not what to call it, a monument of grandeur or ruin! How I have wished this evening for Lord Bute! How I could preach to him! For myself, I do not want to be preached to—I have long considered, how every Balbec must wait for the chance of a Mr Wood.

The servants wanted to lay me in the great apartment—what to make me pass my night as I have my evening! It were like proposing to Margaret Roper to be a Duchess in the court that cut off her father's head, and imagining it would please her. I have chosen to sit in my father's little dressing-room, and am now by his scrutoire, where, in the height of his fortune, he used to receive the accounts of his farmers, and deceive himself—or us, with the thoughts of his economy—how wise a man at once and how weak! For what has he built Houghton? For his grandson to annihilate, or for his son to mourn over! If Lord Burleigh could rise and view his representative driving the Hatfield stage, he would feel as I feel now—poor little Strawberry! At least it will not be snipped to pieces by a descendant!—You will think all these fine meditations dictated by pride, not by philosophy—pray consider, through how many mediums philosophy must pass, before it is purified—

How often must it weep, how often burn!

My mind was extremely prepared for all this gloom, by parting with Mr Conway yesterday morning—moral reflections on commonplaces are the livery one likes to wear, when one has just had a real misfortune—he is going to Germany—I was glad to dress myself up in transitory Houghton, in lieu of very sensible concern. Tomorrow I shall be distracted with thoughts—at least images, of very different complexion—I go to Lynn, and am to be elected on Friday. I shall return hither on Saturday, again alone, to expect Burleighides on Sunday, whom I left at Newmarket—I must once in my life see him on his grandfather's throne—

Epping, Monday night, 31st.

—No, I have not seen him, he loitered on the road, and I was kept at Lynn till yesterday morning. It is plain I never knew for how many trades I was formed, when at this time of day I can begin electioneering and succeed in my new vocation. Think of me, the subject of a mob, who was scarce ever before in a mob! Addressing them in the town-hall, riding at the head of two thousand people through such a town as Lynn, dining with above two hundred of them amid bumpers, huzzas, songs and tobacco, and finishing with country dances at a ball and six-penny whisk! I have borne it all cheerfully; nay, have sat hours in *conversation,* the thing upon earth that I hate, have been to hear misses play on the harpsichord, and to see an alderman's copies of Rubens and Carlo Marat. Yet to do the folks justice, they are sensible and reasonable, and civilized; their very language is polished since I lived among them. I attribute this to their more frequent intercourse with the world and the capital, by the help of good roads and post-chaises, which, if they have abridged the King's dominions, have at least tamed his subjects.—Well! how comfortable it will be tomorrow, to see my perroquet, to play at loo, and not to be obliged to talk seriously—the Heraclitus of the beginning of this letter, will be overjoyed on finishing it to sign himself

Your old friend

Democritus.

PS. I forgot to tell you that my ancient Aunt Hammond came over to Lynn to see me—not from any affection, but curiosity—the first thing she said to me, though we have not met these sixteen years, was, 'Child, you have done a thing today, that your father never did in all his life, you sat as they carried you; he always stood the whole time.' 'Madam,' said I, 'when I am placed in a chair, I conclude I am to sit in it—besides, as I cannot imitate my father in great things, I am not at all ambitious of mimicking him in little ones.'—I am sure she proposes to tell her remark to my uncle Horace's ghost, the instant they meet.

To George Montagu, 5 May 1761

Arlington Street, May 5th, 1761.

We have lost a young genius, Sir William Williams; an express from Belleisle, arrived this morning, brings nothing but his death. He was shot very unnecessarily, riding too near a battery. In sum, he is a sacrifice to his own rashness,—and to ours—for what are we taking Belleisle? I rejoiced at the little loss we had on landing—for the glory, I leave it to the Common Council. I am very willing to leave London to them too, and do pass half the week at Strawberry, where my two passions, lilacs and nightingales are in full bloom. I spent Sunday as if it was Apollo's birthday; Gray and Mason were with me, and we listened to the nightingales till one o'clock in the morning. Gray has translated two noble incantations from the Lord knows who, a Danish Gray, who lived the Lord knows when. They are to be enchased in a history of English bards, which Mason and he are writing, but of which the former has not writ a word yet, and of which the latter, if he rides Pegasus at his usual foot-pace, will finish the first page two years hence—but the true frantic œstrus resides at present with Mr Hogarth; I went t'other morning to see a portrait he is painting of Mr Fox—Hogarth told me he had promised, if Mr Fox would sit as he liked, to make as good a picture as Vandyke or Rubens could. I was silent—'Why now,' said he, 'You think this very vain, but why should not one speak truth?' This *truth* was uttered in the face of his own Sigismonda, which is exactly a maudlin whore tearing off the trinkets that her keeper had given her, to fling at his head. She has her father's picture in a bracelet on her arm, and her fingers are bloody with the heart, as if she had just bought a sheep's pluck in St James's market. As I was going, Hogarth put on a very grave face, and said, 'Mr Walpole, I want to speak to you'; I sat down, and said, I was ready to receive his commands. For shortness, I will mark this wonderful dialogue by initial letters.

H. I am told you are going to entertain the town with something in our way. W. Not very soon, Mr Hogarth. H. I wish you would let me have it, to correct; I should be sorry to have you expose yourself to censure. We painters must know more of those things than other people. W. Do you think nobody understands painting but painters? H. Oh! So far from it, there's Reynolds, who certainly has genius; why, but t'other day he offered £100 for a picture that I would not hang in my cellar; and indeed, to say truth, I have generally found that persons who had studied painting least, were the best judges of it—but what I particularly wanted to say to you was about Sir James Thornhill (you know he married Sir James's daughter) I would not have you say anything against him; there was a book published some time ago, abusing him, and it gave great offence—he was the first that attempted history in England, and I assure you some Germans have said he was a very great painter. W. My work will go no lower than the year 1700, and I really have not considered whether Sir J. Thornhill will come within my plan or not; if he does, I fear you and I shall not agree upon his merits. H. I wish you would let me correct it—besides, I am writing something of the same kind myself, I should be sorry we should clash. W. I believe it is not much known what my work is; very few persons have seen it. H. Why, it is a critical history of painting, is not it? W. No, it is an antiquarian history of it in England; I bought Mr Vertue's MSS, and I believe the work will not give much offence. Besides, if it does, I cannot help it: when I publish anything, I give it to the world to think of it as they please. H. Oh! if it is an antiquarian work, we shall not clash. Mine is a critical work; I don't know whether I shall ever publish it—it is rather an apology for painters—I think it owing to the good sense of the English, that they have not painted better. W. My dear Mr Hogarth, I must take my leave of you, you now grow too wild—and I left him—if I had stayed, there remained nothing but for him to bite me. I give you my honour this conversation is literal, and perhaps, as long as you have known Englishmen and painters, you never met with anything so distracted. I had consecrated a line to his genius (I mean for wit) in my preface; I shall not erase it, but I hope nobody will ask me if he was not mad. Adieu!

Yours ever

H. W.

To Sir Horace Mann, 10 September 1761

Arlington Street, Sept. 10, 1761.

When we least expected the Queen, she came, after being ten days at sea, but without sickness for above half an hour. She was gay the whole voyage, sung to her harpsichord, and left the door of her cabin open. They made the coast of Suffolk last Saturday, and on Monday morning she landed at Harwich; so prosperously has his Majesty's chief eunuch, as they have made the Tripoline ambassador call Lord Anson,[1] executed his commission. She lay

1. Who was suspected of being impotent. (HW's note)

that night at your old friend Lord Abercorn's at Witham, and if she judged by her host, must have thought she was coming to reign in the realm of taciturnity. She arrived at St James's a quarter after three on Tuesday the 8th. When she first saw the palace she turned pale: the Duchess of Hamilton smiled—'My dear Duchess,' said the Princess, '*you* may laugh—you have been married twice; but it is no joke to me.' Is this a bad proof of her sense? On the journey they wanted her to curl her toupet— 'No, indeed,' said she, 'I think it looks as well as those of the ladies that have been sent for me; if the King would have me wear a periwig, I will; otherwise I shall let myself alone.' The Duke of York gave her his hand at the garden gate; her lips trembled, but she jumped out with spirit. In the garden the King met her; she would have fallen at his feet; he prevented and embraced her, and led her into the apartments, where she was received by the Princess of Wales and Lady Augusta; these three princesses only dined with the King. At ten the procession went to chapel, preceded by unmarried daughters of peers, peers and peeresses in plenty. The new princess was led by the Duke of York and Prince William, the Archbishop married them, the King talked to her the whole time with great good humour, and the Duke of Cumberland gave her away. She is not tall, nor a beauty; pale, and very thin, but looks sensible and is genteel. Her hair is darkish and fine, her forehead low, her nose very well, except the nostrils spreading too wide; her mouth has the same fault, but her teeth are good. She talks a good deal, and French tolerably; possesses herself, is frank, but with great respect to the King. After the ceremony, the whole company came into the drawing-room for about ten minutes, but nobody was presented that night. The Queen was in white and silver; an endless mantle of violet-coloured velvet lined with ermine, and attempted to be fastened on her shoulder by a bunch of large pearls, dragged itself and almost the rest of her clothes half way down her waist. On her head was a beautiful little tiara of diamonds; a diamond necklace, and a stomacher of diamonds, worth threescore thousand pounds, which she is to wear at the Coronation too. Her train was borne by the ten bridesmaids, Lady Sarah Lenox, Lady Caroline Russel, Lady Caroline Montagu, Lady Harriot Bentinck, Lady Anne Hamilton, Lady Essex Kerr, daughters of Dukes of Richmond, Bedford, Manchester, Portland, Hamilton and Roxburgh; and four daughters of the Earls of Albemarle, Brook, Harcourt, and Ilchester, Lady Elizabeth Keppel, Louisa Greville, Elizabeth Harcourt, and Susan Fox Strangways; their heads crowned with diamonds, and in robes of white and silver. Lady Caroline Russel is extremely handsome, Lady Elizabeth Keppel very pretty; but with neither features nor air, nothing ever looked so charming as Lady Sarah Lenox; she has all the glow of beauty, peculiar to her family. As supper was not ready, the Queen sat down, sung and played on the harpsichord to the royal family, who all supped with her in private. They talked of the different German dialects; the King asked if the Hanoverian was not pure— 'Oh, no, Sir,' said the Queen, 'it is the worst of all.'—She will not be unpopular. The Duke of Cumberland told the King that himself and Lady Augusta were sleepy— The Queen was very averse to going to bed, and at last articled that nobody should retire with her but the Princess of Wales, and her own two German women, and that nobody should be admitted afterwards but the King—they did not get to bed till between two and three. The Princess Dowager wanted to sit a little at table, and pressed the Duke of Cumberland to stay; he pleaded being tired— 'And besides, Madam,' said he, 'what should I stay for? if she cries out, I cannot help her.'

The next morning the King had a levee; he said to Lord Hardwicke, 'It is a very fine day:' that old gossip replied— 'Yes, Sir, and it was a very fine night.' Lord Bute had told the King that Lord Orford had betted his having a child before Sir James Lowther, who had been married the night before to Lord Bute's eldest daughter; the King told Lord Orford he should be glad to go his halves. The bet was made with Mr Rigby; somebody asked the latter, how he could be so bad a courtier as to bet against the King? He replied, 'Not at all a bad courtier; I betted Lord Bute's daughter against him.'

After the King's levce there was a Drawing-Room; the Queen stood under the throne; the women were presented to her by the Duchess of Hamilton, and then the men by the Duke of Manchester; but as she knew nobody, she was not to speak. At night there was a ball; Drawing-Rooms yesterday and today, and then a cessation of ceremony till the Coronation, except next Monday, when she is to receive the address of the Lord Mayor and aldermen, sitting on the throne attended by the bridesmaids. There was a ridiculous circumstance happened yesterday; Lord Westmorland, not very young nor clear-sighted, mistook Lady Sarah Lenox for the Queen, kneeled to her, and would have kissed her hand if she had not prevented him— People think that a Chancellor of Oxford was naturally attracted by the blood of Stuart. It is as comical to see Kitty Dashwood, the famous old beauty of the Oxfordshire Jacobites, living in the palace as duenna to the Queen— She and Mrs Boughton, Lord Lyttelton's ancient Delia, are revived again in a young Court that never heard of them. There, I think you could not have had a more circumstantial account of a royal wedding from the Herald's office. Adieu!

Yours to serve you

HORACE SANDFORD,
Mecklemburg King-at-Arms

To GEORGE MONTAGU, 24 September 1761

Arlington Street, Sept. 24, 1761.

I am glad you arrived safe in Dublin, and hitherto like it so well; but your trial is not begun yet; when your King comes, the ploughshares will be put into the fire. Bless your stars, that your King is not to be married or crowned: all the vines of Bourdeaux, and all the fumes of Irish brains cannot make a town so drunk as a royal wedding and coronation. I am going to let London cool, and will not venture myself into [it] again this fortnight. Oh! the buzz, the prattle, the crowds, the noise, the hurry! Nay, people are so little come to their senses, that though the Coronation was but the day before yesterday, the Duke of Devonshire[1] had forty messages yesterday desiring tickets for a ball that they fancied was to be at court last night—People had sat up a night and a day and yet wanted to see a dance. If I was to entitle ages, I would call this *the Century of Crowds.* For the Coronation, if a puppet-show could be worth a million, that is. The multitudes, balconies, guards, and procession, made Palace-Yard the liveliest spectacle in the world; the Hall[2] was the most glorious. The blaze of lights, the richness and variety of habits, the ceremonial, the benches of peers and peeresses, *frequent and full,* was as awful as a pageant can be—and yet for the King's sake—and my own I never wish to see another: nor am impatient to have my Lord Effingham's promise fulfilled—the King complained that so few precedents were kept for their proceedings; Lord Effingham owned, the Earl Marshal's office had been strangely neglected; but he had taken such care for the future, that *next Coronation* would be regulated in the most exact manner imaginable. The number of peers and peeresses present was not very great—some of the latter, with no excuse in the world, appeared in Lord Lincoln's gallery, and even walked about the hall indecently in the intervals of the procession. My Lady Harrington, covered with all the diamonds she could borrow, hire, or tease, and with the air of Roxana, was the finest figure at a distance; she complained to George Selwyn, that she was to walk with Lady Portsmouth, who would have a wig, and a stick—'Pho,' said he, 'you will only look as if you was taken up by the constable'—she told this everywhere, thinking the reflection was on my Lady Portsmouth. Lady Pembroke, alone at the head of the Countesses, was the picture of majestic modesty; the Duchess of Richmond, as pretty as nature and dress, with no pains of her own, could make her; Lady Spencer, Lady Sutherland, and Lady Northampton, very pretty figures—Lady Kildare, still beauty itself if not a little too large. The ancient peeresses were by

1. Lord Chamberlain.
2. Westminster Hall, where the Coronation banquet was held.

no means the worst party—Lady Westmorland, still handsome, and with more dignity than all; the Duchess of Queensberry looked well, though her locks milk-white; Lady Albemarle very genteel; nay the middle-aged had some good representatives in Lady Holderness, Lady Rochford, and Lady Strafford, the perfectest little figure of all. My Lady Suffolk ordered her robes and I dressed part of her head, as I made some of my Lord Hertford's dress, for you know, no profession comes amiss to me, from a tribune of the people to a habit-maker. Don't imagine that there were not figures as excellent on the other side: old Exeter, who told the King he was the handsomest young man she ever saw, old Effingham, and a Lady Say and Seal with her hair powdered and her tresses black, were an excellent contrast to the handsome. Lord Bolinbroke put on rouge upon his wife and the Duchess of Bedford in the Painted Chamber; the Duchess of Queensberry told me of the latter, that she looked like an orange-peach, half red and half yellow. The coronets of the peers and their robes disguised them strangely; it required all the beauty of the Dukes of Richmond and Marlborough to make them noticed. One there was, though of another species, the noblest figure I ever saw; the High Constable of Scotland, Lord Errol—as one saw him in a space capable of containing him, one admired him. At the wedding, dressed in tissue, he looked like one of the giants in Guildhall, new-gilt. It added to the energy of his person, that one considered him acting so considerable a part in that very hall where so few years ago one saw his father Lord Kilmarnock condemned to the block. The Champion acted his part admirably; and dashed down his gauntlet with proud defiance. His associates, Lord Effingham, Lord Talbot, and the Duke of Bedford were woeful, yet the last, the least ridiculous of the three. Lord Talbot piqued himself on backing his horse down the Hall, and not turning its rump towards the King, but he had taken such pains to dress it to that duty, that it entered backwards; and at his retreat the spectators clapped, a terrible indecorum, but suitable to such Bartholomew Fair doings. He put me in mind of some King's fool, that would not give his right hand to the King of Spain, because he wiped his backside with it. He had twenty *démêlés* and came out of none creditably. He had taken away the table of the Knights of the Bath, and was forced to admit two in their old place and dine the others in the Court of Requests. Sir William Stanhope said, 'We are ill-treated, for *some of us* are gentlemen.' Beckford told the Earl, it was hard to refuse a table to the City of London, whom it would cost ten thousand pounds to banquet the King, and that his Lordship would repent it, if they had not a table in the Hall—they had. To the Barons of the Cinque Ports, who made the same complaint, he said, 'If you come to me as Lord Steward, I tell you, it is impossible; if, as Lord Talbot, I am a match for any of you.' And then he said to Lord Bute, 'If I was a minister, thus I would talk to France, to Spain, to the Dutch—none of your half measures.' This has brought me to a melancholy topic—Bussy goes tomorrow, a Spanish war is hanging in the air, destruction is taking a new lease of mankind—of the remnant of mankind—I have no prospect of seeing Mr Conway! Adieu! I will not disturb you with my forebodings. You I shall see again in spite of war, and I trust, in spite of Ireland.

Yours ever

H. W.

I was much disappointed at not seeing your brother John; I kept a place for him to the last minute, but have heard nothing of him.

To George Montagu, 8 December 1761

Arlington Street, Dec. 8th, 1761.

I return you the list of prints and shall be glad you will bring me all to which I have affixed this mark X. The rest I have; yet the expense of the whole list would not ruin me. Lord Farnham, who I believe departed this morning, brings you the list of the Duke of Devonshire's pictures.

I had been told that Mr Bourk's history was of England, not of Ireland—I am glad it is the latter, for I am now in Mr Hume's England, and would fain read no more—I not only know what has been written, but what would be written. Our story is so exhausted, that to make it new, they really *make* it *new.* Mr Hume has exalted Edward II and depressed Edward III. The next historian, I suppose, will make James I a hero, and geld Charles II.

Fingal is come out[1]—I have not yet got through it—not but it is very fine—yet I cannot at once compass an epic poem now. It tires me to death to read how many ways a warrior is like the moon, or the sun, or a rock, or a lion, or the ocean. *Fingal* is a brave collection of similes, and will serve all the boys at Eton and Westminster for these twenty years. I will trust you with a secret, but you must not disclose it, I should be ruined with my Scotch friends—in short, I cannot believe it genuine—I cannot believe a regular poem of six books has been preserved, uncorrupted, by oral tradition, from times before Christianity was introduced into the island. What! Preserved unadulterated by savages dispersed among mountains, and so often driven from their dens, so wasted by wars civil and foreign! Has one man ever got all by heart? I doubt it. Were parts preserved by some, other parts by others? Mighty lucky, that the tradition was never interrupted, nor any part lost—not a verse, not a measure, not the sense! Luckier and luckier—I have been extremely qualified myself lately for this Scotch memory; we have had nothing but a coagulation of rain, fogs and frosts, and though they have clouded all understanding, I suppose if I had tried, I should have found that they thickened and gave great consistence to my remembrance.

You want news—I must make it if I send it. To change the dullness of the scene, I went t'other night to the play, where I had not been this winter. They are so crowded, that though I went before six I got no better place than a fifth row, where I heard very ill, and was pent for five hours without a soul near me that I knew. It was *Cymbeline,* and appeared to me as long as if every-

1. The poetical forgery by James Macpherson.

body in it went really to Italy in every act, and came back again. With a few pretty passages and a scene or [two,] it is so absurd and tiresome, that I am persuaded Garrick . . .[1]

To George Montagu, 2 February 1762

Arlington Street, Feb. 2d, 1762.

I scolded you in my last, but I shall forgive you, if you return soon to England, as you talk of doing, for though you are an abominable correspondent, and only write to beg letters, you are good company, and I have a notion, I shall still be glad to see you.

Lady Mary Wortley is arrived; I have seen her; I think her avarice, her dirt, and her vivacity are all increased. Her dress, like her languages, is a galimatias of several countries; the groundwork, rags; and the embroidery, nastiness. She wears no cap, no handkerchief, no gown, no petticoat, no shoes. An old black laced hood represents the first, the fur of a horseman's coat, which replaces the third, serves for the second; a dimity petticoat is deputy and officiates for the fourth, and slippers act the part of the last. When I was at Florence, and she was expected there, we were drawing *Sortes Virgilianas*—for her, we literally drew

Insanam vatem aspices—[2]

it would have been a stronger prophecy now, even than it was then.

You told me not a word of Mr McNaghton, and I have a great mind to be as coolly indolent about our famous ghost in Cock Lane—why should one steal half an hour from one's amusements to tell a story to a friend in another island? I could send you volumes on the ghost, and I believe if I was to stay a little, I might send you its *Life*, dedicated to my Lord Dartmouth, by the Ordinary[3] of Newgate, its two great patrons. A drunken parish clerk

1. The rest of this letter is missing.
2. "Behold the mad prophetess!"
3. Chaplain.

set it on foot out of revenge, the Methodists have adopted it, and the whole town of London think of nothing else. Elizabeth Canning[1] and the rabbit-woman[2] were modest impostors in comparison of this, which goes on without saving the least appearances. The Archbishop, who would not suffer *The Minor* to be acted in ridicule of the Methodists, permits this farce to be played every night, and I shall not be surprised if they perform in the great hall at Lambeth. I went to hear it—for it is not an *apparition,* but an *audition*—we set out from the opera, changed our clothes at Northumberland House, the Duke of York, Lady Northumberland, Lady Mary Coke, Lord Hertford and I, all in one hackney-coach and drove to the spot; it rained torrents; yet the lane was full of mob, and the house so full we could not get in—at last they discovered it was the Duke of York, and the company squeezed themselves into one another's pockets to make room for us. The house, which is borrowed, and to which the ghost has adjourned, is wretchedly small and miserable; when we opened the chamber, in which were fifty people, with no light but one tallow candle at the end, we tumbled over the bed of the child to whom the ghost comes, and whom they are murdering there by inches in such insufferable heat and stench. At the top of the room are ropes to dry clothes—I asked, if we were to have rope-dancing between the acts?—We had nothing; they told us, as they would at a puppet-show, that it would not come that night till 7 in the morning—that is, when there are only prentices and old women. We stayed however till half an hour after one. The Methodists have promised them contributions; provisions are sent in like forage, and all the taverns and alehouses in the neighbourhood make fortunes. The most diverting part, is to hear people wondering *when it will be found out*—as if there was anything to find out; as if the actors would make their noises where they can be discovered. However as this pantomime cannot last much longer, I hope Lady Fanny

1. Elizabeth Canning (1734–73), convicted of perjury for false accusations that she had been kidnapped.

2. Mary Toft (or Tofts) (ca. 1701–63) aroused a storm of discussion in 1726 by pretending that she had given birth to rabbits.

Shirley will set up a ghost of her own at Twickenham, and then you shall *hear* one. The Methodists, as Lord Aylsford assured Mr Chute two nights ago at Lord Dacre's, have attempted ghosts three times in Warwickshire. There! How good I am!

Yours ever

H. W.

To George Montagu, 17 May 1763

Strawberry Hill, May 17th, 1763.

On vient de nous donner une très jolie fête au château de Straberri; tout était tapissé de narcisses, de tulipes, et de lilacs; des cors de chasse, des clarinettes, des petits vers galants faits par des fées, et qui se trouvaient sous la presse, des fruits à la glace, du thé, du café, des biscuits, et force hot-rolls—this is not the beginning of a letter to you, but of one that I might suppose sets out tonight for Paris, or rather which I do not suppose will set out thither, for though the narrative is circumstantially true, I don't believe the actors were pleased enough with the scene, to give so favourable an account of it. The French do not come hither *to see. À l'anglaise* happened to be the word in fashion; and half a dozen of the most fashionable people have been the dupes of it. I take for granted that their next mode will be *à l'iroquoise,* that they may be under no obligation of realizing their pretentions. Madame de Boufflers I think will die a martyr to a taste which she fancied she had, and finds she has not. Never having stirred ten miles from Paris, and having only rolled in an easy coach from one hotel to another on a gliding pavement, she is already worn out with being hurried from morning till night from one sight to another. She rises every morning so fatigued with the toils of the preceding day, that she has not strength, if she had inclination, to observe the least, or the finest thing she sees. She came hither today to a great breakfast I made for her, with her eyes a foot deep in her head, her hands dangling, and scarce able to support her knotting-bag. She had been yesterday to see a ship launched, and went from Greenwich by water to Ranelagh. Madame Dusson, who is Dutch-built, and whose muscles are more pleasure-proof, came with her; there were besides, Lady Mary Coke, Lord and Lady Holderness, the Duke and Duchess of Grafton, Lord Hertford, Lord Villiers, Offley, Messieurs de Fleury, Deon and Duclos. The latter is author of the life of Louis Onze; dresses like a dissenting minister, which I suppose is the livery of a *bel esprit,* and is much more impetuous than agreeable. We breakfasted in the great parlour, and I had filled the hall and large cloister by turns, with French horns and clarinets. As the French ladies had never seen a printing-house, I carried them into mine; they found something ready set, and desiring to see what it was, it proved as follows;

THE PRESS SPEAKS.

For Madame de Boufflers.

The graceful fair, who loves to know,
Nor dreads the North's inclement snow;
Who bids her polish'd accent wear
The British diction's harsher air;
Shall read her praise in ev'ry clime,
Where types can speak, or poets rhyme.

For Madame Dusson.

Feign not an ignorance of what I speak;
You could not miss my meaning, were it Greek.
'Tis the same language Belgium utter'd first,
The same which from admiring Gallia burst.
True sentiment a like expression pours;
Each country says the same to eyes like yours.

You will comprehend that the first speaks English, and that the second does not; that the second is handsome, and the first not; and that the second was born in Holland. This little *gentillesse* pleased, and atoned for the popery of my house, which was not serious enough for Madame de Boufflers, who is Montmorency, and *du sang du premier Chrétien;* and too serious for Madame Dusson, who is a Dutch Calvinist. The latter's husband was not here, nor

Drumgold, who have both got fevers, nor the Duc de Nivernois, who dined at Claremont. The gallery is not advanced enough to give them any idea at all, as they are not apt to go out of their way for one; but the cabinet, and the glory of yellow glass at top, which had a charming sun for a foil, did surmount their indifference, especially as they were animated by the Duchess of Grafton, who had never happened to be here before, and who perfectly entered into the air of enchantment and fairyism, which is the tone of the place, and was peculiarly so today—*à propos,* when do you design to come hither? Let me know that I may have no measures to interfere with receiving you and your Grandisons.

Before Lord Bute ran away, he made Mr Bentley a Commissioner of the Lottery; I don't know whether a single or double one: the latter, which I hope it is, is two hundred a year.

Thursday 19th.

I am ashamed of myself, to have nothing but a journal of pleasures to send you! I never passed a more agreeable day than yesterday. Miss Pelham gave the French an entertainment at Esher, but they have been so feasted and amused that none of them were well enough or reposed enough, to come, but Nivernois and Madame Dusson. The rest of the company were, the Graftons, Lady Rockingham, Lord and Lady Pembroke, Lord and Lady Holderness, Lord Villiers, Count Woronzow the Russian minister, Lady Sondes, Mr and Mrs Pelham, Miss Mary Pelham, Lady Mary Coke, Mrs. Pitt, Mrs Anne Pitt, and Mr Shelley. The day was delightful, the scene transporting, the trees, lawns, concaves, all in the perfection in which the ghost of Kent[1] would joy to see them. At twelve we made the tour of the farm in eight chaises and calashes, horsemen and footmen, setting out like a picture of Wouverman. My lot fell in the lap of Mrs Anne Pitt, which I could have excused, as she was not at all in the style of the day, roman-

1. William Kent (1684–1748), architect and landscape gardener who laid out the grounds.

tic, but political. We had a magnificent dinner, cloaked in the modesty of earthenware: French horns and hautboys on the lawn. We walked to the belvedere on the summit of the hill, where a threatened storm only served to heighten the beauty of the landscape, a rainbow on a dark cloud falling precisely behind the tower of a neighbouring church, between another tower, and the building at Claremont. Monsieur de Nivernois, who had been absorbed all day and lagging behind, translating my verses, was delivered of his version, and of some more lines, which he wrote on Miss Pelham in the belvedere, while we drank tea and coffee. From thence we passed into the wood, and the ladies formed a circle on chairs before the mouth of the cave, which was overhung to a vast height with woodbines, lilacs and laburnums, and dignified by those tall shapely cypresses. On the descent of the hill were placed the French horns; the abigails, servants, and neighbours wandering below by the river—in short, it was Parnassus as Watteau would have painted it. Here we had a rural syllabub, and part of the company returned to town; but were replaced by Giardini and Onofrio, who with Nivernois on the violin and Lord Pembroke on the bass, accompanied Miss Pelham, Lady Rockingham and the Duchess of Grafton who sang. This little concert lasted till past ten; then there were minuets, and as we had seven couple left, it concluded with a country dance—I blush again, for I danced, but was kept in countenance by Nivernois, who has one wrinkle more than I have. A quarter after twelve they sat down to supper, and I came home by a charming moonlight. I am going to dine in town, and to a great ball with fireworks at Miss Chudleigh's—but I return hither on Sunday, to bid adieu to this abominable Arcadian life, for really when one is not young, one ought to do nothing but *s'ennuyer*—I will try, but I always go about it awkwardly. Adieu!

Yours ever

H. W.

PS. I enclose a copy of both the English and French verses.

À Madame de Boufflers.

Boufflers, qu'embellissent les grâces,
Et qui plairait sans le vouloir,
Elle, à qui l'amour du savoir
Fit braver le Nord et les glaces;
Boufflers se plaît en nos vergers,
Et veut à nos sens étrangers
Plier sa voix enchanteresse.
Répétons son nom mille fois,
Sur tous les cœurs Boufflers aura des droits,
  Partout où la rime et la presse
  À l'amour prêteront leur voix.

À Madame D'Usson.

Ne feignez point, Iris, de ne pas nous entendre;
Ce que vous inspirez, en grec doit se comprendre.
  On vous l'a dit d'abord en hollandais,
  Et dans un langage plus tendre
  Paris vous l'a répété mille fois.
  C'est de nos cœurs l'expression sincère;
En tout climat, Iris, à toute heure, en tous lieux,
  Partout où brilleront vos yeux,
  Vous apprendrez combien ils savent plaire.

To the Hon. Henry Seymour Conway, 21 May 1763

Arlington Street, May 21, 1763.

You have now seen the celebrated Madame de Boufflers. I dare say you could in that short time perceive that she is agreeable, but I dare say too that you will agree with me that vivacity is my no means the partage of the French—bating the *étourderie* of the *mousquetaires* and of a high-dried *petit maître* or two, they appear to me more lifeless than Germans. I cannot comprehend how they came by the character of a lively people. Charles Townshend has more *sal volatile* in him than the whole nation. Their King is taciturnity itself, Mirepoix was a walking mummy, Nivernois has about as much life as a sick favourite child, and M. Dusson is a good-humoured country gentleman, who has been drunk the day before, and is upon his good behaviour. If I have the gout next year, and am thoroughly humbled by it again, I will go to Paris, that I may be upon a level with them: at present, I am *trop fou* to keep them company. Mind, I do not insist that, to have spirits, a nation should be as frantic as poor Fanny Pelham, as absurd as the Duchess of Queensbury, or as dashing as the Virgin Chudleigh. Oh that you had been at her ball t'other night! History could never describe it and keep its countenance. The Queen's real birthday, you know, is not kept: this Maid of Honour kept it—nay, while the court is in mourning, expected people to be out of mourning; the Queen's family really was so, Lady Northumberland having desired leave for them. A scaffold was erected in Hyde Park for fireworks. To show the illuminations without to more advantage, the company were received in an apartment totally dark, where they remained for two hours. —If they gave rise to any more birthdays, who could help it? The fireworks were fine, and succeeded well. On each side of the court were two large scaffolds for the Virgin's tradespeople. When the fireworks ceased, a large scene was lighted in the court, representing their Majesties; on each side of which were six obelisks, painted with emblems, and illuminated; mottoes beneath in Latin and English: 1. For the Prince of Wales, a ship, *Multorum spes.* 2. For the Princess Dowager, a bird of paradise, and *two* little ones, *Meos ad sidera tollo.* People smiled. 3. Duke of York, a temple, *Virtuti et honori.* 4. Princess Augusta, a bird of paradise, *Non habet parem*—unluckily this was translated, *I have no peer.* People laughed out, considering where this was exhibited. 5. The three younger Princes, an orange-tree, *Promittit et dat.* 6. The two younger Princesses, the flower crown-imperial. I forget the Latin: the translation was silly enough, *Bashful in youth, graceful in age.* The lady of the house made many apologies for the poorness of the performance, which she said was only oil-paper, painted by one of her servants; but it really was fine and pretty. The Duke of Kingston was in a frock, *comme chez lui.* Behind the house was a cenotaph for the Princess Elizabeth, a kind of illuminated cradle; the motto, *All the honours the dead can receive.* This burying-ground was a strange codicil to a festival; and, what was more strange, about one in the morning, this sarcophagus burst out into crackers and guns. The Margrave of Anspach began the ball with the Virgin. The supper was most sumptuous.

You ask, when I propose to be at Park Place. I ask, shall not you come to the Duke of Richmond's masquerade, which is the 6th of June? I cannot well be with you till towards the end of that month.

The enclosed is a letter which I wish you to read attentively, to give me your opinion upon it, and return it. It is from a sensible friend of mine in Scotland, who has lately corresponded with me on the enclosed subjects, which I little understand; but I promised to communicate his ideas to George Grenville, if he would state them—are they practicable? I wish much that something could be done for those brave soldiers and sailors, who will all come to the gallows, unless some timely provision can be made for them.—The former part of his letter relates to a grievance he complains of, that men who have *not* served are admitted into garrisons, and then into our hospitals, which were designed for meritorious sufferers. Adieu!

Yours ever,

HOR. WALPOLE.

TO SIR HORACE MANN, 12 December 1763

Arlington Street, Dec. 12, 1763.

My last journal was dated the 18th of last month. Since that period we have been totally employed upon Mr Wilkes, or events flowing from him; for he is an inexhaustible source. I shall move regularly, and tell you his history in order.

In the first place he is not dead of his wound, though not yet out of danger, for they think another piece of his coat is to come away, as two have already.

On the 23d we, the Commons, had a debate, that lasted late, whether we should proceed to the question on privilege, as Wilkes could not attend. There was a great defection among the royal troops, and the minority amounted to 166: but the next day on the question itself, it sunk to 133, when we resigned our privilege into the hands of any messengers that should be sent for it. Mr Pitt was brought thither in flannels,[1] and spoke for two hours, but was forced to retire four hours before we came to the question.

These debates were followed by a curious account of the famous blasphemous and bawdy poem, the *Essay on Woman*, published by one Kidgell, a Methodist parson, who had been employed to hunt it out. The man has most deservedly drawn on himself a torrent of indignation and odium, which I suppose he will forget in a deanery.

The next proceeding was in the Lords, who sat till ten at night on the question of agreeing to our resolutions. The Duke of Cumberland, who voted at the head of the minority, was as unsuccessful as he has been in other engagements, and was beaten by *114* to *35*.

So much for within doors. But without, where the minority is the majority, the event was very different. The *North Briton* was ordered to be burned by the hangman at Cheapside on the third of this month. A prodigious riot ensued, the sheriffs were mobbed, the constables beaten, and the paper with much difficulty set on fire by a link, and then rescued. The ministry, some in a panic and some in a rage, fetched the sheriffs before both Houses; but after examinations and conferences for four days, the whole result was, that all the world had appeared to be on the same side, that is, not well disposed to the administration. This dissatisfaction has been increased by a violent attack made by the Duke of Bedford on the Lord Mayor, aldermen, and Common Council, for not discountenancing and suppressing the riot; and though he was abandoned by the rest of the ministry, who paid court to the City at his Grace's expense, they were so exasperated, that a motion being made to thank the sheriffs for their behaviour and to prosecute

1. *The London Chronicle* reported, "He was so infirm with the gout, that he was obliged to be carried."

one of the rioters, who is in prison, it was rejected on a division by the casting vote of the Lord Mayor.

The ministry have received a still greater mortification; the under-secretary, Mr Wood, has been cast in the Common Pleas in damages of a thousand pounds to Mr Wilkes: the printers too have recovered four hundred. And what is still more material, the Solicitor-General could not make out his proof of Wilkes being author of the *North Briton.*

The last scene has been an attempt to assassinate Wilkes. A sea-lieutenant, called Alexander Dun, got into his house on Thursday night last for that purpose; but he is not only mad, but so mad, that he had declared his intention in a coffee-house some nights before; and said twelve more Scotchmen, for he is one, were engaged in the same design.

I have told you all this briefly, but you may imagine what noise so many events have made in the hands of some hundred thousand commentators.

The famous Lord Shelburne, and the no less famous Colonel Barré—I don't know whether their fame has reached you—are turned out for joining the Opposition.

The approaching holidays will suspend farther hostilities for some time, or prepare more. We have scarce any other kind of news than politics. The interlude of Princess Augusta's wedding will be of very short duration.

You have seen some mention in the papers of Monsieur Deon, who from secretary to Monsieur de Nivernois became plenipotentiary; an honour that turned his brain. His madness first broke out upon one Vergy an adventurer, whose soul he threatened to put into the chamber-pot and make him drink it. This rage was carried so far one night at Lord Halifax's, that he was put under arrest. Being told his behaviour was a breach of the peace, he thought it meant the *peace* he had signed, and grew ten times madder. This idea he has thrust into a wild book that he has published, the title-page of which would divert you; he states all his own names, titles and offices, Noble Claude, Geneviève, Louis, Auguste, Cæsar, Alexandre, Hercule, and I don't know what,

Docteur en Droit—the *chute* from Cæsar to Master Doctor is admirable. The conclusion of the story is, that the poor creature has all the papers of the negotiation in his hands, and threescore thousand livres belonging to the Comte de Guerchy, and will deliver neither one nor t'other. He is recalled from home, and forbidden the Court here, but enjoys the papers and lives on the money, and they don't know how to recover either. Monsieur de Guerchy has behaved with the utmost tenderness and humanity to him. This minister is an agreeable man and pleases much.

I have received your long letter of November 12th with your expectations of the Duke of York, the Woronzows and the Garricks, most of whom are I suppose arrived by this time. The Chelsea china, as you guessed, was a present from the Duchess of Grafton: I told her how pleased you was with it, and that you flattered yourself it was her present. She thought you knew it, for she says she had writ you two letters.

Adieu! You must live upon this letter for some time. Our *villeggiatura* begins, when yours ends. The town will be quite empty in a week till the 18th or 20th of January, unless folks come to stare at the Prince of Brunswic—but I don't know when he is to be here. Nay, you will not want English news, while you have English princes, Russian chancellors, and English players.

To George Montagu, 11 January 1764

Arlington Street, Jan. 11th, 1764.

It is an age, I own, since I wrote to you; but, except politics, what was there to send you? And for politics, the present are too contemptible to be recorded by anybody but journalists, gazetteers, and such historians! The Ordinary of Newgate or Mr   , who write for their monthly half-crown, and who are indifferent whether Lord Bute, Lord Melcomb, or Maclean[1] is their hero, may swear they find diamonds on dunghills; but you will excuse *me*, if I let our correspondence lie dormant, rather than deal in

1. A highwayman.

such trash. I am forced to send Lord Hertford and Sir Horace Mann such garbage, because they are out of England, and the sea softens and makes palatable any potion as it does claret; but unless I can divert *you,* I had rather wait till we can laugh together; the best employment for friends, who do not mean to pick one another's pocket, nor make a property of either's frankness. Instead of politics therefore, I shall amuse you today with a fairy tale.

I was desired to be at my Lady Suffolk's on New Year's morn, where I found Lady Temple and others. On the toilette Miss Hotham spied a very small round box. She seized it with all the eagerness and curiosity of eleven years. In it was wrapped up a heart-diamond ring, and a paper in which, in a hand as small as Buckinger's,[1] who used to write the Lord's prayer in the compass of a silver penny, were the following lines,

> Sent by a sylph, unheard, unseen,
> A New Year's gift from Mab our Queen:
> But tell it not, for if you do,
> You will be pinch'd all black and blue.
> Consider well, what a disgrace
> To show abroad your mottled face:
> Then seal your lips, put on the ring,
> And sometimes think of
> Ob: the King.

You will easily guess that Lady Temple was the poetess, and that we were delighted with the genteelness of the thought and execution. The child you may imagine was less transported with the poetry than the present. Her attention however was hurried backwards and forwards from the ring to a new coat that she had been trying on, when sent for down—impatient to revisit her coat and to show the ring to her maid, she whisked upstairs—when she came down again, she found a letter sealed, and lying on the floor—new exclamations! Lady Suffolk bade her open it—here it is;

> Your tongue too nimble for your sense
> Is guilty of a high offence;

1. Matthew Buckinger (1674–1722) who was born without hands.

Hath introduc'd unkind debate,
And topsy-turvy turn'd our state.
In gallantry I sent the ring,
The token of a love-sick king:
Under fair Mab's auspicious name
From me the trifling present came.
You blab'd the news in Suffolk's ear;
The tattling zephyrs brought it here,
As Mab was indolently laid
Under a poppy's spreading shade.
The jealous queen started in rage;
She kick'd her crown and beat her page:
'Bring me my magic wand,' she cries,
'Under that primrose, there it lies:
'I'll change the silly, saucy chit
'Into a flea, a louse, a nit,
'A worm, a grasshopper, a rat,
'An owl, a monkey, hedgehog, bat—
'But hold—why not, by fairy art,
'Transform the wretch into a fart?
'Ixion once a cloud embrac'd,
'By Jove and jealousy well-plac'd.
'What sport to see proud Oberon stare,
'And flirt it with a *pet-en-l'air!*'
Then thrice she stamp'd the trembling ground,
And thrice she wav'd her wand around—
When I, endow'd with greater skill,
And less inclin'd to do you ill,
Mutter'd some words, withheld her arm,
And kindly stopp'd th'unfinish'd charm.
But though not chang'd to owl or bat,
Or something more indelicate;
Yet as your tongue has run too fast,
Your boasted beauty must not last.
No more shall frolic Cupid lie
In ambuscade in either eye,
From thence to aim his keenest dart,
To captivate each youthful heart:
No more shall envious misses pine

At charms now flown that once were thine:
No more, since you so ill behave,
Shall injur'd Oberon be your slave.

There is one word which I could wish had not been there, though it is prettily excused afterwards. The next day my Lady Suffolk desired I would write her a patent for appointing Lady Temple poet laureate to the fairies. I was excessively out of order with a pain in my stomach which I had had for ten days, and was fitter to write verses like a poet laureate, than for making one—however, I was going home to dinner alone, and at six I sent her some lines, which, you ought to have seen how sick I was, to excuse—but first I must tell you my tale methodically. The next morning by nine o'clock Miss Hotham (she must forgive me twenty years hence for saying she was eleven, for I recollect she is but ten) arrived at Lady Temple's, her face and neck all spotted with saffron, and limping. 'Oh! Madam,' said she, 'I am undone forever if you don't assist me!' 'Lord, child,' cried my Lady Temple, 'what is the matter?' thinking she had hurt herself, or lost the ring, and that she was stolen out before her aunt was up—'Oh! Madam,' said the girl, 'nobody but you can assist me.' My Lady Temple protests the child acted her part so well as to deceive her—'What can I do for you?'—'Dear Madam, take this load from my back; nobody but you can'—Lady Temple turned her round, and upon her back was tied a child's wagon. In it were three tiny purses of blue velvet; in one of them a silver cup, in another a crown of laurel, and in the third four new silver pennies; with the patent, signed at top, Oberon Imperator; and two sheets of warrants, strung together with blue silk according to form, and at top an office seal of wax and a chaplet of cut paper on it. The warrants were these;

From the Royal Mews

A wagon with the draught horses delivered by command without fee.

From the Lord Chamberlain's Office

A warrant with the royal sign-manual delivered by command without fee being first entered in the office books.

From the Lord Steward's Office

A butt of sack delivered without fee or gratuity with an order for returning the cask for the use of the office by command.

From the Great Wardrobe

Three velvet bags delivered without fee by command.

From the Treasurer of the Household's Office

A year's salary paid free from land tax poundage or any other deduction whatever by command.

From the Jewel Office

A silver butt, a silver cup, a wreath of bays by command without fee.

Then came the patent;

By these presents be it known
To all who bend before our throne,
Fays and fairies, elves, and sprites,
Beauteous dames and gallant knights,
That we Oberon the grand,
Emperor of Fairy land,
King of moonshine, prince of dreams,
Lord of Aganippe's streams,
Baron of the dimpled isles
That lie in pretty maiden's smiles,
Arch-treasurer of all the graces
Dispers'd through fifty lovely faces
Sov'reign of the Slipper's order,
With all the rites thereon that border,
Defender of the sylphic faith,
Declare—and thus your monarch saith;
  Whereas there is a noble dame,
Whom mortals Countess Temple name,
To whom ourself did erst impart
The choicest secrets of our art,
Taught her to tune th'harmonious line
To our own melody divine,
Taught her the graceful negligence,
Which scorning art, and veiling sense,

Achieves that conquest o'er the heart
Sense seldom gains, and never art:
This lady, 'tis our royal will,
Our laureate's vacant seat should fill:
A chaplet of immortal bays
Shall crown her brow, and guard her lays;
Of nectar-sack an acorn cup
Be at her board each year fill'd up:
And as each quarter feast comes round,
A silver penny shall be found
Within the compass of her shoe—
And so we bid you all adieu!

Given at our palace of Cowslip Castle, the shortest night of the year,

OBERON
and underneath
Hothamina.

Now shall I tell you the greatest curiosity of the story? The whole plan and execution of the second act was laid and adjusted by my Lady Suffolk herself, and Will. Chetwynd, the Master of the Mint, Lord Bolinbroke's Oroonoko-Chetwynd, he fourscore, she past 76—and what is more, much worse than I was, for added to her deafness she has been confined these three weeks with the gout in her eyes, and was actually then in misery and had been without sleep. What spirits and cleverness and imagination at that age and under those afflicting circumstances! You reconnoitre her old court-knowledge; how charmingly she has applied it! Do you wonder I pass so many hours and evenings with her? Alas! I had like to have lost her this morning! They had poulticed her feet to draw the gout downwards, and began to succeed yesterday, but today it flew up into her head, and she was almost in convulsions with the agony, and screamed dreadfully—proof enough how ill she was, for her patience and good breeding makes her forever sink and conceal what she feels. This evening the gout has been driven back to her foot, and I trust she is out of danger. Her loss would be irreparable to me at Twickenham, where she is by far the most rational and agreeable company I have.

I don't tell you that the Hereditary Prince is still expected and not arrived; a royal wedding would be a flat episode after a *real* fairy tale, though the bridegroom is a hero. I have not seen your brother [the] General yet, but have called on him. When come you yourself? Never mind the town and its filthy politics; we can go to the gallery at Strawberry—stay, I don't know whether we can or not, my hill is almost drowned, I don't know how your mountain is—well, we can take a boat, and always be gay there; I wish we may be so at 76 and 80! I abominate politics more and more; we had glories and would not keep them—well! content, that there was an end of blood—then perks prerogative its ass's ears up; we are always to be saving our liberties, and then staking them again! 'Tis wearisome! I hate the discussion, and yet one cannot always sit at a gaming table and never make a bet. I wish for nothing, I care not a straw for the ins or the outs; I determine never to think of them, yet the contagion catches one—can you tell one anything that will prevent infection? Well then, here I swear—no, I won't swear, one always breaks one's oath. Oh! that I had been born to love a court like Sir William Breton! I should have lived and died with the comfort of thinking that courts there will be to all eternity, and the liberty of my country would never once have ruffled my smile or spoiled my bow. I envy Sir William! Good night!

Yours ever

H. W.

To the Rev. William Cole, 9 March 1765

Strawberry Hill, March 9, 1765.

Dear Sir,

I had time to write but a short note with *The Castle of Otranto*, as your messenger called on me at four o'clock as I was going to dine abroad. Your partiality to me and Strawberry have I hope inclined you to excuse the wildness of the story. You will even have found some traits to put you in mind of this place. When you read of the picture quitting its panel, did not you recollect the portrait of Lord Falkland all in white in my gallery? Shall I even confess to you what was the origin of this romance? I waked one morning in the beginning of last June from a dream, of which all I could recover was, that I had thought myself in an ancient castle (a very natural dream for a head filled like mine with Gothic story) and that on the upper-most bannister of a great staircase I saw a gigantic hand in armour. In the evening I sat down and began to write, without knowing in the least what I intended to say or relate. The work grew on my hands, and I grew fond of it—add that I was very glad to think of anything rather than politics—In short I was so engrossed with my tale, which I completed in less than two months, that one evening I wrote from the time I had drunk my tea, about six o'clock, till half an hour after one in the morning, when my hand and fingers were so weary, that I could not hold the pen to finish the sentence, but left Matilda and Isabella talking, in the middle of a paragraph. You will laugh at my earnestness, but if I have amused you by retracing with any fidelity the manners of ancient days, I am content, and give you leave to think me as idle as you please.

You are, as you have long been to me, exceedingly kind, and I should with great satisfaction embrace your offer of visiting the solitude of Blecheley, though my cold is in a manner gone and my cough quite, if I was at liberty: but as I am preparing for my French journey, I have forty businesses upon my hands, and can only now and then purloin a day or half a day to come hither. You know I am not cordially disposed to *your* French journey, which is much more serious, as it is to be much more lasting. However, though I may suffer by your absence, I would not dissuade what may suit your inclination and circumstances. One thing however has struck me which I must mention, though it would depend on a circumstance that would give me the most real concern. It was suggested to me by that great fondness I have for your MSS for your kindness about which I feel the utmost gratitude. You would not, I think, leave them behind you; and are you aware of the danger they would run if you settled entirely in France? Do you know that the King of France is heir to all strangers who die in his dominions, by what they call the *droit d'aubaine?* Sometimes by great interest and favour persons have obtained a remission of this right in their lifetime; and yet that, even that, has not secured their effects from being embezzled. Old Lady Sandwich had obtained this remission, and yet, though she left everything to the present Lord, her grandson, a man for whose rank one should have thought they would have had regard, the King's officers forced themselves into her house, after her death, and plundered. You see, if you go, I shall expect to have your MSS deposited with me—seriously, you must leave them in safe custody behind you.

Lord Essex's trial is printed with the *State Trials.* In return for your obliging offer, I can acquaint you with a delightful publication of this winter, a collection of old ballads and poetry in three volumes, many from Pepys's collection at Cambridge. There were three such published between thirty and forty years ago, but very carelessly, and wanting many in this set: indeed there were others, of a looser sort, which the present editor, who is a clergyman,[1] thought it decent to omit.

When you go into Cheshire and upon your ramble, may I trouble you with a commission, but about which you must promise me not to go a step out of your way. Mr Bateman has a cloister at Old Windsor furnished with ancient wooden chairs, most of them triangular, but all of various patterns, and carved or turned in the most uncouth and whimsical forms. He picked them up one by one, for two, three, five or six shillings apiece from different farmhouses in Herefordshire. I have long envied and coveted them. There may be such in poor cottages in so neighbouring a county as Cheshire. I should not grudge any expense for purchase or carriage; and should be glad even of a couple such for my clois-

1. The Rev. Thomas Percy (1729–1811), later Bishop of Dromore.

ter here. When you are copying inscriptions in a churchyard in any village, think of me, and step into the first cottage you see—but don't take farther trouble than that. I long to know what your bundle of MSS from Cheshire contains.

My bower is determined, but not at all what it is to be. Though I write romances, I cannot tell how to build all that belongs to them. Madame Danois[1] in the fairy tales used to tapestry them with jonquils, but as that furniture will not last above a fortnight in the year, I shall prefer something more huckaback. I have decided that the outside shall be treillage, which however I shall not commence, till I have again seen some of old Louis's old-fashioned *galanteries* at Versailles. Rosamond's bower, you and I and Tom Hearne know was a labyrinth, but as my territory will admit of a very short clue, I lay aside all thoughts of a mazy habitation; though a bower is very different from an arbour, and must have more chambers than one. In short, I both know and don't know what it should be. I am almost afraid I must go and read Spenser, and wade through his allegories and drawling stanzas to get at a picture—but goodnight; you see how one gossips, when one is alone and at quiet on one's own dunghill!— Well! it may be trifling, yet it is such trifling as Ambition never is happy enough to know! Ambition orders palaces, but it is Content that chats for a page or two over a bower.

Yours ever,

H. Walpole

To John Chute, 3 October 1765

Paris, Oct. 3, 1765.

I don't know where you are, nor when I am likely to hear of you. I write at random, and, as I talk, the first thing that comes into my pen.

I am, as you certainly conclude, much more amused than

1. Comtesse d'Aulnoy (d. 1705).

pleased. At a certain time of life, sights and new objects may entertain one, but new people cannot find any place in one's affection. New faces with some name or other belonging to them catch my attention for a minute—I cannot say many preserve it. Five or six of the women that I have seen already are very sensible. The men are in general much inferior, and not even agreeable. They sent us their best, I believe, at first, the Duc de Nivernois. Their authors, who by the way are everywhere, are worse than their own writings, which I don't mean as a compliment to either. In general, the style of conversation is solemn, pedantic, and seldom animated, but by a dispute. I was expressing my aversion to disputes: Mr. Hume, who very gratefully admires the tone of Paris, having never known any other tone, said with great surprise, 'Why, what do you like, if you hate both disputes and whisk?'

What strikes me the most upon the whole is, the total difference of manners between them and us, from the greatest object to the least. There is not the smallest similitude in the twenty-four hours. It is obvious in every trifle. Servants carry their lady's train, and put her into her coach with their hat on. They walk about the streets in the rain with umbrellas to avoid putting on their hats; driving themselves in open chaises in the country without hats, in the rain, too, and yet often wear them in a chariot in Paris when it does not rain. The very footmen are powdered from the break of day, and yet wait behind their master, as I saw the Duc of Praslin's do, with a red pocket-handkerchief about their necks. Versailles, like everything else, is a mixture of parade and poverty, and in every instance exhibits something most dissonant from our manners. In the colonnades, upon the staircases, nay, in the antechambers of the royal family, there are people selling all sorts of wares. While we were waiting in the Dauphin's sumptuous bedchamber, till his dressing-room door should be opened, two fellows were sweeping it, and dancing about in sabots to rub the floor.

You perceive that I have been presented. The Queen took great notice of me; none of the rest said a syllable. You are let into the King's bedchamber just as he has put on his shirt; he dresses and talks good-humouredly to a few, glares at strangers, goes to mass, to dinner, and a-hunting. The good old Queen, who is like Lady Primrose in the face, and Queen Caroline in the immensity of her cap, is at her dressing-table, attended by two or three old ladies, who are languishing to be in Abraham's bosom, as the only man's bosom to whom they can hope for admittance. Thence you go to the Dauphin, for all is done in an hour. He scarce stays a minute; indeed, poor creature, he is a ghost, and cannot possibly last three months. The Dauphiness is in her bedchamber, but dressed and standing; looks cross, is not civil, and has the true Westphalian grace and accents. The four Mesdames, who are clumsy plump old wenches, with a bad likeness to their father, stand in a bedchamber in a row, with black cloaks and knotting-bags, looking good-humoured, not knowing what to say, and wriggling as if they wanted to make water. This ceremony too is very short; then you are carried to the Dauphin's three boys, who you may be sure only bow and stare. The Duke of Berry looks weak and weak-eyed; the Count de Provence is a fine boy; the Count d'Artois[1] well enough. The whole concludes with seeing the Dauphin's little girl dine, who is as round and as fat as a pudding.

In the Queen's antechamber we foreigners and the foreign ministers were shown the famous beast of the Gevaudan, just arrived, and covered with a cloth, which two chasseurs lifted up. It is an absolute wolf, but uncommonly large, and the expression of agony and fierceness remains strongly imprinted on its dead jaws.

I dined at the Duc of Praslin's with four-and-twenty ambassadors and envoys, who never go but on Tuesdays to court. He does the honours sadly, and I believe nothing else well, looking important and empty. The Duc de Choiseul's face, which is quite the reverse of gravity, does not promise much more. His wife is gentle, pretty, and very agreeable. The Duchess of Praslin, jolly, red-faced, looking very vulgar, and being very attentive and civil. I saw the Duc de Richelieu in waiting, who is pale, except his nose, which is red, much wrinkled, and exactly a remnant of that age

1. All three reigned, as Louis XVI, Louis XVIII, and Charles X respectively.

which produced General Churchill, Wilks the player, the Duke of Argyll, &c. Adieu!

Yours ever,

HOR. WALPOLE.

TO THOMAS GRAY, 25 January 1766

Paris, January 25, 1766.

I am much indebted to you for your kind letter and advice; and though it is late to thank you for it, it is at least a stronger proof that I do not forget it. However, I am a little obstinate, as you know, on the chapter of health, and have persisted through this Siberian winter in not adding a grain to my clothes, and in going open-breasted without an under-waistcoat. In short, though I like extremely to live, it must be in my own way, as long as I can: it is not youth I court, but liberty; and I think making one's self tender, is issuing a *general warrant* against one's own person. I suppose I shall submit to confinement, when I cannot help it; but I am indifferent enough to life not to care if it ends soon after my prison begins.

I have not delayed so long to answer your letter, from not thinking of it, or from want of matter, but from want of time. I am constantly occupied, engaged, amused, till I cannot bring a hundredth part of what I have to say into the compass of a letter. You will lose nothing by this: you know my volubility, when I am full of new subjects; and I have at least many hours of conversation for you at my return. One does not learn a whole nation in four or five months; but, for the time, few, I believe, have seen, studied, or got so much acquainted with the French as I have.

By what I said of their religious or rather irreligious opinions, you must not conclude their people of quality, atheists—at least not the men—Happily for them, poor souls! they are not capable of going so far into thinking. They assent to a great deal, because it is the fashion, and because they don't know how to contradict.

They are ashamed to defend the Roman Catholic religion, because it is quite exploded; but I am convinced they believe it in their hearts. They hate the parliaments and the philosophers, and are rejoiced that they may still idolize royalty. At present too they are a little triumphant: the Court has shown a little spirit, and the parliaments much less: but as the Duc de Choiseul, who is very fluttering, unsettled, and inclined to the philosophers, has made a compromise with the Parliament of Bretagne, the parliaments might venture out again, if, as I fancy will be the case, they are not glad to drop a cause, of which they began to be a little weary of the inconveniencies.

The generality of the men, and more than the generality, are dull and empty. They have taken up gravity, thinking it was philosophy and English, and so have acquired nothing in the room of their natural levity and cheerfulness. However, as their high opinion of their own country remains, for which they can no longer assign any reason, they are contemptuous and reserved, instead of being ridiculously, consequently pardonably, impertinent. I have wondered, knowing my own countrymen, that we had attained such a superiority.—I wonder no longer, and have a little more respect for English *heads* than I had.

The women do not seem of the same country: if they are less gay than they were, they are more informed, enough to make them very conversable. I know six or seven with very superior understandings; some of them with wit, or with softness, or very good sense.

Madame Geoffrin, of whom you have heard much, is an extraordinary woman, with more common sense than I almost ever met with. Great quickness in discovering characters, penetration in going to the bottom of them, and a pencil that never fails in a likeness—seldom a favourable one. She exacts and preserves, spite of her birth and their nonsensical prejudices about nobility, great court and attention. This she acquires by a thousand little arts and offices of friendship; and by a freedom and severity which seems to be her sole end of drawing a concourse to her; for she insists on scolding those she inveigles to her. She has little taste and less knowledge, but protects artisans and authors, and courts a few people to have the credit of serving her dependents. She was bred under the famous Madame Tencin, who advised her never to refuse any man; for, said her mistress, though nine in ten should not care a farthing for you, the tenth may live to be an useful friend. She did not adopt or reject the whole plan, but fully retained the purport of the maxim. In short, she is an epitome of empire, subsisting by rewards and punishments. Her great enemy, Madame du Deffand, was for a short time mistress of the Regent, is now very old and stone blind, but retains all her vivacity, wit, memory, judgment, passions and agreeableness. She goes to operas, plays, suppers, and Versailles; gives suppers twice a week; has everything new read to her; makes new songs and epigrams, ay, admirably, and remembers every one that has been made these fourscore years. She corresponds with Voltaire, dictates charming letters to him, contradicts him, is no bigot to him or anybody, and laughs both at the clergy and the philosophers. In a dispute, into which she easily falls, she is very warm, and yet scarce ever in the wrong: her judgment on every subject is as just as possible; on every point of conduct as wrong as possible: for she is all love and hatred, passionate for her friends to enthusiasm, still anxious to be loved, I don't mean by lovers, and a vehement enemy, but openly. As she can have no amusement but conversation, the least solitude and ennui are insupportable to her, and put her into the power of several worthless people, who eat her suppers when they can eat nobody's of higher rank; wink to one another and laugh at her; hate her because she has forty times more parts—and venture to hate her because she is not rich. She has an old friend whom I must mention, a Monsieur Pondevelle, author of the *Fat puni*, and the *Complaisant*, and of those pretty novels, the *Comte de Cominge*, the *Siege of Calais*, and *Les Malheurs de l'amour*. Would not you expect this old man to be very agreeable? He can be so, but seldom is: yet he has another very different and very amusing talent, the art of parody, and is unique in his kind. He composes tales to the tunes of long dances: for instance, he has adapted the Regent's *Daphnis and Chloé* to one, and made it ten times more indecent; but is so old and sings it so well, that it is permitted in all companies. He has succeeded still better in *Les Caractères de la danse*, to which he has adapted words that express all the characters of love. With all this, he has not the least idea of cheerfulness in conversation; seldom speaks but on grave subjects, and not often on them; is a humorist, very supercilious, and wrapped up in admiration of his own country, as the only judge of his merit. His air and look are cold and forbidding; but ask him to sing, or praise his works, his eyes and smiles open and brighten up. In short, I can show him to you: the self-applauding poet in Hogarth's Rake's Progress, the second print, is so like his very features and very wig, that you would know him by it, if you came hither—for he certainly will not go to you.

Madame de Mirepoix's understanding is excellent of the useful kind, and can be so when she pleases of the agreeable kind. She has read, but seldom shows it, and has perfect taste. Her manner is cold, but very civil; and she conceals even the blood of Lorrain, without ever forgetting it. Nobody in France knows the world better, and nobody is personally so well with the King. She is false, artful, and insinuating beyond measure when it is her interest, but indolent and a coward. She never had any passion but gaming, and always loses. Forever paying court, the sole produce of a life of art is to get money from the King to carry on a course of paying debts or contracting new ones, which she discharges as fast as she is able. She advertised devotion to get made Dame du Palais to the Queen and the very next day this Princess of Lorrain was seen riding backwards with Madame Pompadour in the latter's coach. When the King was stabbed and heartily frightened, the mistress took a panic too, and consulted d'Argenson, whether she had not best make off in time. He hated her, and said, 'By all means.' Madame de Mirepoix advised her to stay. The King recovered his spirits, d'Argenson was banished, and *la Maréchale* inherited part of the mistress's credit.—I must interrupt my history of illustrious women with an anecdote of Monsieur de Maurepas, with whom I am much acquainted, and who has one of the few heads that approach to good ones, and who luckily for us was disgraced, and the marine dropped, because it was his favourite object and province. He employed Pondevelle to make a song on the Pompadour: it was clever and bitter, and did not spare even Majesty. This was Maurepas absurd enough to sing at supper at Versailles. Banishment ensued; and lest he should ever be restored, the mistress persuaded the King that he had poisoned her predecessor Madame de Châteauroux. Maurepas is very agreeable, and exceedingly cheerful; yet I have seen a transient silent cloud when politics are talked of.

Madame de Boufflers, who was in England, is a *savante,* mistress of the Prince of Conti, and very desirous of being his wife. She is two women, the upper and the lower. I need not tell you that the lower is *galante,* and still has pretensions. The upper is very sensible too, and has a measured eloquence that is just and pleasing—but all is spoiled by an unrelaxed attention to applause. You would think she was always sitting for her picture to her biographer.

Madame de Rochfort is different from all the rest. Her understanding is just and delicate; with a finesse of wit that is the result of reflection. Her manner is soft and feminine, and though a *savante,* without any declared pretensions. She is the *decent* friend of Monsieur de Nivernois, for you must not believe a syllable of what you read in their novels. It requires the greatest curiosity, or the greatest habitude, to discover the smallest connection between the sexes here. No familiarity, but under the veil of friendship, is permitted, and love's dictionary is as much prohibited, as at first sight one should think his ritual was. All you hear, and that pronounced with nonchalance, is, that *monsieur un tel* has had *madame une telle.* The Duc de Nivernois has parts, and writes at the top of the mediocre, but, as Madame Geoffrin says, is *manqué par tout; guerrier manqué, ambassadeur manqué, homme d'affaires manqué,* and *auteur manqué*—no, he is not *homme de naissance manqué.* He would think freely, but has some ambition of being governor to the Dauphin, and is more afraid of his wife and daughter, who are ecclesiastic fagots. The former out-chatters the Duke of Newcastle; and the latter, Madame de Gisors, exhausts Mr Pitt's eloquence in defence of the Archbishop of Paris. Monsieur de Nivernois lives in a small circle of dependent admirers, and Madame de Rochfort is high priestess for a small salary of credit.

The Duchess of Choiseul, the only young one of these heroines, is not very pretty, but has fine eyes, and is a little model in waxwork, which not being allowed to speak for some time as incapable, has a hesitation and modesty, the latter of which the Court has not cured, and the former of which is atoned for by the most interesting sound of voice, and forgotten in the most elegant turn and propriety of expression. Oh! it is the gentlest, amiable, civil, little creature that ever came out of a fairy egg! So just in its phrases and thoughts, so attentive and good-natured! Everybody loves it, but its husband, who prefers his own sister the Duchesse de Grammont, an Amazonian, fierce, haughty dame, who loves and hates arbitrarily, and is detested. Madame de Choiseul, passionately fond of her husband, was the martyr of this union, but at last submitted with a good grace; has gained a little credit with him, and is still believed to idolize him—But I doubt it—she takes too much pains to profess it.

I cannot finish my list without adding a much more common character—but more complete in its kind than any of the foregoing, the Maréchale de Luxembourg. She has been very handsome, very abandoned, and very mischievous. Her beauty is gone, her lovers are gone, and she thinks the Devil is coming. This dejection has softened her into being rather agreeable, for she has wit and good breeding; but you would swear, by the restlessness of her person and the horrors she cannot conceal, that she had signed the compact, and expected to be called upon in a week for the performance.

I could add many pictures, but none so remarkable. In those I send you, there is not a feature bestowed gratis or exaggerated. For the beauties, of which there are a few considerable, as Mesdames de Brionne, de Monaco, et d'Egmont, they have not yet lost their characters, nor got any.

You must not attribute my intimacy with Paris to curiosity alone. An accident unlocked the doors for me. That *passe-partout,* called the fashion, has made them fly open—and what do you think was that fashion?—I myself—Yes, like Queen Elinor in the ballad, I sunk at Charing Cross, and have risen in the Faubourg St Germain. A *plaisanterie* on Rousseau,[1] whose arrival here in his way to you brought me acquaintanced with many anecdotes comformable to the idea I had conceived of him, got about, was liked much more than it deserved, spread like wild-fire, and made me the subject of conversation. Rousseau's devotees were offended. Madame de Boufflers, with a tone of sentiment, and the accents of lamenting humanity, abused me heartily, and then complained to myself with the utmost softness. I acted contrition, but had like to have spoiled all, by growing dreadfully tired of a second lecture from the Prince of Conti, who took up the ball, and made himself the hero of a history wherein he had nothing to do. I listened, did not understand half he said (nor he neither), forgot the rest, said 'yes' when I should have said 'no,' yawned when I should have smiled, and was very penitent when I should have rejoiced at my pardon. Madame de Boufflers was more distressed, for he owned twenty times more than I had said: she frowned, and made him signs; but she had wound up his clack, and there was no stopping it. The moment she grew angry, the [lord of the house] grew charmed, and it has been my fault if I am not at the head of a numerous sect:—but when I left a triumphant party in England, I did not come hither to be at the head of a fashion. However, I have been sent for about like an African prince or a learned canary-bird, and was, in particular, carried by force to the Princess of Talmond, the Queen's cousin, who lives in a charitable apartment in the Luxembourg, and was sitting on a small bed hung with saints and Sobieskis, in a corner of one of those vast chambers, by two blinking tapers. I stumbled over a cat, a foot-stool, and a chamber-pot in my journey to her presence. She could not find a syllable to say to me, and the visit ended with her begging a lap-dog. Thank the Lord! though this is the first month, it is the last week, of my reign; and I shall resign my crown with great sat-

1. HW wrote a pretended letter from the King of Prussia to Rousseau that ridiculed the latter.

isfaction to a *bouillie* of chestnuts, which is just invented, and whose annals will be illustrated by so many indigestions, that Paris will not want anything else these three weeks. I will enclose the fatal letter[1] after I have finished this enormous one; to which I will only add, that nothing has interrupted my Sévigné researches but the frost. The Abbé de Malesherbes has given me full power to ransack Livry. I did not tell you, that by great accident, when I thought on nothing less, I stumbled on an original picture of the Comte de Grammont. Adieu! You are generally in London in March: I shall be there by the end of it.

Yours ever,

HOR. WALPOLE

TO JOHN CHUTE, 10 October 1766

Bath, Oct. 10, 1766.

I am impatient to hear that your charity to me has not ended in the gout to yourself—all my comfort is, if you have it, that you have good Lady Brown to nurse you.

My health advances faster than my amusement. However, I have been at one opera, Mr. Wesley's. They have boys and girls with charming voices, that sing hymns, in parts, to Scotch ballad tunes; but indeed so long, that one would think they were already in eternity, and knew how much time they had before them. The chapel is very neat, with true Gothic windows (yet I am not converted); but I was glad to see that luxury is creeping in upon them before persecution: they have very neat mahogany stands for branches, and brackets of the same in taste. At the upper end is a broad *haut-pas* of four steps, advancing in the middle: at each end of the broadest part are two of *my* eagles[2] with red cushions for the parson and clerk. Behind them rise three more steps, in the midst

1. To Rousseau.

2. Eagles in the attitude of the marble one at Strawberry Hill.

of which is a third eagle for pulpit. Scarlet armed-chairs to all three. On either hand, a balcony for elect ladies. The rest of the congregation sit on forms. Behind the pit, in a dark niche, is a plain table within rails; so you see the throne is for the apostle. Wesley is a lean elderly man, fresh-coloured, his hair smoothly combed, but with a *soupçon* of curl at the ends. Wondrous clean, but as evidently an actor as Garrick. He spoke his sermon, but so fast, and with so little accent, that I am sure he has often uttered it, for it was like a lesson. There were parts and eloquence in it; but towards the end he exalted his voice, and acted very ugly enthusiasm; decried learning, and told stories, like Latimer, of the fool of his college, who said, 'I *thanks* God for everything.' Except a few from curiosity, and *some honourable women,* the congregation was very mean. There was a Scotch Countess of Buchan, who is carrying a pure rosy vulgar face to heaven, and who asked Miss Rich, if that was *the author of the poets.* I believe she meant me and the *Noble Authors.*

The Bedfords came last night. Lord Chatham was with me yesterday two hours; looks and walks well, and is in excellent political spirits.

Yours ever,

HOR. WALPOLE.

TO THOMAS GRAY, 18 February 1768

Arlington Street, February 18, 1768.

You have sent me a long and very obliging letter, and yet I am extremely out of humour with you. I saw *Poems by Mr Gray* advertised: I called directly at Dodsley's to know if this was to be more than a new edition? He was not at home himself, but his foreman told me he thought there were some new pieces, and notes to the whole. It was very unkind, not only to go out of town without mentioning them to me, without showing them to me, but not to say a word of them in this letter. Do you think I am indifferent, or not curious, about what you write? I have ceased to ask you, because you have so long refused to show me anything. You could not suppose I thought that you never write. No; but I concluded you did not intend, at least yet, to publish what you had written. As you did intend it, I might have expected a month's preference. You will do me the justice to own that I had always rather have seen your writings than have shown you mine; which you know are the most hasty trifles in the world, and which, though I may be fond of the subject when fresh, I constantly forget in a very short time after they are published. This would sound like affectation to others, but will not to you. It would be affected, even to you, to say I am indifferent to fame—I certainly am not, but I am indifferent to almost anything I have done to acquire it. The greater part are mere compilations; and no wonder they are, as you say, incorrect, when they are commonly written with people in the room, as *Richard*[1] and the *Noble Authors* were. But I doubt there is a more intrinsic fault in them; which is, that I cannot correct them. If I write tolerably, it must be at once; I can neither mend nor add. The articles of Lord Capel and Lord Peterborough, in the second edition of the *Noble Authors*, cost me more trouble than all the rest together: and you may perceive that the worst part of *Richard*, in point of ease and style, is what relates to the papers you gave me on Jane Shore, because it was tacked on so long afterwards, and when my impetus was chilled. If some time or other you will take the trouble of pointing out the inaccuracies of it, I shall be much obliged to you: at present I shall meddle no more with it. It has taken its fate; nor did I mean to complain. I found it was condemned indeed beforehand, which was what I alluded to. Since publication (as has happened to me before) the success has gone beyond my expectation.

Not only at Cambridge, but here, there have been people wise enough to think me too free with the King of Prussia! A newspaper has talked of my known inveteracy to him.—Truly, I love him as well as I do most kings. The greater offence is my reflection on Lord Clarendon. It is forgotten that I had overpraised him before.

1. HW's *Historic Doubts of the Life and Reign of King Richard the Third* had just been published by James Dodsley.

Pray turn to the new State Papers from which, *it is said,* he composed his history. You will find they are the papers from which he did *not* compose his history. And yet I admire my Lord Clarendon more than these pretended admirers do. But I do not intend to justify myself. I can as little satisfy those who complain that I do not let them know what *really did* happen. If this inquiry can ferret out any truth, I shall be glad. I have picked up a few more circumstances. I now want to know what Perkin Warbeck's proclamation was, which Speed in his *History* says is preserved by Bishop Leslie. If you look in Speed, perhaps you will be able to assist me.

The Duke of Richmond and Lord Lyttelton agree with you, that I have not disculpated Richard of the murder of Henry VI. I own to you, it is the crime of which in my own mind I believe him most guiltless. Had I thought he committed it, I should never have taken the trouble to apologize for the rest. I am not at all positive or obstinate on your other objections, nor know exactly what I believe on many points of this story. And I am so sincere, that, except a few notes hereafter, I shall leave the matter to be settled or discussed by others. As you have written much too little, I have written a great deal too much, and think only of finishing the two or three other things I have begun—and of those, nothing but the last volume of painters is designed for the present public. What has one to do when turned fifty, but really think of *finishing?*

I am much obliged and flattered by Mr Mason's approbation, and particularly by having had almost the same thought with him. I said, 'People need not be angry at my excusing Richard; I have not diminished their fund of hatred, I have only transferred it from Richard to Henry.'—Well, but I have found you close with Mason—No doubt, cry prating I, something will come out. —Oh! no—leave us, both of you, to Annabellas and epistles to Ferney, that give Voltaire an account of his own tragedies, to *Macarony Fables* that are more unintelligible than Pilpay's are in the original, to Mr Thornton's hurdy-gurdy poetry, and to Mr ———, who has imitated himself worse than any fop in a magazine would have done. In truth, if you should abandon us, I could not wonder—when Garrick's prologues and epilogues, his own Cymons and farces, and the comedies of the fools that pay court to him, are the delight of the age, it does not deserve anything better.

Pray read the new *Account of Corsica.*[1] What relates to Paoli will amuse you much. There is a deal about the island and its divisions that one does not care a straw for. The author, Boswell, is a strange being, and, like———, has a rage of knowing anybody that ever was talked of. He forced himself upon me at Paris in spite of my teeth and my doors, and I see has given a foolish account of all he could pick up from me about King Theodore.[2] He then took an antipathy to me on Rousseau's account, abused me in the newspapers, and exhorted Rousseau to do so too: but as he came to see me no more, I forgave all the rest. I see he now is a little sick of Rousseau himself, but I hope it will not cure him of his anger to me. However, his book will I am sure entertain you.

I will add but a word or two more. I am criticized for the expression *tinker up* in the Preface. Is this one of those that you object to? I own I think such a low expression, placed to ridicule an absurd instance of wise folly, very forcible. Replace it with an elevated word or phrase, and to my conception it becomes as flat as possible.

George Selwyn says I may, if I please, write historic doubts on the present Duke of G[loucester][3] too. Indeed they would be doubts, for I know nothing certainly.

Will you be so kind as to look into Leslie *De rebus Scotorum,* and see if Perkin's proclamation is there, and if there, how authenticated. You will find in Speed my reason for asking this.

I have written in such a hurry, I believe you will scarce be able to read my letter—and as I have just been writing French, perhaps the sense may not be clearer than the writing. Adieu!

Yours ever,

HOR. WALPOLE

1. By James Boswell.

2. Theodore (1690–1756), Baron de Neuhoff, proclaimed King of Corsica April–September 1736, died a prisoner in the Fleet. HW wrote about him in *The World* (22 Feb. 1753) and erected a tablet to him at the west door of St. Anne's, Soho.

3. Who had secretly married HW's niece, Maria Waldegrave.

To Sir Horace Mann, 31 March 1768

Arlington Street, Thursday, March 31, 1768.

I have received your letter with the extract of that from Mr M. You know it was not agreeable to my opinion that you should hear of the new promise, because when it is not immediately executed, I look upon it as little preferable to an old one, and because I thought it would be raising the quicksilver of your impatience unnecessarily. I do not think any honours will be bestowed yet. The peerages are all postponed to an indefinite time— If you are in a violent hurry, you may petition the ghosts of your neighbours Massaniello and the Gracchi. The spirit of one of them walks here—nay, I saw it go by my window yesterday at noon in a hackney chair—

Friday.

I was interrupted yesterday. The ghost is laid for a time in a red sea of port and claret. This spectre is the famous Wilkes. He appeared the moment the Parliament was dissolved. The ministry despised him. He stood for the City of London, and was the last on the poll of seven candidates, none but the mob, and most of them without votes, favouring him. He then offered himself to the county of Middlesex. The election came on last Monday. By five in the morning a very large body of weavers, etc. took possession of Piccadilly, and the roads and turnpikes leading to Brentford, and would suffer nobody to pass without blue cockades, and papers inscribed *No. 45, Wilkes and Liberty*. They tore to pieces the coaches of Sir W. Beauchamp Proctor, and Mr Cooke, the other candidates, though the latter was not there, but in bed with the gout—and it was with difficulty that Sir William and Mr Cooke's cousin got to Brentford. There, however, lest it should be declared a void election, Wilkes had the sense to keep everything quiet. But about five, Wilkes being considerably ahead of the other two, his mob returned to town and behaved outrageously. They stopped every carriage, scratched and spoiled several, with writing all over them No. 45, pelted, threw dirt and stones, and forced everybody to huzza for Wilkes. I did but cross Piccadilly at eight in my coach with a French Monsieur D'Angeul whom I was carrying to Lady Hertford's; they stopped us, and bid us huzza. I desired him to let down the glass on his side, but as he was not alert, they broke it to shatters. At night they insisted in several streets on houses being illuminated, and several Scotch refusing, had their windows broken. Another mob rose in the City, and Harley the present Mayor being another Sir William Walworth, and having acted formerly and now with great spirit against Wilkes, and the Mansion House not being illuminated and he out of town, they broke every window and tried to force their way into the house. The trained bands were sent for, but did not suffice. At last a party of guards from the Tower and some lights erected, dispersed the tumult. At one in the morning a riot began before Lord Bute's house in Audley Street, though illuminated. They flung two large flints into Lady Bute's chamber who was in bed, and broke every window in the house. Next morning Wilkes and Cooke were returned members. The day was very quiet, but at night they rose again, and obliged almost every house in town to be lighted up, even the Duke of Cumberland's and Princess Amelie's. About one o'clock they marched to the Duchess of Hamilton's in Argyle Buildings (Lord Lorn being in Scotland). She was obstinate and would not illuminate, though with child and as they hope of an heir to the family, and with the Duke her son and the rest of her children in the house. There is a small court and parapet-wall before the house: they brought iron crows, tore down the gates, pulled up the pavement, and battered the house for three hours. They could not find the key of the back door, nor send for any assistance. The night before they had obliged the Duke and Duchess of Northumberland to give them beer and appear at the windows and drink Wilkes's health. They stopped and opened the coach of Count Seilern the Austrian ambassador, who has made a formal complaint, on which the Council met on Wednesday night, and were going to issue a proclamation, but hearing all was quiet, and that only a few houses were illuminated in Leicester

Fields from the terror of the inhabitants, a few constables were sent with orders to extinguish the lights, and not the smallest disorder has happened since. In short, it has ended like other election riots, and with not a quarter of the mischief that has been done in some other towns.

There are, however, difficulties to come. Wilkes has notified that he intends to surrender himself to his outlawry the beginning of next term, which comes on the 17th of this month. There is said to be a flaw in the proceedings, in which case his election will be good, though the King's Bench may fine or imprison him on his former sentence. In my own opinion the House of Commons is the place where he can do the least hurt, for he is a wretched speaker, and will sink to contempt, like Admiral Vernon, whom I remember just such an illuminated hero, with two birthdays in one year. You will say he can write better than Vernon—true; and therefore his case is more desperate. Besides, Vernon was rich: Wilkes is undone, and though he has had great support, his patrons will be sick of maintaining him. He must either sink to poverty and a jail, or commit new excesses, for which he will get knocked on the head. The Scotch are his implacable enemies to a man. A Rienzi cannot stop—their histories are summed up in two words, a triumph and an assassination.

I must finish, for Lord Hertford is this moment come in, and insists on my dining with the Prince of Monaco, who is come over to thank the King for the presents his Majesty sent him on his kindness and attention to the late Duke of York. You shall hear the suite of the above histories, which I sit quietly and look at, having nothing more to do with the storm, and sick of politics, but as a spectator while they pass over the stage of the world. Adieu!

To George Montagu, 15 April 1768

Strawberry Hill, April 15, 1768.

Mr Chute tells me that you have taken a new house in Squireland, and have given yourself up for two years more to port and parsons. I am very angry, and resign you to the works of the devil or the church, I don't care which. You will get the gout, turn Methodist, and expect to ride to heaven upon your own great toe. I was happy with your telling me how well you love me, and though I don't love loving, I could have poured out all the fullness of my heart to such an old and true friend—but what am I the better for it, if I am to see you but two or three days in the year? I thought you would at last come and while away the remainder of life on the banks of the Thames in gaiety and old tales. I have quitted the stage, and the Clive is preparing to leave it. We shall neither of us ever be grave: dowagers roost all around us, and you could never want cards or mirth. Will you end like a fat farmer, repeating annually the price of oats, and discussing stale newspapers? There have you got, I hear, into an old gallery, that has not been glazed since Queen Elizabeth, and under the nose of an infant Duke and Duchess, that will understand you no more than if you wore a ruff and a coif, and talked to them of a call of sergeants the year of the Spanish Armada! Your wit and humour will be as much lost upon them as if you talked the dialect of Chaucer: for with all the divinity of wit, it grows out of fashion like a fardingale. I am convinced that the young men at White's already laugh at George Selwyn's bon mots only by tradition. I avoid talking before the youth of the age as I would dancing before them: for if one's tongue don't move in the steps of the day, and thinks to please by its old graces, it is only an object of ridicule, like Mrs Hobart in her cotillion. I tell you we should get together, and comfort ourselves with reflecting on the brave days that we have known—not that I think people were a jot more clever or wise in our youth, than they are now; but as my system is always to live in a vision as much as I can, and as visions don't increase with years, there is nothing so natural as to think one remembers what one does not remember.

I have finished my tragedy,[1] but as you would not bear the subject,[2] I will say no more of it, but that Mr Chute, who is not easily pleased, likes it, and Gray who is still more difficult, approves it. I am not yet intoxicated enough with it, to think it would do for the stage, though I wish to see it acted: but as Mrs Pritchard leaves the stage next month, I know nobody could play the Countess; nor am I disposed to expose myself to the impertinences of that jackanapes Garrick, who lets nothing appear but his own wretched stuff, or that of creatures still duller, who suffer him to alter their pieces as he pleases. I have written an epilogue *in character* for the Clive, which she would speak admirably—but I am not so sure that she would like to speak it. Mr Conway, Lady Ailesbury, Lady Lyttelton and Miss Rich are to come hither the day after tomorrow, and Mr Conway and I are to read my play to them, for I have not strength enough to go through the whole alone.

My press is revived, and is printing a French play written by the old President Hénault. It was damned many years ago at Paris, and yet I think is better than some that have succeeded, and much better than any of *our* modern tragedies. I print it to please the old man, as he was exceedingly kind to me at Paris; but I doubt whether he will live till it is finished. He is to have an hundred copies, and there are to be but an hundred more, of which you shall have one.

Adieu! Though I am very angry with you, I deserve all your friendship, by that I have for you, witness my anger and disappointment.

Yours ever

H. W.

PS. Send me your new direction, and tell me when I must begin to use it.

1. *The Mysterious Mother.*

2. A double incest.

To George Montagu, 15 June 1768

Strawberry Hill, June 15, 1768.

No, I cannot be so false as to say I am glad you are pleased with your situation. You are so apt to take root, that it requires ten years to dig you out again when you once begin to settle. As you go pitching your tent up and down, I wish you was still more a Tartar, and shifted your quarters perpetually. Yes, I *will* come and see you; but tell me first, when do your Duke and Duchess travel to the north? I know he is a very amiable lad, and I do not know that she is not as amiable a lad*dess*, but I had rather see their house comfortably when they are not there.

I perceive the deluge fell upon you before it reached us: it began here but on Monday last, and then rained near eight and forty hours without intermission. My poor hay has not a dry thread to its back. I have had a fire these three days. In short, every summer one lives in a state of mutiny and murmur, and I have found the reason. It is because we will affect to have a summer, and we have no title to any such thing. Our poets learned their trade of the Romans, and so adopted the terms of their masters. They talk of shady groves, purling streams, and cooling breezes, and we get sore throats and agues with attempting to realize these visions. Master Damon writes a song and invites Miss Chloe to enjoy the cool of the evening, and the deuce a bit have we of any such thing as a cool evening. Zephyr is a northeast wind, that makes Damon button up to the chin, and pinches Chloe's nose till it is red and blue; and then they cry *this is a bad summer*—as if we ever had any other! The best sun we have, is made of Newcastle coal, and I am determined never to reckon upon any other. We ruin ourselves with inviting over foreign trees, and make our houses clamber up hills to look at prospects. How our ancestors would laugh at us, who knew there was no being comfortable, unless you had a high hill before your nose, and a thick warm wood at your back! Taste is too freezing a commodity for us, and depend upon it will go out of fashion again.

There is indeed a natural warmth in this country, which, as you say, I am very glad not to enjoy any longer—I mean the hothouse in St Stephen's chapel. My own sagacity makes me very vain, though there was very little merit in it. I had seen so much of all parties, that I had little esteem left for any; it is most indifferent to me who is in or who is out, nor which is set in the pillory, Mr Wilkes or my Lord Mansfeld. I see the country going to ruin, and no man with brains enough to save it. That is mortifying—but what signifies who has the undoing of it? I seldom suffer myself to think on this subject: *my* patriotism could do no good, and my philosophy can make me be at peace.

I am sorry you are likely to lose your poor cousin Lady Hinchinbrook; I heard a very bad account of her when I was last in town. Your letter to Madame Roland shall be taken care of—but as you are so scrupulous of making me pay postage, I must remember not to overcharge you, as I can frank my idle letters no longer—therefore, good night!

Yours ever

H. W.

PS. I was in town last week, and found Mr Chute still confined. He had a return in his shoulder, but I think it more rheumatism than gout.

To George Montagu, 11 May 1769

Arlington Street, May 11th, 1769.

You are so wayward, that I often resolve to give you up to your humours. Then something happens with which I can divert you, and my good nature returns. Did not you say you should return to London long before this time? At least could not you tell me you had changed your mind? Why am I to pick it out from your absence and silence, as Dr Warburton found a future state in Moses's saying nothing of the matter? I could go on with a chapter of severe interrogatories; but I think it more cruel to treat you as a hopeless reprobate—yes, you are graceless, and as I have a respect for my own scolding, I shall not throw it away upon you.

Strawberry has been in great glory—I have given a *festino* there that will almost mortgage it. Last Tuesday all France dined there. Monsieur and Madame du Châtelet, the Duc de Liancour, three more French ladies whose names you will find in the enclosed paper, eight other Frenchmen, the Spanish and Portuguese ministers, the Holdernesses, Fitzroys, in short we were four and twenty. They arrived at two. At the gates of the castle I received them dressed in the cravat of Gibbins's carving, and a pair of gloves embroidered up to the elbows that had belonged to James I. The French servants stared and firmly believed this was the dress of English country gentlemen. After taking a survey of the apartments, we went to the printing-house where I had prepared the enclosed verses, with translations by Monsieur de Lisle, one of the company. The moment they were printed off, I gave a private signal and French horns and clarinets accompanied the compliment. We then went to see Pope's grotto and garden, and returned to a magnificent dinner in the refectory. In the evening we walked, had tea, coffee and lemonade in the gallery, which was illuminated with a thousand, or thirty candles, I forget which, and played at whisk and loo till midnight. Then there was a cold supper, and at one the company returned to town saluted by fifty nightingales, who as tenants of the manor came to do honour to their lord.

I cannot say last night was equally agreeable. There was what they called a *ridotto al fresco* at Vauxhall, for which one paid half a guinea, though except some thousand more lamps and a covered passage all round the garden which took off from the gardenhood, there was nothing better than on a common night. Mr Conway and I set out from his house at eight o'clock—the tide and torrent of coaches was so prodigious, that it was half an hour after nine before we got halfway from Westminster Bridge. We then alighted, and after scrambling under bellies of horses, through wheels, and over posts and rails, we reached the gardens, where were already many thousand persons. Nothing diverted me but a

Strawberry Hill from the southeast, by Paul Sandby

man in a Turk's dress and two nymphs, in masquerade without masks, who sailed amongst the company, and which was surprising, seemed to surprise nobody. It had been given out that people were desired to come in fancied dresses without masks. We walked twice round, and were rejoiced to come away, though with the same difficulties as at our entrance, for we found three strings of coaches all along the road who did not move half a foot in half an hour. There is to be a rival mob in the same way at Ranelagh tomorrow, for the greater the folly and imposition, the greater is the crowd. I have suspended the *vestimenta* that were torn off my back to the god of repentance, and shall stay away. Adieu! I have not a word more to say to you.

Yours etc.

H. W.

PS. I hope you will not regret paying a shilling for this packet.

To the Rev. William Cole, 14 June 1769

Strawberry Hill, June 14, 1769.

Dear Sir,

Among many agreeable passages in your last, there is nothing I like so well as the hope you give me of seeing you here in July. I will return that visit immediately—don't be afraid, I do not mean to incommode you at Waterbeach, but if you will come, I promise I will accompany you back as far as Cambridge; nay, carry you on to Ely, for thither I am bound. The Bishop has sent a Dr Nichols to me to desire I would assist him in a plan for the east window of his cathedral, which he intends to *benefactorate* with painted glass. The window is the most untractable of all Saxon uncouthnesses; nor can I conceive what to do with it, but by taking off the bottoms for arms and mosaic, splitting the crucifixion into three compartments, and filling the five lights at top with prophets, saints, martyrs or such-like, after shortening the windows like the great ones. This I shall propose; however, I choose to see the spot myself, as it will be a proper attention to the Bishop after his civility, and I really would give the best advice I could. The Bishop, like Alexander VIII, feels that the clock has struck half an hour past eleven, and is impatient to be let depart in peace after his eyes shall have seen his vitrification; at least he is impatient to give his eyes that treat—and yet it will be pity to precipitate the work. If you can come to me first, I shall be happy; if not, I must come to you, that is, will meet you at Cambridge. Let me know your mind, for I would not press you unseasonably. I am enough obliged to you already, though by mistake you think it is you that are obliged to me. I do not mean to plunder you of any more prints; but shall employ a little collector to get me all that are *gettable;* the rest, the greatest collectors of us all must want.

I am very sorry for the fever you have had; but Goodman Frog, if you will live in the fens, do you expect to be as healthy as if you were a fat Dominican at Naples? You and your MSS will all grow mouldy. When our climate is subject to no sign but Aquarius and Pisces, would one choose the dampest county under the heavens? I do not expect to persuade you, and so I will say no more. I wish you joy of the treasure you have discovered. Six Saxon bishops and a Duke of Northumberland! You have had fine sport this season. Thank you much for wishing to see my name on a plate in the history—but seriously I have no such vanity. I did my utmost to dissuade Mr Granger from the dedication, and took especial pains to get *my virtues* left out of the question; till I found he would be quite hurt if I did not let him express his gratitude as he called it; so to satisfy him, I was forced to accept of *his present,* for I doubt I have few virtues but what he has presented me with; and in a dedication you know one is permitted to have as many as the author can afford to bestow. I really have another objection to the plate, which is, the ten guineas. I have so many draughts on my extravagance for trifles that I like better than vanity, that I should not care to be at that expense. But I should think either the Duke or Duchess of Northumberland would rejoice at such opportunity of buying incense—and I will tell you what you shall do. Write to Mr Percy, and vaunt the discovery of Duke Brythnoth's bones, and ask him to move their Graces to contribute a plate. They could not be so unnatural as to refuse—especially if the Duchess knew the size of his thigh-bone.

I was very happy to show civilities to your friends, and should have asked them to stay and dine, but unluckily expected other company. Dr Ewin seems a very good sort of man and Mr Rawlinson a very agreeable one. Pray do not think it was any trouble to me to pay respect to your recommendation.

I have been eagerly reading Mr Shenstone's letters, which though containing nothing but trifles, amused me extremely, as they mention so many persons I know, particularly myself. I found there what I did not know, and what I believe Mr Gray himself never knew, that his ode on my cat was written to ridicule Lord Lyttelton's monody. It is just as true, as that the latter will survive and the former be forgotten. There is another anecdote equally vulgar and void of truth: that my father, *sitting in George's Coffee-house* (I suppose Mr Shenstone thought that after he quitted his place, he went to coffee-houses to learn news) was asked to contribute to a figure of himself that was to be beheaded by the mob. I do remember something like it, but it happened to myself. I met a mob, just after my father was out, in Hanover Square, and drove up to it to know what was the matter. They were carrying about a figure of my sister. This probably gave rise to the other story. That on my uncle I never heard, but it is a good story and not at all improbable. I felt great pity on reading these letters for the narrow circumstances of the author, and the passion for fame that he was tormented with; and yet he had much more fame than his talents entitled him to. Poor man, he wanted to have all the world talk of him for the pretty place he had made, and which he seems to have made only that it might be talked of. The first time a company came to see my house, I felt his joy. I am now so tired of it, that I shudder when the bell rings at the gate. It is as bad as keeping an inn, and I am often tempted to deny its being shown, if it would not be ill-natured to those that come, and to my housekeeper. I own, I was one day too cross. I had been plagued all the week with staring crowds. At last it rained a deluge. Well!

said I, at least nobody will come today. The words were scarce uttered, before the bell rang; a company desired to see the house—I replied, tell them they cannot possibly see the house, but they are very welcome to walk in the garden.

Observe: nothing above alludes to Dr Ewin and Mr Rawlinson; I was not only much pleased with them, but quite glad to show them how entirely you command my house and your most sincere friend and servant,

HOR. WALPOLE

TO SIR HORACE MANN, 27 February 1770

Arlington Street, Feb. 27, 1770.

It is very lucky, seeing how much of the tiger enters into the human composition, that there should be a good dose of the monkey too. If Æsop had not lived so many centuries before the introduction of masquerades and operas, he would certainly have anticipated my observation, and worked it up into a capital fable. As we still trade upon the stock of the ancients, we seldom deal in any other manufacture; and though nature, after new combinations, lets forth new characteristics, it is very rarely that they are added to the old fund; else how could so striking a remark have escaped being made, as mine on the joint ingredients of tiger and monkey? In France the latter predominates, in England the former; but like Orozmades and Arimanius[1] they get the better by turns. The bankruptcy in France and the rigours of the new Comptroller-General, are half forgotten in the expectation of a new opera at the new theatre. Our civil war has been lulled asleep by a subscription masquerade, for which the House of Commons literally adjourned yesterday. Instead of Fairfax's and Cromwells, we have had a crowd of Henrys the Eighth, Wolseys, Vandykes, and harlequins; and because Wilkes was not mask enough, we

1. Ormuzd and Ahriman, the rival principles of good and evil in the system of Zoroaster.

had a man dressed like him with a vizor in imitation of his squint, and a cap of liberty on a pole. In short, sixteen or eighteen young lords have given the town a masquerade, and politics for the last fortnight were forced to give way to habit-makers. The ball was last night at Soho, and if possible, was more magnificent than the King of Denmark's. The bishops opposed; he of London formally remonstrated to the King, who did not approve it, but could not help him. The consequence was that four divine vessels belonging to the holy fathers, alias, their wives, were at this masquerade. Monkey again. A fair widow, who once bore my whole name and now bears half of it, was there with one of those whom the newspapers call *great personages;* he dressed like Edward IV she like Elizabeth Woodville in grey and pearls with a black veil. Methinks it was not very difficult to find out the meaning of those masks. As one of my ancient passions formerly was masquerades, I had a large trunk of dresses by me; I dressed out a thousand young Conways and Cholmondeleys, and went with more pleasure to see them pleased than when I formerly delighted in that diversion myself. It has cost me a great headache, and I shall probably never go to another. A symptom appeared of the change that has happened in the people. The mob was beyond all belief; they held flambeaux to the windows of every coach, and demanded to have the masks pulled off and put on at their pleasure, but with extreme good humour and civility. I was with my Lady Hertford and two of her daughters in their coach; the mob took me for Lord Hertford, and huzzaed and blessed me! One fellow cried out, 'Are you for Wilkes?' Another said, 'Damn you, you fool, what has Wilkes to do with a masquerade?' In good truth, that stock is fallen very low. The Court has recovered a majority of 75 in the House of Commons; and the party has succeeded so ill in the Lords, that my Lord Chatham has betaken himself to the gout, and appears no more. What Wilkes may do at his enlargement in April, I don't know, but his star is certainly much dimmed. The distress of France, the injustice they have been reduced to commit on public credit, immense bankruptcies, and great bankers hanging and drowning themselves, are comfortable objects in our prospect, for one tiger is charmed if another tiger loses his tail.

There was a stroke of the monkey last night that will sound ill in the ears of your neighbour the Pope. The heir apparent of the house of Norfolk, a drunken old mad fellow, was, though a Catholic, dressed like a cardinal—I hope he was scandalized at the wives of our bishops.

So you agree with me, and don't think that the *crusado* from Russia will recover the Holy Land! It is a pity, for if the Turks keep it a little longer, I doubt it will be the Holy Land no longer. When Rome totters, poor Jerusalem! As to your Count Orloff's denying the murder of the late Czar, it is no more than every felon does at the Old Bailey. If I could write like Shakespeare, I would make Peter's ghost perch on the dome of Sancta Sophia, and when the Russian fleet comes in sight, roar with a voice of thunder, that should reach to Petersburgh,

> Let me sit heavy on thy soul tomorrow!

We have had two or three simpletons return from Russia, charmed with the murderess, and believing her innocent, *because* she spoke graciously to *them* in the drawing-room. I don't know what the present Grand Signior's name is, Osman or Mustapha, or what, but I am extremely on his side against Catherine of Zerbst; and I never intend to ask him for a farthing, nor write panegyrics on him for pay, like Voltaire and Diderot; so you need not say a word to him of my good wishes. Benedict XIV deserved my friendship, but being a sound Protestant, one would not, you know, make all Turk and pagan and infidel princes too familiar. Adieu!

To George Montagu, 7 July 1770

Strawberry Hill, Saturday night, July 7th, 1770.

After making an inn of your house, it is but decent to thank you for my entertainment, and to acquaint you with the result of my journey. The party passed off much better than I expected. A Princess[1] at the head of a very small set for five days together did not promise well. However she was very good-humoured, and easy, and dispensed with a large quantity of etiquette. Lady Temple is good-nature itself, my Lord was very civil, Lord Besborough is made to suit all sorts of people, Lady Mary Coke respects royalty too much not to be very condescending, Lady Ann Howard and Mrs Middleton[2] filled up the drawing-room, or rather made it out, and I was determined to carry it off as well as I could, and happened to be in such good spirits, and took such care to avoid politics, that we laughed a great deal, and had not a cloud the whole time.

We breakfasted at half an hour after nine; but the Princess did not appear till it was finished; then we walked in the garden or drove about it in cabriolets, till it was time to dress: dined at three, which though properly proportioned to the smallness of the company to avoid ostentation, lasted a vast while, as the Princess eats and talks a great deal; then again into the garden till past seven, when we came in, drank tea and coffee, and played at pharaoh till ten, when the Princess retired, and we went to supper, and before twelve to bed. You see there was great sameness and little vivacity in all this. It was a little broken by fishing, and going round the park one of the mornings; but in reality the number of buildings and variety of scenes in the garden made each day different from the rest: and my meditations on so historic a spot prevented my being tired. Every acre brings to one's mind some instance of parts or pedantry, of the taste or want of taste, of the ambition, or love of fame, or greatness, or miscarriages of those that have inhabited, decorated, planned or visited the place. Pope, Congreve, Vanbrugh, Kent, Gibbs, Lord Cobham, Lord Chesterfield, the mob of nephews, the Lytteltons, Grenvilles, Wests, Leonidas Glover and Wilkes, the late Prince of Wales, the King of Denmark, Princess Amelie, and the proud monuments of

1. Princess Amelia.
2. Ladies-in-waiting.

Lord Chatham's services, now enshrined there, then anathematized there, and now again commanding there, with the Temple of Friendship like the temple of Janus, sometimes open to war, and sometimes shut up in factious cabals, all these images crowd upon one's memory and add visionary personages to the charming scenes, that are so enriched with fanes and temples, that the real prospects are little less than visions themselves.

On Wednesday night a small Vauxhall was acted for us at the grotto in the Elysian fields, which was illuminated with lamps, as were the thickets and two little barks on the lake. With a little exaggeration I could make you believe that nothing ever was so delightful. The idea was really pretty, but as my feelings have lost something of their romantic sensibility, I did not quite enjoy such an entertainment *al fresco* so much as I should have done twenty years ago. The evening was more than cool, and the destined spot anything but dry. There were not half lamps enough, and no music but an ancient militia-man who played cruelly on a squeaking tabor and pipe. As our procession descended the vast flight of steps into the garden, in which was assembled a crowd of people from Buckingham and the neighbouring villages to see the Princess and the show, the moon shining very bright, I could not help laughing, as I surveyed our troop, which instead of tripping lightly to such an Arcadian entertainment, were hobbling down, by the balustrades, wrapped up in cloaks and great-coats for fear of catching cold. The Earl you know is bent double, the Countess very lame, I am a miserable walker, and the Princess, though as strong as a Brunswic lion, makes no figure in going down fifty stone stairs. Except Lady Ann—and by courtesy, Lady Mary, we were none of us young enough for a pastoral. We supped in the grotto, which is as proper to this climate, as a sea-coal fire would be in the dog-days at Tivoli.

But the chief entertainment of the week, at least what was so to the Princess, is an arch which Lord Temple has erected to her honour in the most enchanting of all picturesque scenes. It is inscribed on one side *Ameliæ Sophiæ Aug.* and has a medallion of her on the other. It is placed on an eminence at the top of the Elysian fields, in a grove of orange trees. You come to it on a sudden, and are startled with delight on looking through it: you at once see through a glade the river winding at bottom; from which a thicket rises, arched over with trees, but opened, and discovering a hillock full of haycocks, beyond which in front is the Palladian bridge, and again over that, a larger hill crowned with the castle. It is a tall landscape, framed by the arch and the overbowering trees, and comprehending more beauties of light, shade and buildings, than any picture of Albano I ever saw.

Between the flattery and the prospect the Princess was really in Elysium: she visited her arch four and five times every day, and could not satiate herself with it. The statues of Apollo and the Muses stand on each side of the arch. One day she found in Apollo's hand the following lines, which I had written for her and communicated to Lord Temple;

> T'other day with a beautiful frown on her brow
> To the rest of the gods said the Venus of Stow,[1]
> 'What a fuss is here made with that arch just erected!
> How *our* temples are slighted, our altars neglected!
> Since yon nymph has appear'd, *we* are noticed no more:
> All resort to *her* shrine, all *her* presence adore.
> And what's more provoking, before all our faces
> Temple thither has drawn both the Muses and Graces.'
> 'Keep your temper, dear child,' Phoebus cried with a smile,
> 'Nor this happy, this amiable festival spoil.
> Can your shrine any longer with garlands be drest?
> When a true goddess reigns, all the false are supprest.'

If you will keep my counsel, I will own to you, that originally the two last lines were much better, but I was forced to alter them out of decorum, not to be too pagan upon the occasion; in short, here they are as in the first sketch,

> Recollect, once before that our oracles ceas'd,
> When a real divinity rose in the East.

1. One of the buildings at Stowe was a temple to her.

So many heathen temples around, had made me talk as a Roman poet would have done; but I corrected my verses, and have made them insipid enough to offend nobody. Good night. I am rejoiced to be once more in the gay solitude of my own little Tempe.

Yours ever

H. W.

To John Chute, 5 August 1771

Paris, Aug. 5, 1771.

It is a great satisfaction to me to find by your letter of the 30th that you have had no return of your gout. I have been assured here that the best remedy is to cut one's nails in hot water. It is, I fear, as certain as any other remedy! It would at least be so here, if their bodies were of a piece with their understandings; or if both were as curable as they are the contrary. Your prophecy, I doubt, is not better founded than the prescription. I may be lame; but I shall never be a duck, nor deal in the garbage of the Alley.

I envy your *Strawberry tide,* and need not say how much I wish I was there to receive you. Methinks, I should be as glad of a little grass, as a seaman after a long voyage. Yet English gardening gains ground here prodigiously—not much at a time, indeed—I have literally seen one that is exactly like a tailor's paper of patterns. There is a Monsieur Boutin, who has tacked a piece of what he calls an English garden to a set of stone terraces, with steps of turf. There are three or four very high hills, almost as high as, and exactly in the shape of, a tansy pudding. You squeeze between these and a river, that is conducted at obtuse angles in a stone channel, and supplied by a pump; and when walnuts come in, I suppose it will be navigable. In a corner enclosed by a chalk wall are the samples I mentioned; there is a stripe of grass, another of corn, and a third *en friche,* exactly in the order of beds in a nursery. They have translated Mr. Whatcly's[1] book, and the Lord knows

1. Thomas Whateley, author of *Observations on Modern Gardening.*

what barbarism is going to be laid at our door. This new *Anglomanie* will literally be *mad English.*

New *arrêts,* new retrenchments, new misery, stalk forth every day. The Parliament of Besançon is dissolved; so are the *Grenadiers de France.* The King's tradesmen are all bankrupt; no pensions are paid, and everybody is reforming their suppers and equipages. Despotism makes converts faster than Christianity did. Louis *Quinze* is the true *rex Christianissimus,* and has ten times more success than his dragooning great-grandfather. Adieu, my dear Sir!

Yours most faithfully,

HOR. WALPOLE.

Friday, 9th.

This was to have gone by a private hand, but cannot depart till Monday; so I may be continuing my letter till I bring it myself. I have been again at the Chartreuse; and, though it was the sixth time, I am more enchanted with those paintings[1] than ever. If it is not the first work in the world, and must yield to the Vatican, yet in simplicity and harmony it beats Raphael himself. There is a vapour over all the pictures, that makes them more natural than any representation of objects—I cannot conceive how it is effected. You see them through the shine of a south-east wind. These poor folks do not know the inestimable treasure they possess—but they are perishing these pictures, and one gazes at them as at a setting sun. There is the purity of Racine in them, but they give me more pleasure—and I should much sooner be tired of the poet than of the painter.

It is very singular that I have not half the satisfaction in going into churches and convents that I used to have. The consciousness that the vision is dispelled, the want of fervour so obvious in the religious, the solitude that one knows proceeds from contempt, not from contemplation, make those places appear like abandoned theatres destined to destruction. The monks trot about as if they had not long to stay there; and what used to be holy gloom is now

1. Le Sueur's paintings of incidents in the life of St. Bruno.

but dirt and darkness. There is no more deception than in a tragedy acted by candle-snuffers. One is sorry to think that an empire of common sense would not be very picturesque; for, as there is nothing but taste that can compensate for the imagination of madness, I doubt there will never be twenty men of taste for twenty thousand madmen. The world will no more see Athens, Rome, and the Medici again, than a succession of five good emperors, like Nerva, Trajan, Adrian, and the two Antonines.

Aug. 13.

Mr. Edmonson has called on me; and, as he sets out to-morrow, I can safely trust my letter to him. I have, I own, been much shocked at reading Gray's death[1] in the papers. 'Tis an hour that makes one forget any subject of complaint, especially towards one with whom I lived in friendship from thirteen years old. As self lies so rooted in self, no doubt the nearness of our ages made the stroke recoil to my own breast; and having so little expected his death, it is plain how little I expect my own. Yet to you, who of all men living are the most forgiving, I need not excuse the concern I feel. I fear most men ought to apologize for their want of feeling, instead of palliating that sensation when they have it. I thought that what I had seen of the world had hardened my heart; but I find that it had formed my language, not extinguished my tenderness. In short, I am really shocked—nay, I am hurt at my own weakness, as I perceive that when I love anybody, it is for my life; and I have had too much reason not to wish that such a disposition may very seldom be put to the trial. You, at least, are the only person to whom I would venture to make such a confession.

Adieu! my dear Sir! Let me know when I arrive, which will be about the last day of the month, when I am likely to see you. I have much to say to you. Of being here I am most heartily tired, and nothing but this dear old woman should keep me here an hour—I am weary of them to death—but that is not new!

Yours ever,

HOR. WALPOLE.

1. Gray died at Cambridge of gout in the stomach on July 30, 1771.

To Lady Mary Coke, 22 August 1771

Paris, Aug. 22, 1771.

I never trouble your Ladyship with common news. The little events of the world are below the regard of one who steps from throne to throne, and converses only with demigods and demigoddesses. Parliaments are broken here every day about our ears, but their splinters are not of consequence enough to send you. I waited for something worthy of being entered in your imperial archives—little thinking that I should be happy enough to be the first to inform you, at least to ascertain you, of the most extraordinary discovery that ever was made, and far more important than the forty dozen of islands, which Dr Solander has picked up the Lord knows where, as he went to catch new sorts of fleas and crickets; and which said islands, if well husbanded, may produce forty more wars. The discovery I mean will occasion great desolation too: it will produce a violent change in the empire of Parnassus, it will be very prejudicial to the eyes, and considerably reduce the value of what Cibber called *the Paraphonalia of a Woman of Quality.* It is difficult not to moralize on so trist an event! Can we wonder at that fleeting condition of human life, when the brightest and most durable of essences is proved to be but a vapour! No, Madam, I do not mean angels. They have indeed been in some danger; but have been saved, at least for some time, by Madame du Barry, and the late edicts that wink at the return of the Jesuits. The radiances in question have undergone a more fiery trial, and their nothingness is condemned without reprieve. Yes, Madam, diamonds are a bubble, and adamant itself has lost its obduracy! I am sorry to say that it would be a greater compliment now to tell a beauty that she had ruby eyes, than to compare them to a diamond, and if your Ladyship's heart were no harder than adamant, I should be sure of finding it no longer irresistible. As this memorable process took its rise at Vienna, your Ladyship may perhaps have heard something of it. Public experiences have now been made here; and the day before yesterday, the ordeal trial was executed. A diamond was put into a crucible over a moderate fire, and in an hour was absolutely annihilated. No ashes were left, not enough to enclose in a fancy ring. An emerald mounted the scaffold next—its verdure suffered, but not its essence. The third was a ruby, who triumphed over the flames, and came forth from the furnace as unhurt as Shadrac, Meshac, and Abednego—to the immortal disgrace of the diamond: a crystal behaved with as much heroism as the ruby, and not a hair of its head was singed. Nobody can tell how far this revolution will go. For my part as I foresee that no woman of quality will deign to wear any more diamonds, and that next to rubies, crystal will be the principal ornament in a lady's dress, I am buying up all the old lustres I can meet with. I have already got a piece of two thousand weight, and that I hope to sell for fifty thousand pounds to the first nabob's daughter that is married, for a pair of earrings; and I have another still larger, that I am taking to pieces, and intend to have set in a stomacher, large enough for the most prominent slope of the present age. Madame du Barry they say has already given Pitt's diamond to her chambermaid; and if Lord Pigot is wise, he will change his at Betts's glass shop for a dozen strong beer glasses. As to Lord Clive and the Lady of Loretto, I do not feel much pity for them; they are rich enough to stand this loss. The reflections one might make on this disaster are infinite, but I will take up no more of your Ladyship's time—nor do I condole with you, Madam; your philosophy is incapable of being shaken by so sublunary a consideration, as a decrease in the value of your large ring. It has a secret and inestimable merit, which is out of the power of a crucible to assail; and you and it will remain or become stars, when the fashion of this world passeth away.

I am, Madam,

Your Ladyship's most faithful, humble servant,

HOR. WALPOLE

To the Rev. William Mason, 25 September 1771

Strawberry Hill, Sept. 25, 1771.

I have received both your letters, Sir, by Mr Stonhewer and by the post from York. I direct this to Aston rather than to York, for fear of any miscarriage, and will remember to insert *near Sheffield.*

I not only agree with your sentiments, but am flattered that they countenance my own practice. In some cases I have sold my works, and sometimes have made the impressions at my own press pay themselves, as I am not rich enough to treat the public with all I print there; nor do I know why I should; some editions have been given to charities, to the poor of Twickenham, etc. Mr Spence's life of Magliabecchi was bestowed on the reading tailor. I am neither ashamed of being an author, or a bookseller. My mother's father was a timber-merchant, I have many reasons for thinking myself a worse man, and none for thinking myself better: consequently I shall never blush at doing anything he did. I print much better than I write, and love my trade, and hope I am not one of those *most undeserving of all objects* printers and booksellers, whom I confess you lash with justice. In short, Sir, I have no notion of poor Mr Gray's delicacy; I would not sell my talents as orators and senators do, but I would keep a shop, and sell any of my own works that would gain me a livelihood, whether books or shoes, rather than be tempted to sell myself. 'Tis an honest vocation to be a scavenger—but I would not be Solicitor-General. Whatever method you fix upon for the publication of Mr Gray's works, I dare answer I shall approve, and will, therefore, say no more on it till we meet. I will beg you, Sir, when you come to town to bring me what papers or letters he had preserved of mine—for the answer to Dr Milles it is not worth asking you to accept or to take the trouble of bringing me, and, therefore, you may fling it aside where you please.

The epitaph is very unworthy of the subject. I had rather anybody should correct my works than take the pains myself. I thank you very sincerely for criticizing it, but indeed I believe you would with much less trouble write a new one than mend that. I abandon it cheerfully to the fire, for surely bad verses on a great poet are the worst of panegyrics. The sensation of the moment dictated the epitaph, but though I was concerned, I was not inspired; your corrections of my play I remember with the greatest gratitude, because I confess I liked it enough to wish it corrected, and for that friendly act, Sir, I am obliged to you. For writing, I am quitting all thoughts of it—and for several reasons—the best is because it is time to remember that I must quit the world. Mr Gray was but a year older and he had much more the appearance of a man to whom several years were promised. A contemporary's death is the Ucalegon[1] of all sermons: in the next place his death has taught me another truth. Authors are said to labour for posterity; for my part I find I did not write even for the rising generation. Experience tells me it was all for those of my own, or near my own, time. The friends I have lost were I find more than half the public to me. It is as difficult to write for young people, as to talk to them; I never, I perceive, meant anything about them in what I have written, and cannot commence an acquaintance with them in print.

Mr Gray was far from an agreeable confidant to self-love, yet I had always more satisfaction in communicating anything to him, though sure to be mortified, than in being flattered by people whose judgment I do not respect. We had besides known each other's ideas from almost infancy, and I was certain he would *understand* precisely whatever I said, whether it was well or ill expressed. This is a kind of feeling that every hour of age increases. Mr Gray's death, I am persuaded, Sir, has already given you this sensation, and I make no excuse for talking seemingly so much of myself, but though I am the instance of these reflections, they are only part of the conversation, which that sad event occasions, and which I trust we shall renew. I shall sincerely be a little consoled if our common regret draws us nearer together; you will find all possible esteem on my side; as there has been much similarity in

1. Ucalegon was one of the elders of Troy, whose house stood next to that of Deiphobus and was burned with it ("Proximus ardet Ucalegon": *Æneid* ii.311–12).

some of our pursuits, it may make some amends for other defects. I have done with the business, the politics, the pleasures of the world, without turning hermit or morose. My object is to pass the remainder of my life tranquilly and agreeably, with all the amusements that will gild the evening, and are not subject to disappointment; with cheerfulness, for I have very good spirits, and with as much of the company, as I can obtain, of the few persons I value and like [value and like is one word]. If you have charity enough or inclination to contribute to such a system you will add much to the happiness of it, and if you have not, you will still allow me to say I shall be ever, with great regard, Sir,

Your obedient humble servant,

HOR. WALPOLE

TO THE REV. WILLIAM MASON, 27 March 1773

Strawberry Hill, [March] 27, 1773.

I received your letter, dear Sir, your MS and Gray's letters to me, by Mr Alderson. Twenty things crowd about my pen and jostle and press to be said: as I came hither today (my first flight since my illness) for a little air and to read you undisturbed, they shall all have their place in good time; but having so safe a conveyance for my thoughts, I must begin with the uppermost of them, the *Heroic Epistle*.[1] I have read it so very often that I have got it by heart, and as I am now master of all its beauties, I profess I like it infinitely better than I did, and yet I thought I liked it infinitely before; there is more wit, ten times more delicacy of irony, as much poetry and greater facility than, and as, in the *Dunciad*. But what signifies what I think? all the world thinks the same, except a dark corner, where its being so much disliked is still better praise. No soul, as I have heard, has guessed within an hundred miles. I catched at Anstey's name and I believe contributed to spread that notion. It has since been called Temple Lutterel's,

1. By Mason, who published it anonymously.

and to my infinite honour mine. Lord Nuneham swears he should think so, if I did not commend it so excessively! oh how very vain I am! Sir William Chambers consoles himself with its having sold him three hundred copies of his book—I do not hear that the patron of arts consoles himself with anything, but is heartily sore—He *would* read it insultingly to Chambers, but soon flung it down in a passion. It is already of the fourth edition. Thank you for giving my impatient heir, Sam. Martin, a niche. There is published a defence of Negro slavery by his father.

But now, my dear Sir, as you have tapped this mine of talent, and it runs so richly and easily, for Heaven's and England's sake do not let it rust. You have a vein of irony and satire that the best of causes bleeds for having wanted. Point all your lightnings at that wretch Dalrymple, and yet make him but the footstool to the throne as you made poor simple Chambers. We are acting the very same scene Dalrymple has brought to fuller light, sacrificing friends to stab heroes and martyrs. There are repeated informations from France that preliminaries of strict union are signed between that Court and ours; Lord Stormont is the negotiator, and Lord Mansfield, who has not courage enough even to be Chancellor, hopes the Chancellor of France has courage and villainy enough to assist him in enslaving us, as the French Chancellor has enslaved his own country! if you mind not me, depend upon it you will meet the indignant shade of Sidney in your moonlight walk by your cold bath, who will frown inspiration. You see what you can do, what Milton trusted to prose, what Pope had not principles elevated enough to do, and for doing what Gray's bards will bless you. In short you have seated yourself close to all three, and you must now remain in full display of your dignity. When Gray's life is finished, you are not permitted to write anything inferior to the *Dispensary*.[1] Thank you for your admirable remark on Barillon's letter; I will communicate it to Mrs Macaulay (without naming you); she will defend Sidney in her next volume—but he demands a higher pen.

1. By Samuel Garth.

I am extremely pleased with the easy unaffected simplicity of your MS,[1] nor have found anything scarce I would wish added, much less retrenched—unless the paragraph on Lord Bute, which I do not think quite clearly expressed, and yet perhaps too clearly, while you choose to remain unknown for author of the *Epistle*. The paragraph I mean might lead to a suspicion: might it not look a little too, as if Gray, at least his friends for him, had been disappointed? especially as he asked for the place, and accepted it afterwards from the Duke of Grafton? Since Gray (and I am sorry he did not) has left no marks of indignation against the present times, I do not know whether it were so well to mix politics with a life so unpolitical: but I only suggest this—you are sure I do not speak from disinclination to the censure, but from infinite regard both for him and you. The page and reflections on poor West's death are new, most touching, most exquisitely worded.

I send you Mr Andrew Stuart's book; and as I had two given to me, I beg you will accept that I send. It will be a great curiosity, for after all his heroism, fear or nationality have preponderated, and it will not be published.

I can add nothing to your account of Gray's going abroad with me. It was my own thought and offer, and was cheerfully accepted; thank you for inserting my alteration; as I survive, any softening would be unjust to the dead; and nobody can justify him so well as my confession and attestation. It must be believed that I was in the wrong, not he, when I allow it; in things of that nature, the survivor has the better chance of being justified: and for your sake, dear Sir, as well as his, I choose you should do justice to your friend. I am sorry I had a fault towards him; it does not wound me to own it.

I return you Mr Trollop's verses, of which many are excellent, and yet I cannot help thinking the best were Gray's, not only as they appear in his writing, but as they are more nervous and less diffuse than the others; when we meet, why should not we select the best, and make a complete poem?

1. Of his *Memoirs of Gray*.

Dr Goldsmith has written a comedy[1]—no, it is the lowest of all farces; it is not the subject I condemn, though very vulgar, but the execution. The drift tends to no moral, no edification of any kind—the situations however are well imagined, and make one laugh in spite of the grossness of the dialogue, the forced witticisms, and total improbability of the whole plan and conduct. But what disgusts me most, is that though the characters are very low, and aim at low humour, not one of them says a sentence that is natural or marks any character at all. It is set up in opposition to sentimental comedy, and is as bad as the worst of them. Garrick would not act it, but bought himself off by a poor prologue. I say nothing of the Home's *Alonzo* and Murphy's *Alzuma*, because as the latter is sense and poetry compared to the former, you cannot want an account of either.

Mr Nicoll is returned, transported with Italy: I hope he will come hither with me next week, Gothic ground may sober him a little from pictures and statues, which he will not meet with in his village, and which, I doubt, will at first be a little irksome. His friend Mr Barrett stands for Dover, I suppose on the Court-interest, for Wilkes has sent down a remonstrating candidate. I like the *Parliamentary right* in his City remonstrance. I forgot to tell you too, that I believe the Scotch are heartily sick of their Dalrymplyan publication. It has reopened all the mouths of clamour; and the *Heroic Epistle* arrived in the critical minute to furnish clamour with quotations. You cannot imagine how I used it as fumigation. Whenever I was asked, have you read Sir J. Dalrymple? I replied, have *you* read the *Heroic Epistle*? Betty is in raptures on being immortalized; the Elephant and Ass are become constellations, and *he has stolen the Earl of Denbigh's handkerchief* is the proverb in fashion—good night.

Pope—Garth—Boileau—you may guess whether I am or not

Your sincere admirer,

HOR. WALPOLE

1. *She Stoops to Conquer.*

To Sir Horace Mann, 13 July 1773

Strawberry Hill, July 13th, 1773.

I have delayed writing to you from day to day, my dear Sir, that I might be able at last to say something precisely to you about my poor nephew,[1] and myself with regard to his affairs, chiefly for the information of his mother, who has not allured me to write to herself.

Her son has had a terrible relapse, and for above a fortnight kept me under dreadful alarms by attempting to destroy himself. He is now quieter, and is settled at Hampstead in a house I have taken for him, and with which he is pleased. He was to have gone to a farm he has near Newmarket, but as I am much upon my guard, I asked whether there was water near it, and being answered, yes, a millpond and wet ditches, I would not hear of it. Dr Jebbe reckons this relapse favourable, as opposite to idiotism, into which he seemed sinking. It may be so—but idiotism would guarantee his life, and such relapses, (after recovering from the immediate cause of his malady, the violent quack medicines) indicate strongly to me a radical cause. It is not for his mother's ear, but she knows that he may have inherited the seeds from her own family.

Mr Sharpe, her lawyer, will give, I hope has given, her a circumstantial account of the bad posture of his affairs. He has promised me to tell her, that, perplexing and almost desperate as they are, I have offered to undertake the management of them, and to endeavour by inspection, control and economy to put them on a better foot. Mr Sharpe has assured me this will be agreeable to her Ladyship; but I demand and insist on her giving me a positive confirmation of that request under her own hand, or I will immediately throw up the trust, which must be part of my warrant to Chancery, or no consideration shall prevent my relinquishing so difficult and intricate a charge, so fatiguing and troublesome to one of my shattered constitution, and to my love of ease. This, my good friend, for my sake, for the salvation of the

1. Lord Orford, whose mother lived at Florence.

family, for the only chance of unravelling the perplexities of affairs in which your own family is concerned, nay, for her own sake, as the whole burthen or whole shame will fall on herself, you must persuade her to comply with immediately. The whole world will justify me in refusing, if she refuses. My brother, Lord Walpole[1] and his next brother,[2] have signed to me this request in form. The whole family is happy that I will sacrifice myself to this duty, and everybody approves my conduct—I will say to you, that I have but too much reason to think, that neither Lord Orford nor a distant view to my own interest call upon me, or even Sir Edward, who is nearer, to thrust ourselves into an invidious situation. We have been told by one that ought to know, that my Lord has disinherited us both— Indeed I have the less repugnance for that very reason. My behaviour can then be influenced only by duty. I was a very untractable nephew myself, but I will be a just uncle, though my uncle was not so.

I will trouble you with no more details, though my head and heart are full of them. They have jostled out every other idea, and I fear will occupy the rest of my life, for the vanity of restoring my family engrosses me. My father, excellent and wise as he was, ruined it by pushing this vanity too far. It will be mine to try to repair the havoc of three generations—and this I have had the confidence to call *duty*.— But it would please my father, and that thought will be my reward—or I shall cease from this labour and all other thoughts in that small spot that puts an end to vainglory!

When my mind reposes a little, I smile at myself. I intended to trifle out the remnant of my days—and lo! they are invaded by lawyers, stewards, physicians, and jockeys! Yes, this whole week past I have been negotiating a sale of race-horses at Newmarket, and to the honour of my transactions the sale has turned out greatly. My Gothic ancestors are forgotten; I am got upon the turf. I give orders about game, dispark Houghton, have plans of farming, vend colts, fillies, bullocks and sheep, and have not yet

1. HW's cousin Horatio Walpole, Lord Walpole of Wolterton.
2. The Hon. Thomas Walpole.

confounded terms, nor ordered pointers to be turned to grass. I read the part of the newspapers I used to skip, and peruse the lists of sweepstakes—not the articles of intelligence, nor the relations of the shows at Portsmouth for the King, or at Oxford for the Viceroy North. I must leave Europe and its kings and queens to you; we do not talk of such folks at the Inns of Court. I sold *Stoic* for five hundred guineas: I shall never get five pence by the monarchs of the empire, and therefore we jockeys of the Temple, and we lawyers of Newmarket, hold them to be very insignificant individuals. The only political point that touches me at present, is what does occasion much noise and trouble, the new act that decries guineas under weight. Though I have refused to receive a guinea myself of Lord Orford's income, yet I must see it all paid into my Lady's banker's hands, and I am now in a fright lest the purchase money of the racers should be made in light coin—not from suspicion of such *honourable* men, but from their inattention to money. I must tell you a story apropos, which I had this morning from the person to whom it happened last summer. My deputy Mr Tullie has an estate in Yorkshire, where clipping and *de*-coining is most practised. He was to pay an hundred guineas to a farmer there, and desired the man to stay till he could send for them to the next market town. The man was in haste, and as Mr Tullie was just arrived from London, was sure he must have money in the house. With much persuasion he opened his bureau and took out an hundred new pieces, which he did not care to part with in that county where there were none but bad. The man started, and refused to take them—'Sir,' said he, 'there are so many coiners in these parts, that if I was seen to have so many new guineas, I should be sent to prison as one of the gang'—and he literally waited till an hundred bad guineas could be fetched from Gisborough. They say the Bank is to issue five-pound notes—at present all trade is at a stop, and the confusion is extreme. Yea, verily, the villainy and iniquities of the age are bringing things rapidly to a crisis! Ireland is drained and has not a shilling. The explosion of the Scotch banks has reduced them almost as low, and sunk their flourishing manufactures to low water ebb. The Maccaronis are at their *ne plus ultra:* Charles Fox is already so like Julius Cæsar, that he owes an hundred thousand pounds. Lord Carlisle pays fifteen hundred and Mr Crewe twelve hundred a year for him—literally for him, being bound for him, while he, as like Brutus as Cæsar, is indifferent about such paltry counters—one must talk of Clodius, when one has no Scipio. Yet if the merit of some historian does not interest posterity by the beauty of his narration, this age will be as little known as the annals of the Byzantine Empire, marked only by vices and follies. What is England now?—A sink of Indian wealth, filled by nabobs and emptied by Maccaronis! A senate sold and despised! A country overrun by horse-races! A gaming, robbing, wrangling, railing nation, without principles, genius, character or allies; the overgrown shadow of what it was! —Lord bless me, I run on like a political barber—I must go back to my shop—I shall let farms well, if I attend to the state of the nation—What's Hecuba to me?— Don't read the end of my letter to the Countess; she will think I am as mad as her son.

PS. St John Donatello comes down tomorrow to occupy his niche in my new chapel in the garden. With Houghton before my eyes, I am indulging myself in making this place delightful!

Monday, 19th.

This letter was to have set out last Friday; but was mislaid by an accident. I heard yesterday that the brother and sister-in-law of one who gave you so much uneasiness near a year ago, are going to Italy for some time; first to Milan. You are at least safe from having them for guests, which you must not even offer. The moment you hear of their approach, you had better write for specific directions. The person, on whose account you was so ill-treated, has no reason to alter his opinion on that transaction; except in being convinced that a want of sense was *not* the cause, which does not add to the opinion of the heart.

To Lady Ossory, 9 August 1773

Strawberry Hill, Aug. 9, 1773.

Here is a pause from my journeyings, Madam! I returned yesterday from Park Place[1] and Nuneham,[2] and hope for a letter before I go to Houghton on Thursday sennight. Nuneham astonished me with the first *coup d'œil* of its ugliness and the next day charmed me. It is as rough as a bear, but capable of being made a most noble scene. There is a fine apartment, some few very good pictures, the part of a temple acted by a church, and a flower-garden that would keep all Maccaronia in nosegays. The comfort was a little damped by the constant presence of Sir William Lee, and Dame Elizabeth his wife, with a prim Miss, whose lips were stuffed into her nostrils. They sat bolt upright, like macaws on their perches in a menagerie, and scarce said so much—I wanted to bid them *call a coach!* The morning and the evening was the first day, and the morning and the evening was the second day, and still they were just in their places! I made a discovery that was more amusing; Lady Nuneham is a poetess, and writes with great ease and sense and some poetry, but is as afraid of the character, as if it was a sin to make verses. You will be more entertained with what I heard of Lord Edgcumbe—stay, I dare not tell it your Ladyship—well, Lord Ossory must read this paragraph. Every scrap of Latin Lord Edgcumbe heard at the Encænia at Oxford, he translated ridiculously; one of the themes was 'Ars Musica'—he Englished it, 'Bumfiddle.'

I wish you joy, Madam, of the sun's settling in England. Was ever such a southern day as this? My house is a bower of tuberoses, and all Twitnamshire is passing through my meadows to the races at Hampton Court. The picture is incredibly beautiful—but I must quit my joys for my sorrows. My poor Rosette is dying. She relapsed into her fits the last night of my stay at Nuneham;

1. In Berkshire; the seat of HW's cousin and correspondent, Henry Seymour Conway.

2. The seat of HW's friend and correspondent, Lord Nuneham, later (1777) Lord Harcourt; in Oxfordshire, about sixteen miles from Park Place.

and has suffered exquisitely ever since. You may believe I have too—I have been out of bed twenty times every night, have had no sleep, and sat up with her till three this morning—but I am only making you laugh at me: I cannot help it, I think of nothing else. Without weaknesses I should not be I, and I may as well tell them, as have them tell themselves.

PS. I am going to make a postscript of a very old riddle, but if you never saw it, you will like it, and revere the riddle-maker, which was, I am told, one Sir Isaac Newton, a great star-gazer and conjuror;

> Four people sat down at a table to play;
> They play'd all that night, and some part of next day:
> This one thing observ'd, that when they were seated,
> Nobody play'd with them and nobody betted:
> Yet when they got up, each was winner a guinea;
> Who tells me this riddle, I'm sure is no ninny.

To Lady Ossory, 1 September 1773

Strawberry Hill, Sept. 1, 1773.

Your Ladyship was particularly kind in letting me meet so agreeable a letter at my return, which made me for some minutes forget the load of business and mortification that I have brought from Houghton, where I was detained four days longer than I intended. You would I fear repent your love of details, were I to enter on particulars of all I have seen and heard! far worse than my worst apprehensions! You know, Madam, I do not want a sufficient stock of family pride, yet perhaps do not know, though I think it far from a beautiful place, how very fond I am of Houghton, as the object of my father's fondness. Judge then what I felt at finding it half a ruin, though the pictures, the glorious pictures, and furniture are in general admirably well preserved. All the rest is destruction and desolation! The two great staircases exposed to all weathers; every room in the wings rotting with wet; the ceiling of the gallery in danger; the chancel of the church unroofed; the water-house, built by Lord Pembroke, tumbling down; the garden a common; the park half covered with nettles and weeds; the walls and pales in ruin; perpetuities of livings at the very gates sold; the interest at Lynn gone; mortgages swallowing the estate, and a debt of above forty thousand pounds heaped on those of my father and brother. A crew of banditti were harboured in the house, stables, town and every adjacent tenement; and I have but too great reason to say that the outpensioners have committed as great spoil—much even since my nephew's misfortune. The high treasurer who paid this waste, and shared it, is a steward that can neither read nor write—This worthy prime minister I am forced to keep from particular circumstances—I mean if I continue in office myself—but though I have already done something, and have reduced an annual charge of near twelve hundred a year, the consequences of which I believe were as much more, I mean the waste made and occasioned by bad servants, dogs and horses, still I very much doubt whether I must not resign, from causes not proper for a letter.

In the shock and vexation of such a scene was I forced to act as if my mind was not only perfectly at ease, but as if I, who never understood one useful thing in my days, was master of every country business, and qualified to be a surveyor-general. Though you would have pitied my sensations, you would have smiled, Madam, I am sure, at my occupations, which lasted without interruption from nine every morning till twelve at night, except that, a few times, I stole from the steward and lawyer I carried with me, to peep at a room full of painters, who you and Lord Ossory will like to hear, are making drawings from the whole collection, which Boydell is going to engrave. Well, the morning was spent in visiting the kennels, in giving away pointers, greyhounds and foreign beasts, in writing down genealogies of horses—with all my heraldry I never thought to be the Anstis[1] of Newmarket—in selling bullocks, sheep, Shetland horses, and all kind of stock—

1. John Anstis (1669–1744), Garter King-of-Arms, was succeeded by his son of the same name.

in hearing petitions and remonstrances of old servants, whom I pitied though three were drunk by the time I had breakfasted; in listening to advice on raising leases; in ordering repairs, sending two teams to Lynn for tiles; in limiting expense of coals, candles, soap, brushes, etc., and in forty other such details. About one or two arrived farmers to haggle on leases, and though I did not understand one word in a score that they uttered, I was forced to keep them to dinner, and literally had three, four, and five to dine with me six days of the eight that I stayed there—nor was I quit so, for their business literally lasted most days till eight or nine at night. They are not laconic, nor I intelligent; and the stupidity and knavery of the steward did their utmost to perplex me, and confound the map of the estate, every name in which he miscalled, as if he was interpreting to an Arabian ambassador. The three last hours of the night were employed in reducing and recording the transactions of the day, in looking over accounts, and methodizing debts, demands, and in drawing plans of future conduct—Oh! I am weary even with the recollection—is not your Ladyship with the recapitulation? For the first four days I was amazed at the quickness of my own parts, and almost lamented that such talents had lain so long unemployed. I improved two leases an hundred and fifty pounds, and thought I had raised another more; and let a farm, which my Lord kept in his own hands and has received not a shilling from for seven years, for five hundred a year—Alas! I soon found I had been too obstinate or too sanguine, and absolutely had done nothing but blunder—my farmers broke off when I thought them ready to sign, and the second lease I found my Lord had been overreached in, and had engaged for four hundred pounds, though I was offered six by two different persons. I came away chagrined and humbled. As King Phyz says in *The Rehearsal*, if I am turned off, nobody will take me. I am glad therefore your Ladyship did this time resist your propensity to praising me—I am glad to have done with my own chapter, and to come to your Ladyship's entertaining letter—I should not say entertaining, as you have been a month in apprehensions of *you know not what.* I hope Lord Ossory will soon be without apprehension, and see *what* he wishes—good Madam, do not scamper about like some ladies of antiquity, I forget their country, who thought fatigue went half way in the procreation of a son and heir. I was not so much frightened at Mrs Page's news —on the contrary, I was diverted, concluding the antiquated beauty was a lady famous for making ducal captives, and was going to be restored.

Lady Barrymore has, I think, two thousand a year, and I believe will not break her little heart, as you may see I thought by this stanza to the tune of *Green grow the rushes ho!*

O my Lady Barrymore,
O my Lady Barrymore,
If I was you,
I'd bill and coo,
But I would never marry more.

I promise you I will not myself, nor do I think the lady in question will choose another skeleton.

You guessed right, Madam. *Musicians* is the key to the riddle. If it is too easy, which I am bound not to think as I could not guess it, remember Sir Isaac was more famous for solving problems than for wrapping them in obscurity. . . .

To the Rev. William Mason, 27 November 1773

Arlington Street, Nov. 27, 1773.

Dear Sir,
Mr Stonhewer has sent me, and I have read, your first part of Gray's life, which I was very sorry to part with so soon. Like everything of yours, I like it ten times better upon reading it again: you have with most singular art displayed the talents of my two departed friends to the fullest advantage; and yet there is a simplicity in your manner, which, like the frame of a fine picture, seems a frame only, and yet is gold. I should say much more in praise, if, as I have told Mr Stonhewer, I was not aware that I myself must be far more interested in the whole of the narrative, than

any other living mortal, and therefore may suppose it will please the world still more than it will—And yet if wit, parts, learning, taste, sense, friendship, information can strike or amuse mankind, must not this work have that effect?—and yet, though *me* it may affect far more strongly, self-love certainly has no share in my affection to many parts. Of my two friends and me, I only make a most indifferent figure. I do not mean with regard to parts or talents. I never one instant of my life had the superlative vanity of ranking myself with them. They not only possessed genius, which I have not, great learning which is to be acquired, and which I never acquired; but both Gray and West had abilities marvellously premature; what wretched boyish stuff would my contemporary letters to them appear, if they existed; and which they both were so good-natured as to destroy! [1]—what unpoetic things were mine at that age, some of which unfortunately do exist, and which I yet could never surpass; but it is not in that light I consider my own position. We had not got to Calais before Gray was dissatisfied, for I was a boy, and he, though infinitely more a man, was not enough so to make allowances. Hence am I never mentioned once with kindness in his letters to West. This hurts me for him, as well as myself. For the oblique censures on my want of curiosity, I have nothing to say. The fact was true; my eyes were not purely classic; and though I am now a dull antiquary, my age then made me taste pleasures and diversions merely modern: I say this to you, and to you only, in confidence. I do not object to a syllable. I know how trifling, how useless, how blamable I have been, and submit to hear my faults, both because I have had faults, and because I hope I have corrected some of them; and though Gray hints at my unwillingness to be told them, I can say truly that to the end of his life, he neither spared the reprimand nor mollified the terms, as you and others know, and I believe have felt.

These reflections naturally arose on reading his letters again,

1. Twenty of HW's letters to West have been found, but only one to Gray before 1755.

and arose in spite of the pleasure they gave me, for self will intrude, even where self is not so much concerned. I am sorry to find I disobliged Gray so very early. I am sorry for him that it so totally obliterated all my friendship for him; a remark the world probably, and I hope, will not make, but which it is natural for me, dear Sir, to say to you. I am so sincerely zealous that all possible honour should be done to my two friends, that I care not a straw for serving as a foil to them. And as confession of faults is the only amendment I can now make to the one disobliged, I am pleased with myself for having consented and for consenting as I do, to that public reparation. I thank you for having revived West and his alas! stifled genius, and for having extended Gray's reputation. If the world admires them both as much as they deserved, I shall enjoy their fame—if it does not, I shall comfort myself for standing so prodigiously below them, as I do even without comparison.

There are a few false printings I could have corrected, but of no consequence, as 'Grotto del Cane,' for 'Grotta,' and a few notes I could have added, but also of little consequence. Dodsley, who is printing Lord Chesterfield's letters, will hate you for this publication. I was asked to write a preface—*Sic notus Ulysses?* I knew Ulysses too well. Besides, I have enough to burn without adding to the mass. Forgive me, if I differ with you, but I cannot think Gray's Latin poems inferior even to his English, at least as I am not a Roman. I wish too that in a note you had referred to West's ode on the Queen in Dodsley's miscellanies. Adieu! go on and prosper; my poor friends have an historian worthy of them, and who satisfies their and your friend

HOR. WALPOLE[1]

TO SIR HORACE MANN, 28 November 1773

Arlington Street, Nov. 28, 1773.

Don't commend me yet, my dear Sir; I will be a good man before I die, if it is possible—but at present I am only learning virtues at

1. A postscript has been omitted.

the expense of all the world. For some time I had wrapped myself up in my indifference and integrity, and hoped the former, like cedar chips, would preserve the latter, as it lay useless by me in my drawer. The swarms of rogues that my nephew's affairs have let loose upon me, oblige me to produce all my little stock of honesty, and all the service I intend to do myself by my endless fatigue, shall be to make myself better. The possession of one vice, pride, and the want of two more, ambition and self-interest, have preserved me from many faults—but into how many more have I fallen! The fruit is past—but the soil shall be improved. I do not talk with a lawyer, that at the same time I am not looking into him as a glass and setting my mind into a handsomer attitude. When he gives me advice, I often say silently, 'This I will be sure *not* to follow;' for if many try to cheat me, some are as zealous to make me defraud *for* my family, which though more likely to tempt me than if it was for myself, shall not make me swerve from that narrow middle path, that does exist, but is seldom perceptible, especially as we rarely look for it but through spectacles that we take care should not magnify. Oh, my dear Sir,—we are wretched and contemptible creatures! Have I not been writing a panegyric here, when I meant a satire on myself, and did not dare to finish it? I am not mercenary, and therefore lash those that are. I pick out a single negative quality, which I happened to be born without, and think that like charity it is to cover a multitude of sins! I am a Pharisee, and affect the modest humility of the publican! Well! I give up all pretensions—but I will try to have some positive merit. I never thought of it, while I was idle—my life is now a scene of incessant business—I shall never learn my business, but thank God! virtue is not so intricate as law and farming. My honesty shall not be a sinecure like my places. I will learn economy for my nephew's estate, though I never had it for the care of my own fortune— My pride—no, pray let me keep that—if I expel it, seven worse devils will enter in, and I should sell another passion, a very predominant one, the love of liberty. While all the world is selling the thing, pray let me, if but as a virtuoso, preserve the affection, which is already a curiosity, and will soon, I believe, be an unique— Luckily for you, I have not time to talk any longer about myself, which you see one loves to do, even though it be to rail at one's self— Indeed, like Montaigne, one contrives to specify no failings without giving them a foil that makes them look like virtues. For my part, I forswear any good qualities, I am mortified at knowing I have none, or if I have had, and virtue fathered them, pride was their mother, and whoever she laid them to, hypocrisy was her gallant. Still, if she is not past child-bearing, her husband shall yet have some lawful issue. . . .

Lord Holland is dying, is paying Charles Fox's debts, or most of them, for they amount to ONE HUNDRED AND THIRTY THOUSAND POUNDS—aye, aye; and has got a grandson and heir. I thought this child a Messiah, who came to foretell the ruin and dispersion of the *Jews,* but while there is a broker or a gamester upon the face of the earth, Charles will not be out of debt. Pray do your crews of English at Florence, emulate their countrymen? I saw a letter t'other day from Aix, which said a young Englishman there had lost £22,000 at one sitting. Madness and perdition are gone forth! Is it possible we should not be undone? I can tell you of two English above the common standard coming to you. The great Indian Verres, or Alexander if you please, Lord Clive, is one. The other, Lady Mary Coke. She was much a friend of mine, but a late marriage,[1] which *she* particularly disapproved, having flattered herself with the hopes of one[2] just a step higher, has a little cooled our friendship. In short, though she is so greatly born, she has a frenzy for royalty, and will fall in love with and at the feet of the Great Duke and Duchess, especially the former, for next to being an empress herself, she adores the Empress Queen, or did—for perhaps that passion not being quite reciprocal, may have waned. However, bating every English person's madness, for every English person must have their madness, Lady Mary has a thousand virtues and good qualities: she is noble, generous, high-spirited,

1. Of the Duke of Gloucester and Lady Waldegrave. (HW's note)

2. She had flattered herself that Edward Duke of York, elder brother of the Duke of Gloucester, would marry her. (HW's note)

undauntable, is most friendly, sincere, affectionate, and above any mean action. She loves attention, and I wish you to pay it even for my sake, for I would do anything to serve her. I have often tried to laugh her out of her weakness, but as she is very serious, she was so in that, and if all the sovereigns in Europe combined to slight her, she still would put her trust in the next generation of princes. Her heart is excellent, and deserves and would become a crown, and that is the best of all excuses for desiring one. I am glad you will have so little trouble with those that are nearer.

Thank you a thousand times for your anecdotes of the Jesuits. It is comfortable to see the world ever open its eyes— If it had all Argus's, it would have need to stare with every pair—but I think it was said of them, that some watched, while others slept— Just so would the world's, and would say with the sluggard in the Psalms, 'A little more slumber, a little more sleep, a little more folding of the arms to sleep.' The Jesuits have many collaterals, besides other monks. Adieu!

PS. We have just heard that the tax on Irish absentees has been thrown out even at Dublin.

To the Rev. William Mason, ca. May 1774

I have been reading a new French translation of the elder Pliny, of whom I never read but scraps before; because, in the poetical manner in which we learn Latin at Eton, we never become acquainted with the names of the commonest things, too undignified to be admitted into verse; and therefore I never had patience to search in a dictionary for the meaning of every substantive. I find I shall not have a great deal less trouble with the translation, as I am not more familiar with their common *drogues* than with the Latin. However, the beginning goes off very glibly, as I am not yet arrived below the planets. But do you know that this study, of which I have never thought since I learnt astronomy at Cambridge, has furnished me with some very entertaining ideas! I have long been weary of the common jargon of poetry. You bards have exhausted all the nature we are acquainted with; you have treated us with the sun, moon, and stars, the earth and the ocean, mountains and valleys, etc., etc., under every possible aspect. In short, I have longed for some American poetry, in which I might find new appearances of nature, and consequently of art. But my present excursion into the sky has afforded me more entertaining prospects, and newer phenomena. If I was as good a poet as you are, I would immediately compose an idyll, or an elegy, the scene of which should be laid in Saturn or Jupiter; and then, instead of a niggardly soliloquy by the light of a single moon, I would describe a night illuminated by four or five moons at least, and they should be all in a perpendicular or horizontal line, according as Celia's eyes (who probably in that country has at least two pair) are disposed in longitude or latitude. You must allow that this system would diversify poetry amazingly.—And then Saturn's belt! which the translator says in his notes, is not round the planet's waist, like the shingles, but is a globe of crystal that encloses the whole orb, as you may have seen an enamelled watch in a case of glass. If you do not perceive what infinitely pretty things may be said, either in poetry or romance, on a brittle heaven of crystal, and what furbelowed rainbows they must have in that country, you are neither the Ovid nor natural philosopher I take you for. Pray send me an eclogue directly upon this plan—and I give you leave to adopt my idea of Saturnian Celias having their everything quadrupled—which would form a much more entertaining rhapsody than Swift's thought of magnifying or diminishing the species in his *Gulliver*. How much more execution a fine woman would do with two pair of *piercers!* or four! and how much longer the honeymoon would last, if both the sexes have (as no doubt they have) four times the passions, and four times the means of gratifying them!—I have opened new worlds to you—You must be four times the poet you are, and then you will be above Milton, and equal to Shakespeare, the only two mortals I am acquainted with, who ventured beyond the visible diurnal sphere, and preserved their intellects. Dryden himself would have talked nonsense, and, I fear, bawdy, on my plan; but you are too good a divine, I am sure, to treat my quadruple love but Platonically. In Saturn, notwithstanding their glass case, they are supposed to be very cold; but Platonic love of itself produces frigid conceits enough, and you need not augment the dose—But I will not dictate. The subject is new; and you, who have so much imagination, will shoot far beyond me. Fontenelle would have made something of the idea even in prose; but Algarotti would dishearten anybody from attempting to meddle with the system of the universe a second time in genteel dialogue. Good night! I am going to bed.—Mercy on me! if I should dream of Celia with four times the usual attractions!

To the Rev. William Cole, 28 May 1774

Strawberry Hill, May 28, 1774.

Nothing will be more agreeable to me, dear Sir, than a visit from you in July. I will try to persuade Mr Granger to meet you; and if you had any such thing as summer in the fens, I would desire you to bring a bag with you. We are almost freezing here in the midst of beautiful verdure with a profusion of blossoms and flowers: but I keep good fires, and seem to feel warm weather while I look through the window, for the way to insure summer in England, is to have it framed and glazed in a comfortable room.

I shall be still more glad to hear you are settled in your living. Burnham is almost in my neighbourhood, and its being in that of Eton and Windsor, will more than console you I hope for leaving Ely and Cambridge. Pray let me know the moment you are certain. It would now be a disappointment to me as well as you. You shall be inaugurated in my chapel, which is much more venerable than your parish church, and has the genuine air of antiquity. I bought very little at poor Mr Bateman's. His nephew disposed of little that was worth house-room, and yet pulled the whole to pieces.

Mr Pennant has published a new tour to Scotland and the Hebrides, and though he has endeavoured to paint their dismal isles and rocks in glowing colours, they will not be satisfied, for he seems no bigot about Ossian, at least in some passages, and is free in others, which their intolerating spirit will resent. I cannot say the book is very entertaining to me, as it is more a book of rates than of antiquities. The most amusing part was communicated to him by Mr Banks, who found whole islands that bear nothing but columns, as other places do grass and barley. There is a beautiful cave called Fingal's, which proves that Nature loves Gothic architecture. Mr Pennant has given a new edition of his former *Tour* with more cuts. Among others is the vulgar head called the Countess of Desmond. I told him I had discovered and proved past contradiction that it is Rembrandt's mother; he owned it and said he would correct it by a note—but he has not. This is a brave way of being an antiquary: as if there could be any merit in giving for genuine what one knows is spurious. He is indeed a superficial man, and knows little of history or antiquity—but he has a violent rage for being an author. He set out with ornithology and a little natural history, and picks up his knowledge as he rides. I have a still lower idea of Mr Gough, for Mr Pennant at least is very civil. The other is a hog. Mr Fenn, another smatterer in antiquity, but a very good sort of man, told me Mr Gough desired to be introduced to me—but as he has been such a bear to you, he shall not come. The Society of Antiquaries put me in mind of what the old Lord Pembroke said to Anstis the herald: 'Thou, silly fellow, thou dost not know thy own silly business.' If they went beyond taste by poking into barbarous ages when there was no taste, one could forgive them—but they catch at the first ugly thing they see, and take it for old because it is new to them, and then usher it pompously into the world as if they had made a discovery, though they have not yet cleared up a single point that is of the least importance, or that tends to settle any obscure passage in history.

I will not condole with you on having had the gout, since you find it has removed other complaints. Besides as it begins late, you are never likely to have it severely. I shall be in terrors in two or three months, having had the four last fits periodically and biennially. Indeed the two last were so long and severe, that my remaining and shattered strength could ill support such. I must repeat how glad I shall be to have you at Burnham. When people grow old as you and I do, they should get together. Others do not care for us, but we seem wiser to one another by finding fault with them—not that I am apt to dislike young folks, whom I think everything becomes; but it is a kind of self-defence to live in a body. I dare to say that monks never find out that they grow old fools. Their age gives them authority and nobody contradicts them. In the world one cannot help perceiving one is out of fashion. Women play at cards with women of their own standing, and censure others between the deals, and thence conclude themselves Gamaliels. I who see many young men with better parts than myself, submit with a good grace, or retreat hither to my castle, where I am satisfied with what I have done and am always in good humour; but I like to have one or two old friends with me—I do not much invite the juvenile, who think my castle and me of equal antiquity, for no wonder if they suppose that George I lived in the time of the Crusades. Adieu! my good Sir, and pray let Burnham Wood and Dunsinane be good neighbours.

Yours ever,

HOR. WALPOLE

TO LADY OSSORY, 14 September 1774

Strawberry Hill, Sept. 14, 1774.

Madam,

Methinks an Æsop's fable you relate, as Dryden says in *The Hind and Panther*. A mouse that wraps itself in a French cloak and sleeps on a couch; and a goldfinch that taps at the window and swears it will come in to quadrille at eleven o'clock at night! no, no, these are none of Æsop's cattle; they are too fashionable to have lived so near the creation. The mouse is neither Country Mouse, nor

City Mouse; and whatever else he may be, the goldfinch must be a Maccaroni, or at least of the sçavoir vivre.[1] I do not deny but I have some skill in expounding types and portents; and could give a shrewd guess at the identical persons who have travestied themselves into a quadruped and biped—but the truth is, I have no mind, Madam, to be prime minister. King Pharaoh is mighty apt on emergencies to send for us soothsayers, and put the whole kingdom into our hands, if his butler or baker, with whom he is wont to gossip, does but tell him of a cunning man. I have no ambition to supplant Lord North—especially as the season approaches when I dread the gout; and I should be very sorry to be fetched out of my bed to pacify America. To be sure, Madam, you give me a fair field for uttering oracles—however all I will unfold is, that the emblematic animals have no views on Lady Louisa. The omens of her fortune are in herself; and I will burn my books, if beauty, sense and merit do not bestow all the happiness on her they prognosticate. . . .

I like the blue eyes, Madam, better than the denomination of Lady Gertrude Fitzpatrick, which, all respectable as it is, is very harsh and rough-sounding: pray let her change it with the first goldfinch that offers. Nay, I do not even trust to the blueth of the eyes. I do not believe they last once in twenty times. One cannot go into any village fifty miles from London without seeing a dozen little children with flaxen hair and eyes of sky-blue. What becomes of them all? One does not see a grown Christian with them twice in a century, except in poetry.

The Strawberry Gazette is very barren of news. Mr Garrick has the gout, which is of more consequence to the metropolis than to Twitnamshire. Lady Hertford dined here last Saturday, brought her loo party and stayed supper; there were Lady Mary Cooke, Mrs Howe, and the Colonels Maude and Keene. This was very heroic, for one is robbed every hundred yards. Lady Hertford herself was attacked last Wednesday on Hounslow Heath at three in the afternoon, but she had two servants on horseback, who would not let her be robbed, and the highwayman decamped.

1. A social club.

The greatest event I know was a present I received last Sunday, just as I was going to dine at Lady Blanford's, to whom I sacrificed it. It was a bunch of grapes as big—as big—as that the two spies carried on a pole to Joshua—for spies in those days when they robbed a vineyard were not at all afraid of being overtaken. In good truth this bunch weighed three pounds and a half, *côte rôtie* measure; and was sent to me by my neighbour Prado of the tribe of Issachar, who is descended from one of foresaid spies, but a good deal richer than his ancestor. Well, Madam, I carried it to the Marchioness, but gave it to the maître d'hôtel, with injunctions to conceal it till the dessert. At the end of dinner, Lady Blanford said, she had heard of three immense bunches of grapes at Mr Prado's at a dinner he had made for Mr Ellis. I said, those things were always exaggerated. She cried, oh! but Mrs Ellis told it, and it weighed I don't know how many pounds, and the Duke of Argyle had been to see the hothouse, and she wondered as it was so near I would not go and see it. 'Not I, indeed,' said I; 'I dare to say there is no curiosity in it.' Just then entered the gigantic bunch. Everybody screamed. 'There,' said I, 'I will be shot if Mr Prado has such a bunch as yours'—In short, she suspected Lady Egremont, and the adventure succeeded to admiration. If you will send the Bedfordshire wagon, Madam, I will beg a dozen grapes for you.

Mr Barker may pretend what he will, but if he liked Strawberry so well, he would have visited it again, and by daylight. He could see no more of it at nine o'clock at night, than he does at this moment.

Pray, Madam, is not it Farming-Woods-tide? Who is to have the care of the dear mouse in your absence? I wish I could spare Margaret, who loves all creatures so well that she would have been happy in the Ark, and sorry when the Deluge ceased—unless people had come to see Noah's old house, which she would have liked still better than cramming his menagerie. . . .

To John Craufurd,[1] 26 September 1774

Strawberry Hill, Sept. 26, 1774.

You tell me to write to you, and I am certainly disposed to do anything I can to amuse you; but that is not so easy a matter, for two very good reasons: you are not the most amusable of men, and I have nothing to amuse you with, for you are like electricity, you attract and repel at once; and though you have at first a mind to know anything, you are tired of it before it can be told. I don't go to Almack's nor amongst your acquaintance. Would you bear to hear of mine? of Lady Blandford, Lady Anne Conolly, and the Duchess of Newcastle? for by age and situation I live at this time of year with nothing but old women. They do very well for me who have little choice left, and who rather prefer common nonsense to wise nonsense—the only difference I know between old women and old men. I am out of all politics, and never think of elections, which I think I should hate even if I loved politics; just as if I loved tapestry I do not think I could talk over the manufacture of worsteds. Books I have almost done with too; at least, read only such as nobody else would read. In short, my way of life is too insipid to entertain anybody but myself, and though I am always employed, I must say I think I have given up everything in the world only to be at liberty to be very busy about the most arrant trifles.

Well! I have made out half a letter with a history very like the journal in the *Spectator*, of the man, the chief incidents of whose life were stroking his cat, and walking to Hampstead. Last night, indeed, I had an adventure that would make a great figure in such a narrative. *You* may be enjoying bright suns and serene horizons under the Pole, but in this dismal southern region it has rained for this month without interruption. Lady Browne and I dined as usually on Sundays with Lady Blandford. Our gentle Thames was swelled in the morning to a very respectable magnitude, and we had thought of returning by Kew Bridge; however, I persuaded

1. John Craufurd of Auchinames (d. 1814). He was well known in French and English society, and was a friend and correspondent of Madame du Deffand.

her to try if we could not ferry, and when we came to the foot of the hill, the bargemen told us the water was sunk. We embarked and had four men to push the ferry. The night was very dark, for though the moon was up, we could neither see her, nor she us. The bargemen were drunk, the poles would scarce reach the bottom, and in five minutes the rapidity of the current turned the barge round, and in an instant we were at Isleworth. The drunkest of the men cried out, 'She is gone, she is lost!' meaning they had lost the management. Lady Browne fell into an agony, began screaming and praying to Jesus, and every land and water god and goddess, and I, who expected not to stop till we should run against Kew Bridge, was contriving how I should get home; or what was worse, whether I must not step into some mud up to my middle, be wet through, and get the gout. With much ado they recovered the barge and turned it; but then we ran against the piles of the new bridge, which startled the horses, who began kicking. My Phillis's terrors increased, and I thought every minute she would have begun confession. Thank you, you need not be uneasy; in ten minutes we landed very safely, and if we had been drowned, I am too exact not to have dated my letter from the bottom of the Thames. There! there's a letter; I think you would not want to read such another, even if written to somebody else.

Yours ever,

H. W.[1]

To the Hon. Henry Seymour Conway and the Countess of Ailesbury, 15 January 1775

Arlington Street, Jan. 15, 1775.

You have made me very happy by saying your journey to Naples is laid aside. Perhaps it made too great an impression on me; but you must reflect, that all my life I have satisfied myself with your being perfect, instead of trying to be so myself. I don't ask you to

1. Two postscripts have been omitted.

return, though I wish it: in truth, there is nothing to invite you. I don't want you to come and breathe fire and sword against the Bostonians, like that second Duke of Alva, the inflexible Lord George Germain; or to anathematize the court and all its works, like the incorruptible Burke, who scorns lucre, except when he can buy a hundred thousand acres from naked Caribs for a song. I don't want you to do anything like a party-man. I trust you think of every party as I do, with contempt, from Lord Chatham's mustard-bowl down to Lord Rockingham's hartshorn. All, perhaps, will be tried in their turns, and yet, if they had genius, might not be mighty enough to save us. From some ruin or other I think nobody can, and what signifies an option of mischiefs?

An account is come of the Bostonians having voted an army of sixteen thousand men, who are to be called *minute-men,* as they are to be ready at a minute's warning. Two directors or commissioners, I don't know what they are called, are appointed. There has been too a kind of mutiny in the Fifth Regiment. A soldier was found drunk on his post. Gage, in this time of *danger,* thought rigour necessary, and sent the fellow to a court-martial. They ordered two hundred lashes. The General ordered them to improve their sentence. Next day it was published in the *Boston Gazette.* He called them before him, and required them on oath to abjure the communication: three officers refused. Poor Gage is to be scapegoat, not for this, but for what was a reason against employing him, incapacity. I wonder at the precedent! Howe is talked of for his successor.—Well, I have done with *you!*—Now I shall gossip with Lady Ailesbury.

You must know, Madam, that near Bath is erected a new Parnassus, composed of three laurels, a myrtle-tree, a weeping-willow, and a view of the Avon, which has been new christened Helicon. Ten years ago there lived a Madam Riggs, an old rough humourist who passed for a wit; her daughter, who passed for nothing, married to a Captain Miller, full of good-natured officiousness. These good folks were friends of Miss Rich, who carried me to dine with them at Bath-Easton, now Pindus. They caught a little of what was then called taste, built and planted, and begot children, till the whole caravan were forced to go abroad to retrieve. Alas! Mrs. Miller is returned a beauty, a genius, a Sappho, a tenth Muse, as romantic as Mademoiselle Scudéri, and as sophisticated as Mrs. Vesey. The Captain's fingers are loaded with cameos, his tongue runs over with *virtù*, and that both may contribute to the improvement of their own country, they have introduced *bouts-rimés* as a new discovery. They hold a Parnassus fair every Thursday, give out rhymes and themes, and all the flux of quality at Bath contend for the prizes. A Roman vase dressed with pink ribbons and myrtles receives the poetry, which is drawn out every festival; six judges of these Olympic games retire and select the brightest compositions, which the respective successful acknowledge, kneel to Mrs. Calliope Miller, kiss her fair hand, and are crowned by it with myrtle, with—I don't know what. You may think this is fiction, or exaggeration. Be dumb, unbelievers! The collection is printed, published.—Yes, on my faith! There are *bouts-rimés* on a buttered muffin, made by her Grace the Duchess of Northumberland; receipts to make them by Corydon the venerable, *alias* George Pitt; others very pretty, by Lord Palmerston; some by Lord Carlisle; many by Mrs. Miller herself, that have no fault but wanting metre; and immortality promised to her without end or measure. In short, since folly, which never ripens to madness but in this hot climate, ran distracted, there never was anything so entertaining or so dull—for you cannot read so long as I have been telling.

To Robert Jephson, February 1775

February 1775.

You have drawn more trouble on yourself, Sir, than you expected; and would probably excuse my not performing the rest of my promise: but though I look upon myself as engaged to send you my thoughts, you are neither bound to answer them, nor regard them. They very likely are not new, and it is presumption in me to send hints to a much abler writer than myself. I can only plead in apology, that I interest myself in your fame; and as you are the only man capable of restoring and improving our stage, I really mean no more than to exhort and lead you on to make use of your great talents.

I have told you, as is true, that I am no poet. It is as true that you are a genuine one; and therefore I shall not say one word on that head. For the construction of a drama—it is mechanic, though much depends on it. A by-stander may be a good director at least; for mechanism certainly is independent of, though easily possessed by, a genius. Banks never wrote six tolerable lines, yet disposed his fable with so much address, that I think three plays have been constructed on his plot of the Earl of Essex, not one of which is much better than the original. The disposition is the next step to the choice of a subject, on which I have said enough in a former letter. A genius can surmount defects in both. If there is art in *Othello* and *Macbeth*, it seems to have been by chance; for Shakespeare certainly took no pains to adjust a plan, and in his historic plays seems to have turned Hollinshed and Stowe into verse and scenes as fast as he could write—though every now and then divine genius flashed upon particular scenes and made them immortal; as in his *King John*, where nature itself has stamped the scenes of Constance, Arthur and Hubert with her own impression, though the rest is as defective as possible. He seems to recall the Mahometan idea of lunatics, who are sometimes inspired, oftener changelings. Yet what signifies all his rubbish? He has scenes, and even speeches, that are infinitely superior to all the correct elegance of Racine. I had rather have written the two speeches of Lady Percy, in the second part of *Henry IV*, than all Voltaire, though I admire the latter infinitely, especially in *Alzire*, *Mahomet*, and *Semiramis*. Indeed, when I think over all the great authors of the Greeks, Romans, Italians, French, and English (and I know no other languages), I set Shakespeare first and alone, and then begin anew.

Well, Sir, I give up Shakespeare's dramas; and yet prefer him to every man. Why? For his exquisite knowledge of the passions and nature; for his simplicity, too, which he possesses too when most natural. Dr. Johnson says he is bombast whenever he attempts to be sublime: but this is never true but when he aims at sublimity in the expression; the glaring fault of Johnson himself. —But as simplicity is the grace of sublime, who possesses it like Shakespeare? Is not the

'Him, wondrous Him!'

in Lady Percy's speech, exquisitely sublime and pathetic too? He has another kind of sublime which no man ever possessed but he; and this is, his art in dignifying a vulgar or trivial expression. Voltaire is so grossly ignorant and tasteless as to condemn this, as to condemn *the bare bodkin*.—But my enthusiasm for Shakespeare runs away with me.

I was speaking of the negligence of his construction. You have not that fault. I own I do not admire your choice of *Braganza*, because in reality it admits of but two acts, the conspiracy and the revolution. You have not only filled it out with the most beautiful dialogue, but made the interest rise, though the revolution has succeeded. I can never too much admire the appearance of the friar, which disarms Velasquez: and yet you will be shocked to hear that, notwithstanding all I could say at the rehearsal, I could not prevail to have Velasquez drop the dagger instantly, the only artful way of getting it out of his hand; for as Lady P—— observed, if he kept it two moments, he would recollect that it was the only way of preserving himself. But actors are not always judges. They persisted, for show-sake, against my remonstrances, to exhibit the Duke and Duchess on a throne in the second act; which could not but make the audience conclude that the revolution had even then taken place.

If I could find a fault in your tragedy, Sir, it would be a want of more short speeches, of a sort of serious repartee, which gives great spirit. But I think the most of what I have to say may be comprised in a recommendation of keeping the audience in suspense, and of touching the passions by the pathetic familiar. By the latter, I mean the study of Shakespeare's strokes of nature, which, soberly used, are alone superior to poetry, and, with your ear, may easily be made harmonious.

If there is any merit in my play,[1] I think it is in interrupting the spectator's fathoming the whole story till the last, and in making every scene tend to advance the catastrophe. These arts are mechanic, I confess; but at least they are as meritorious as the scrupulous delicacy of the French in observing, not only the unities, but a fantastic decorum, that does not exist in nature, and which consequently reduce all their tragedies, wherever the scene may lie, to the manners of modern Paris. Corneille could be Roman; Racine, never but French, and consequently, though a better poet, less natural and less various. Both indeed have prodigious merit. *Phèdre* is exquisite, *Britannicus* admirable; and both excite pity and terror. Corneille is scarce ever tender, but always grand; yet never equal in a whole play to Racine. *Rodogune*, which I greatly admire, is very defective; for the two Princes are so equally good, and the two women so very bad, that they divide both our esteem and indignation. Yet I own, Racine, Corneille, and Voltaire ought to rank before all our tragedians, but Shakespeare. *Jane Shore* is perhaps our best play after his. I admire *All for Love* very much; and some scenes in *Don Sebastian* and Young's *Revenge. The Siege of Damascus* is very pure—and *Phaedra and Hippolitus* fine poetry, though wanting all the nature of the original. We have few other tragedies of signal merit, though the four first acts of *The Fair Penitent* are very good. It is strange that Dryden, who showed such a knowledge of nature in *The Cock and Fox*, should have so very little in his plays—he could rather describe it than put into action. I have said all this, Sir, only to point out to you what a field is open to you—and though so many subjects, almost all the known, are exhausted, nature is inexhaustible, and genius can achieve anything. We have a language far more energic, and more sonorous too, than the French. Shakespeare could do what he would with it in its unpolished state. Milton gave it pomp from the Greek, and softness from the Italian; Waller now and then,

1. *The Mysterious Mother.*

here and there, gave it the elegance of the French. Dryden poured music into it; Prior gave it ease; and Gray used it masterly for either elegy or terror. Examine, Sir, the powers of a language you command, and let me again recommend to you a diction of your own,[1] at least in some one play. The majesty of Paradise Lost would have been less imposing, if it had been written in the style of *The Essay on Man*. Pope pleases, but never surprises; and astonishment is one of the Springs of tragedy. *Coups de théâtre,* like the sublime one in *Mahomet*, have infinite effect. The incantations in *Macbeth*, that almost border on the burlesque, are still terrible. What French criticism can wound the ghosts of Hamlet or Banquo? Scorn rules, Sir, that cramp genius, and substitute delicacy to imagination in a barren language. Shall we not soar, because the French dare not rise from the ground?

You seem to possess the *tender*. The *terrible* is still more easy, at least I know to me. In all my tragedy, Adeliza contents me the least. Contrasts, though mechanic too, are very striking; and though Molière was a comic writer, he might give lessons to a tragic. But I have passed all bounds; and yet shall be glad if you can cull one useful hint out of my rhapsodies. I here put an end to them; and wish, out of all I have said, that you may remember nothing, Sir, but my motives in writing, obedience to your commands, and a hearty eagerness for fixing on our stage so superior a writer.

I am, Sir,

With great esteem and truth,

Your most obedient humble servant

HOR. WALPOLE.

P. S.—I must beg you, Sir, not to let these letters go out of your hands; for they are full of indigested thoughts, some perhaps capricious, as those on novel diction—but I wish to tempt genius out of the beaten road; and originality is the most captivating evidence of it.

1. Mr. Jephson followed this advice in his *Law of Lombardy*—but was not happy in his attempt. (HW's note)

To the Rev. William Mason, 3 April 1775

Arlington Street, April 3, 1775.

Well! your book[1] is walking the town in mid-day. How it is liked, I do not yet know. Were I to judge from my own feelings, I should say there never was so entertaining or interesting a work: that it is the most perfect model of biography; and must make Tacitus, and Agricola too, detest you. But as the world and simple I are not often of the same opinion, it will perhaps be thought very dull. If it is, all we can do, is to appeal to that undutiful urchin, posterity, who commonly treats the judgment of its parents with contempt, though it has so profound a veneration for its most distant ancestors. As you have neither imitated the teeth-breaking diction of Johnson, nor coined slanders against the most virtuous names in story, like modern historians, you cannot expect to please the *reigning* taste. Few persons have had time, from their politics, diversions and gaming, to have read much of so large a volume, which they will keep for the summer, when they have full as much of nothing to do. Such as love poetry, or think themselves poets, will have hurried to the verses and been disappointed at not finding half a dozen more Elegies in a Churchyard. A few fine gentlemen will have read one or two of the shortest letters, which not being exactly such as they write themselves, they will dislike or copy next post; they who wish or intend to find fault with Gray, you, or even me, have, to be sure, skimmed over the whole, except the Latin, for even spite, *non est tanti*—. The reviewers no doubt are already writing against you; not because they have read the whole, but because one's own name is always the first thing that strikes one in a book. The Scotch will be more deliberate, but not less angry; and if not less angry, not more merciful. Every Hume, however spelt, will I don't know what do; I should be sorry to be able to guess what. I have already been asked, why I did not prevent publication of the censure on David? The truth is (as you know) I never saw the whole together till now, and not that part; and if I had, why ought I to have prevented it: Voltaire will cast

1. His *Memoirs of Gray*.

an *imbelle* javelin *sine ictu* at Gray, for he loves to depreciate a *dead* great author, even when unprovoked,—even when he has commended him alive, or before he was so vain and so envious as he is now. The Rousseaurians will imagine that I interpolated the condemnation of his *Eloïse*. In short, we shall have many sins laid to our charge, of which we are innocent; but what can the malicious say against the innocent, but what is not true? I am here in brunt to the storm; you sit serenely aloof and smile at its sputtering. So should I too, were I out of sight, but I hate to be stared at, and the object of whispers before my face. The macaronies will laugh out, for you say I am still in the fashionable world.—What! they will cry, as they read while their hair is curling,—that old soul;—for old and old-fashioned are synonymous in the vocabulary of mode, alas! Nobody is so sorry as I to be in the world's fashionable purlieus; still, in truth, all this is a joke and touches me little. I seem to myself a Stralbrug, who have lived past my time, and see almost my own life written before my face while I am yet upon earth, and as it were the only one of my contemporaries with whom I began the world. Well; in a month's time there will be little question of Gray, and less of me. America and feathers and masquerades will drive us into libraries, and there I am well content to live as an humble companion to Gray and you; and, thank my stars, not on the same shelf with the Macphersons and Dalrymples.

One omission I have found, at which I wonder; you do not mention Gray's study of physic, of which he had read much, and I doubt to his hurt. I had not seen till now that delightful encomium on Cambridge, when empty of its inhabitants. It is as good as anything in the book, and has that true humour, which I think equal to any of his excellencies. So has the apostrophe to Nicols, 'Why, you monster, I shall never be dirty and amused as long as I live,' but I will not quote any more, though I shall be reading it and reading it for the rest of my life. . . .

To the Rev. William Cole, 25 April 1775

Arlington Street, April 25, 1775.

The least I can do, dear Sir, in gratitude for the cargo of prints I have received today from you, is to send you a medicine. A pair of bootikins will set out tomorrow morning in the machine that goes from the Queen's Head in Gray's Inn Lane. To be certain, you had better send for them where the machine inns, lest they should neglect delivering them at Milton. My not losing a moment, shows my zeal—but if you can bear a little pain, I should not press you to use them. I have suffered so dreadfully, that I constantly wear them to diminish the stock of gout in my constitution; but as your fit is very slight, and will not last, and as you are pretty sure by its beginning so late, that you will never have much; and as the gout certainly carries off other complaints, had not you better endure a little, when it is rather a remedy than a disease? I do not desire to be entirely delivered from the gout, for all reformations do but make room for some new grievance; and in my opinion, a disorder that requires no physician is preferable to any that does. However I have put relief in your power and you will judge for yourself. You must tie them as tight as you can bear, the flannel next to the flesh; and when you take them off, it should be in bed. Rub your feet with a warm cloth, and put on warm stockings, for fear of catching cold while the pores are open. It would kill anybody but me, who am of adamant, to walk out into the dew in winter in my slippers in half an hour after pulling off the bootikins. A physician sent me word good-naturedly that there was danger of catching cold after the bootikins, unless one was careful. I thanked him, but told him my precaution was, never taking any. All the winter I pass five days in a week without walking out, and sit often by the fireside till seven in the evening. When I do go out, whatever the weather is, I go with both glasses of the coach down, and so I do at midnight out of the hottest room. I have not had a single cold however slight, these two years.

You are too candid in submitting at once to my defence of Mr Mason. It is true I am more charmed with his book than I almost ever was with one. I find more people like the grave letters than those of humour, and some think the latter a little affected, which is as wrong a judgment as they could make, for Gray never wrote anything easily but things of humour. Humour was his natural and original turn—and though from his child[hood] he was grave, and reserved, his genius led him to see things ludicrously and satirically; and though his health and dissatisfaction gave him low spirits, his melancholy turn was much more affected than his pleasantry in writing. You knew him enough to know I am in the right—but the world in general always wants to be told how to think as well as what to think. The print,[1] I agree with you, though like, is a very disagreeable likeness, and the worst likeness of him. It gives the primness he had when under constraint; and there is a blackness in the countenance which was like him only the last time I ever saw him, when I was much struck with it; and though I did not apprehend him in danger, it left an impression on me that was uneasy and almost prophetic of what I heard but too soon after leaving him. Wilson drew the picture under much such impression, and I could not bear it in my room; Mr Mason altered it a little, but still it is not well, nor gives any idea of the determined virtues of his heart. It just serves to help the reader to an image of the person, whose genius and integrity they must admire, if they are so happy as to have a taste for either.

The *Peep into the Gardens at Twickenham* is a silly little book, of which a few little copies were printed some years ago for presents, and which now sets up for itself as a vendible book. It is a most inaccurate, superficial, blundering account of Twickenham and other places, drawn up by a Jewess, who has married twice and turned Christian, poetess and authoress. She has printed her poems too, and one complimentary copy of mine which in good breeding I could not help sending her in return for violent compliments in verse to me. I do not remember that hers were good; mine I know were very bad, and certainly never intended for the press.

1. The frontispiece to the *Memoirs*.

I bought the first volume of Manchester,[1] but could not read it; it was much too learned for me; and seemed rather an account of Babel than Manchester, I mean in point of antiquity. To be sure it is very kind in an author to promise one the history of a country town, and give one a circumstantial account of the antediluvian world into the bargain. But I am simple and ignorant, and desire no more than I pay for. And then for my progenitors Noah and the Saxons, I have no curiosity about them. Bishop Lyttelton used to plague me to death with barrows and tumuli and Roman camps, and all those bumps in the ground that do not amount to a most imperfect ichnography; but in good truth I am content with all arts when perfected, nor inquire how ingeniously people contrived to do without them—and I care still less for remains of arts that retain no vestiges of art. Mr Bryant, who is sublime in unknown knowledge, diverted me more, yet I have not finished his work,[2] no more than he has. There is a great ingenuity in discovering all history (though it has never been written) by etymologies. Nay he convinced me that the Greeks had totally mistaken all they went to learn in Egypt, etc., by doing, as the French do still, judge wrong by the ear—but as I have been trying now and then for above forty years to learn something, I have not time to unlearn it all again, though I allow this is our best sort of knowledge. If I should die when I am not clear in the history of the world below its first three thousand years, I should be at a sad loss on meeting with Homer and Hesiod or any of those *moderns* in the Elysian fields, before I knew what I ought to think of them.

Pray do not betray my ignorance: the reviewers and such *literati* have called me *a learned and ingenious gentleman*. I am sorry they ever heard my name, but don't let them know how irreverently I speak of the erudite, whom I dare to say they admire. These wasps, I suppose, will be very angry at the just contempt Mr Gray had for them, and will, as insects do, attempt to sting, in hopes that their twelvepenny readers will suck a little venom from the momentary

1. John Whitaker, *History of Manchester* (1771).
2. Jacob Bryant, *A New System or Analysis of Ancient Mythology* (1774–76).

tumor they raise—but good-night—and once more thank you for the prints.

Yours ever,

H. W.

To the Countess of Ailesbury, 20 August 1775

Paris, Aug. 20, 1775.

I have been sea-sick to death; I have been poisoned by dirt and vermin; I have been stifled by heat, choked by dust, and starved for want of anything I could touch: and yet, Madam, here I am, perfectly well, not in the least fatigued; and, thanks to the rivelled parchments, formerly faces, which I have seen by hundreds, I find myself almost as young as when I came hither first in the last century. In spite of my whims, and delicacy, and laziness, none of my grievances have been mortal: I have borne them as well as if I had set up for a philosopher, like the sages of this town. Indeed, I have found my dear old woman[1] so well, and looking so much better than she did four years ago, that I am transported with pleasure, and thank your Ladyship and Mr. Conway for driving me hither. Madame du Deffand came to me the instant I arrived, and sat by me whilst I stripped and dressed myself; for, as she said, since she cannot see, there was no harm in my being stark. She was charmed with your present; but was so kind as to be so much more charmed with my arrival, that she did not think of it a moment. I sat with her till half an hour after two in the morning, and had a letter from her before my eyes were open again. In short, her soul is immortal, and forces her body to bear it company.

This is the very eve of Madame Clotilde's wedding; but Monsieur Turgot, to the great grief of Lady Mary, will suffer no cost, but one banquet, one ball, and a play at Versailles. Count Virri gives a banquet, a *bal masqué,* and a firework. I think I shall see little but the last, from which I will send your Ladyship a rocket in

1. Madame du Deffand.

my next letter. Lady Mary, I believe, has had a private audience of the ambassador's leg, but *en tout bien et honneur,* and only to satisfy her ceremonious curiosity about any part of royal nudity. I am just going to her, as she is at Versailles; and I have not time to add a word more to the vows of your Ladyship's

Most faithful,

HOR. WALPOLE.

TO SIR HORACE MANN, 10 October 1775

Paris, Oct. 10, 1775.

I am still here, though on the wing. Your answer to mine from hence was sent back to me from England, as I have loitered here beyond my intention—in truth from an indisposition of mind: I am not impatient to be in a frantic country that is stabbing itself in every vein. The delirium still lasts, though I believe kept up by the quacks that caused it. Is it credible that five or six of the great *trading* towns have presented addresses against the Americans? I have no doubt but those addresses are procured by those boobies the country gentlemen their members, and bought of the aldermen—but is it not amazing that the merchants and manufacturers do not duck such tools in a horsepond? When the storm will recoil I do not know, but it will be terrible in all probability—though too late! Never shall we be again what we have been! Other powers, who sit still and wisely suffer us to plunge over head and ears, will perhaps be alarmed at what they write from England, that we are to buy twenty thousand Russian assassins at the price of Georgia—how deep must be our game when we pursue it at the expense of establishing a new maritime power, and aggrandize that engrossing throne, which threatens half Europe, for the satisfaction of enslaving our own brethren! horrible policy! If the Americans, as our papers say, are on the point of seizing Canada, I should think that France would not long remain neuter, when she may regain her fur trade with the Canadians, or obtain Canada from the Americans—but it is endless to calculate what we may lose. Our Court has staked everything against despotism; and the nation which must be a loser whichever side prevails, takes part against the Americans, who fight for the nation as well as for themselves! what Egyptian darkness!

This country is far more happy. It is governed by benevolent and beneficent men under a Prince who has not yet betrayed a fault; and who will be as happy as his people if he always employs such men. Messieurs de Turgot and Malesherbes are philosophers in the true sense, that is, legislators—but as their plans tend to serve the public, you may be sure they do not please interested individuals. The French too are light and fickle, and designing men, who have no weapon against good men but ridicule, already employ it to make a trifling nation laugh at its benefactors—and if it is the fashion to laugh, the laws of fashion will be executed preferably to those of common sense.

There is a great place just vacant. The Maréchal de Muy, *secrétaire d'état pour la guerre,* died yesterday, having been cut the day before for the stone. The operation lasted thirty-five ages, that is, minutes!

Our Parliament meets on the 26th—and I suppose will act as infamously as it did last year— It cannot do worse—scarce so ill, for now it cannot act inconsiderately. To joke in voting a civil war is the *comble* of infamy. I hope it will present flattering addresses on our disgraces, and heap taxes on those who admire the necessity of them. If the present generation alone would be punished by inviting the yoke, it were pity but it were already on their necks! Do not wonder at my indignation, nor at my indulging it. I can write freely hence—from England, where I may find the Inquisition, it would not be so prudent—but judge of our situation, when an Englishman to speak his mind must come to France!—and hither I will come, unless the times alter—I had rather live where a Maupeou is banished, than where he is Chief Justice.[1] . . .

1. Alluding to Lord Mansfield. (HW's note)

To the Rev. William Mason, 27 November 1775

Nov. 27, 1775.

I thought it long since I heard from you; it is plain you did not forget me, for the first moment of an opportunity to show me kindness, made you show it; fortunately I had written to Lord Strafford the very day you wrote to me, and our letters passed each other, though without bowing. I think it still more fortunate that I had not written sooner, because I like to be obliged to you; I had delayed because in truth I had nothing to say but what I thought; and when my friends and I do not think alike,[1] I prefer silence to contradiction or disputes, for I cannot say what I do not think, especially to my friends; to other people one can talk a good deal of nonsense which serves instead of thinking.

Your delay of coming displeases me, because what I wish, I wish for immediately; when spring comes, I shall be glad my joy was postponed, and I like better to see you at Strawberry than in town, especially when Strawberry is in its beauty; and as you and it are two chiefs of the few pleasures I have left, or to come, I am luxurious and love a complete banquet.

What shall I say more? talk politics? no; we think too much alike. England was, Scotland is—indeed by the blunders the latter has made one sees its Irish origin,—but I had rather talk of anything else. I see nothing but ruin whatever shall happen, and what idle solicitude is that of childless old people, who are anxious about the first fifty years after their death, and do not reflect that in the eternity to follow, fifty or five hundred years are a moment, and that all countries fall sooner or later.

Naturally I fly to books, there is a finis too, for I cannot read Dean Tucker, nor newspapers. We have had nothing at all this winter but Sterne's letters, and what are almost as nothingly,—Lady Luxborough's. She does not write ill, or, as I expected affectedly, like a woman, but talks of *scrawls,* and of her letters being *stupid.* She had no spirit, no wit, knew no events; she idolizes poor Shenstone, who was scarce above her, and flatters him, to be flat-

1. HW and Strafford differed on the American War.

tered. A stronger proof of her having no taste is, that she says coldly, she likes Gray's Churchyard *well;* in good truth the productions of this country and age are suited to its natives. Mr Cumberland, the maker of plays, told me lately, it *was pity Gray's letters were printed; they had disappointed him much;* no doubt he likes Sterne's, and Shenstone's, and Lady Luxborough's. Oh! Dodsley, print away: you will never want authors or readers, unless a classic work like Gray's life should, as Richardson said of Milton, be born two thousand years after its time!

I approve your printing in manuscript, that is, not for the public, for who knows how long the public will be able, or be permitted to read? Bury a ſew copies against this island is rediscovered, some American versed in the old English language will translate it, and revive the true taste in gardening; though he will smile at the diminutive scenes on the little Thames when he is planting a forest on the banks of the Oroonoko. I love to skip into futurity and imagine what will be done on the giant scale of a new hemisphere; but I am in little London, and must go and dress for a dinner with some of the inhabitants of that ancient metropolis, now in ruins, which was really for a moment the capital of a large empire, but the poor man who made it so, outlived himself and the duration of the empire.

To the Rev. William Mason, 18 February 1776

Feb. 18, 1776.

As my illness prevented my answering your delightful letter I do not see why the leisure and solitude of convalescence should not be employed in replying to it, not poetically; for the current of the blood, frozen by age and chalk-stoned by the gout, does not, though loosened from disease, flow over the smooth pebbles of Helicon; mine at best were factitious rills that, like the artificial cascatelle of Hagley, played for moments to entertain visitors, and were not the natural bounty of the soil; *you* are forced to restrain your torrent and the dikes of prudence must be borne down before it overflows the country. Not so Mr Anstey; because his muddy mill-pool had in one point of view, the roar and lustre of a cascade when it fell over a proper wheel, he thinks every pail full of its water, though soused down by a ploughman, has the same effect. His Somersetshire dialogue is stupidity itself, you described it prophetically before you saw it.

Somebody or other has given us an epistle of another kind by the late Lord Melcombe, not different from having more meaning, for Phœbus knows it has none at all, but so civil, so harmless, and so harmonious, that it is the ghost of one of Pope's tunes. How the puffy Peer must have sweated when learning to sing of Pope, whom he could have strangled! The whole and sole drift of this cantata is to call Lord Bute Pollio, and to beg to be his vicegerent upon earth. I should like to have heard Lord Bute asking Sir Harry Erskine who Pollio was.

Mr Whitehed has just published a pretty poem called *Variety*, in which there is humour and ingenuity, but not more poetry than is necessary for a laureate; however the plan is one [*sic*], and is well wound up. I now pass to prose.

Lo, there is just appeared a truly classic work: a history, not majestic like Livy, nor compressed like Tacitus; not stamped with character like Clarendon; perhaps not so deep as Robertson's *Scotland*, but a thousand degrees above his *Charles*; not pointed like Voltaire, but as accurate as he is inexact; modest as he is *tranchant* and sly as Montesquieu without being so *recherché*. The style is as smooth as a Flemish picture, and the muscles are concealed and only for natural uses, not exaggerated like Michael Angelo's to show the painter's skill in anatomy; nor composed of the limbs of clowns of different nations, like Dr Johnson's heterogeneous monsters. This book is Mr Gibbon's *History of the Decline and Fall of the Roman Empire*. He is son of a late foolish alderman, is a member of Parliament, and called a whimsical one because he votes variously as his opinion leads him; and his first production was in French, in which language he shines too. I know him a little, never suspected the extent of his talents, for he is perfectly modest, or I want penetration, which I know too, but I intend to know him a great deal more—there! there is food for your residence at York.

Do I know nothing superior to Mr Gibbon? yes, but not what will entertain you at York. Mr Gibbon's are good sense and polished art. I talk of great original genius. Lady Di Beauclerc has made seven large drawings in soot-water (her first attempt of the kind) for scenes of my *Mysterious Mother*. Oh! such drawings! Guido's grace, Albano's children, Poussin's expression, Salvator's boldness in landscape and Andrea Sacchi's simplicity of composition might perhaps have equalled them had they wrought all together very fine; how an author's vanity can bestow bombast panegyric on his flatterers! Pray, Sir, when did I take myself for an original genius! Did not Shakespeare draw Hamlet from Olaus Ostrogothus, or some such name? did Le Sœur conceive the Chartreuse from any merit in the legend of St Bruno? seeing is believing, miracles are not ceased; I know how prejudiced I am apt to be; some time or other you will see whether I am so in this instance.

Now for specific answers to your queries—many of which answers will not be specific, for I know little more than if I were at York. I know nothing of Garrick's sale of patent, but I know forty stories of his envy and jealousy, that are too long to tell you by mouth of pen—of a Monsieur Le Texier, another real prodigy, who acts whole plays, in which every character is perfect—and pray observe he has not read *my* play. In sum, Garrick says when he quits the stage, he will read plays too, but they will be better than Monsieur Texier's (who only reads those of other authors) for he shall write them himself. This I know he has said twice. *Ex pede Herculem.*

The Duchess of Kingston only knows whether she will be tried. The Earl's zeal against her was as marvellous to me as to you; I know reasons why he should have done the reverse, and cannot reconcile contradictions. Why should not Sayre's affair sleep? what, who is awake? For your hundred other queries which you have not put to me, I shall not attempt to guess them, not from idleness, but from the probable incapacity of my being able to answer them. The womb of time is big; we shall see, whether she is delivered of mice or mountains.

One word about myself and I have done. I know you disliked my answer to Dr Milles,[1] and I know I was angry both at him and Mr Hume. The latter had acted very treacherously by the story I have hinted at of the Swiss reviewer. Dr Milles is a fool, who had been set on by Lord Hardwicke and that set, and at whom I have glanced. I have received many indirect little mischiefs from the Earl, who has of late courted me as much, and I have been civil to him. But my answers shall some time or other appear when I only shall be blamed and my antagonists will be dead, and not hurt by them. For Mr Masters, he is a dirty simpleton, who began by flattering me, and because I neglected him joined the pack. The arguments in the answers are very essential to the question, and I shall not give myself the trouble of extracting the ridicule on the answerers, as they deserved it.

My hands you see are well, but I could not have written so long an epistle with my feet, which are still in their flannels. As my spirits always revive in proportion as pain subsides, I shall take the liberty, Sir Residentiary, to trespass on your decorum by sending you an impromptu I wrote yesterday, to pretty Lady Craven, who sent me an eclogue of her own, every stanza of which ended with *January,* and which she desired me not to criticize, as some of the rhymes were incorrect, a license I adopted in my second line:

> Though lame and old, I do not burn
> With fretfulness to scare ye;
> And charms and wit like yours would turn
> To May my January.
>
> The God who can inspire and heal
> Sure breathed your lines, sweet fairy;
> For as I read, I feel, I feel,
> I am not quite January.

Probably you would have liked better to have the eclogue, but I had not leave to send it.

1. Who had attacked HW's *Historic Doubts of . . . Richard III.*

To Sir Horace Mann, 27 May 1776

Strawberry Hill, May 27th, 1776.

This fatal year puts to the proof the nerves of my friendship! I was disappointed of seeing you when I had set my heart on it—and now I have lost Mr Chute! It is a heavy blow; but such strokes reconcile one's self to parting with this pretty vision, life! What is it, when one has no longer those to whom one speaks as confidentially as to one's own soul? Old friends are the great blessing of one's latter years—half a word conveys one's meaning. They have memory of the same events, and have the same mode of thinking. Mr Chute and I agreed invariably in our principles; he was my counsel in my affairs, was my oracle in taste, the standard to whom I submitted my trifles, and the genius that presided over poor Strawberry! His sense decided me in everything, his wit and quickness illuminated everything—I saw him oftener than any man; to him in every difficulty I had recourse, and him I loved to have here, as our friendship was so entire, and we knew one another so entirely, that he alone never was the least constraint to me. We passed many hours together without saying a syllable to each other, for we were both above ceremony. I left him without excusing myself, read or wrote before him, as if he were not present— Alas! alas!—and how *self* presides even in our grief! I am lamenting myself, not him!—no, I am lamenting my other self. Half is gone; the other remains solitary. Age and sense will make me bear my affliction with submission and composure—but forever—that little *forever* that remains, I shall miss him. My first thought will always be, *I will go talk to Mr Chute on this*—the second, *alas! I cannot*—and therefore judge how my life is poisoned! I shall only seem to be staying behind one that is set out a little before me.

Mr Chute for these last two or three years was much broken by his long and repeated shocks of gout, yet was amazingly well, considering he had suffered by it from twenty to seventy-three. Still as he never had had it in his head or stomach, I never was alarmed till last summer, when he had a low lingering fever, and sickness and pain in his breast, with returns of an excessive palpitation at his heart, which formerly much alarmed me, but of which he had been free for some years. He got better and went to the Bath, which gave him the gout, and he returned quite well—so well, that alarmed at our situation, he thought of drawing some money out of the stocks and buying an annuity, saying he thought his life as good as any man's for five years—I am sure I thought so too. On Thursday last, being surprised at his not calling on me for three days, which was unusual, I went to him and was told he was very ill. I found him in bed; he had so violent a pain in his breast that two days before he had sent for Dr Thomas, whom he had consulted in the summer, though of all men the most averse to physicians. Thomas had given him an hundred drops of laudanum and asafœtida. Mr Chute said, 'It is not the gout, I have had my palpitation, and fear it is something of a polypus.' Thus, perfectly reasonable, though with much more indifference than he who was all spirit and eagerness used to have, I attributed it to the laudanum, and indeed he desired me to leave him, as he was heavy and wanted to sleep. He dozed all that evening, and had no return of pain. On Friday morning still without pain, I saw him again. He had taken more asafœtida, but no more laudanum; yet when I said I trusted the pain was gone, he said, 'I do not know, the effects of the laudanum are not yet gone.' I said I thought that impossible, that the pain would have surmounted the laudanum by that time, if the pain were not removed. I was coming hither on business, and charged his gentleman to send for me, if the pain returned. On Saturday morning I rejoiced at not receiving even a letter by the post, and concluded all was well. This dream of satisfaction lasted all that day and Saturday night. I knew he would take no more laudanum, unless the pain returned, and that then I should be advertised—but, oh! unhappy! Yesterday just as I had breakfasted and was in the garden, I heard the bell at the gate ring, and wondered, as it was but ten o'clock, who could come to me so early—I went to see and met my valet-de-chambre with a letter in his hand, who said, 'Oh, Sir, Mr Chute is dead!'— In a word, he had continued quite easy till three that morning, when he said, 'Who is in the room!' His own gentleman replied, 'I, Sir' —and going to the bed, found him very ill, ran to call help, and returning as quick as possible, saw him dead!— It was certainly a polypus; his side immediately grew black as ink. A charming death for him, dearest friend!—and why should I lament? His eyes, always short-sighted, were grown dimmer, his hearing was grown imperfect, his hands were all chalk-stones and of little use, his feet very lame—yet how not lament? The vigour of his mind was strong as ever; his powers of reasoning clear as demonstration, his rapid wit astonishing as at forty, about which time you and I knew him first. Even the impetuosity of his temper was not abated, and all his humane virtues had but increased with his age. He was grown sick of the world, saw very, very few persons, submitted with unparalleled patience to all his sufferings, and in five and thirty years I never once saw or heard him complain of them, nor, passionate as he was, knew him fretful. His impatience seemed to proceed from his vast sense, not from his temper: he saw everything so clearly and immediately, that he could not bear a momentary contradiction from folly or defective reasoning. Sudden contempt broke out, particularly on politics, which having been fixed in him by a most sensible father, and matured by deep reflection, were rooted in his inmost soul. His truth, integrity, honour, spirit, and abhorrence of all dirt, confirmed his contempt; and even I, who am pretty warm and steady, was often forced to break off politics with him, so impossible was it to be zealous enough to content him, when I most agreed with him. Nay, if I disputed with him, I learnt something from him, and always saw truth in a stronger and more summary light. His possession of the quintessence of argument reduced it at once into axioms, and the clearness of his ideas struck out flashes of the brightest wit. He saw so suddenly and so far, that, as Mr Bentley said of him long ago, 'his wit strikes, the more you analyse it, and more than at first hearing: he jumps over two or three intermediate ideas, and couples the first with the third or fourth'— Don't wonder I pour out my heart to you; you knew him, and know how faithfully true all I say of him. My loss is most irreparable. To me he was the most faithful and secure of friends, and a delightful companion. I shall not seek to replace him. Can I love any that are old, more than I have had reason for loving them—and is it possible to love younger as one loved an habitual old friend of thirty-five years standing? I have young relations that may grow upon me, for my nature is affectionate, but can they grow *old* friends? My age forbids that. Still less can they grow companions. Is it friendship to explain half one says? One must relate the history of one's memory and ideas—and what is that to the young, but old stories? No, my dear Sir, *you* could be that resource, but I must not think of it, I must not be selfish. I must do what I ought to do, while I remain here; pass my time as amusingly as I can, enjoy the friends I have left; drink my grief in silence, it is too sincere for parade; and what cares the world about my private sensations? Or what has an old man to do but to try to be forgotten; and to remember how soon he will be so? Forgive this expansion of my heart; it was necessary to me. I will not often mention poor Mr Chute, even to you. His loss is engraven on my soul, and real grief does not seek for applause. Could the world's plaudit comfort me, sit with me, hear me, advise me? Did it know Mr Chute's worth as well as I did? Does it love me as well? When it does, I will beg its compassion—I have done, and will now show you I am master of myself, and remember *you,* and consider that at this distance of time you cannot feel what I do, and must be anxious about public affairs. If I indulged my own feelings, I should forswear thinking of the public. *He* is gone to whom I ran with every scrap of news I heard—but I promised to forget myself: I will go take a walk, shed a tear, and return to you more composed.

I take up my pen again, and fear my last sentences have made you expect some news. I know none; except that I think the intoxication of this country begins to wear off. The stocks have taken the alarm, and the ministers have felt it some time. The change in the French councils has changed the spirits of ours. I believe almost any peace would be welcome to them. I doubt the Americans have experienced too much our inability to hurt them: and as I have no great faith in virtue tempted by power, I expect that the American leaders having too fair a field before them, will not easily part with dictatorships and consulships to retire to their private ploughs. Oh! Madness, to have squandered away such an empire!—Now we tremble at France, which America enabled us to resist. How naturally our ideas hang on our country, even when all future ages are the same to one who is going to leave it! What will it be to me a few years hence, whether England shrinks back to its little insular insignificance under George the Third or George the Tenth? Yet as our minds seldom roam into the future affairs of the world, we rejoice or grieve over the state of our country according to the condition in which we leave it at our departure. Else why do people nurse visions of pride about their own descendants? How long do the greatest and most ancient families last? What a speck in rolling ages does the longest genealogy occupy!—but I will moralize no more. Today's misfortune has given a wise cast to my mind. Spirits and folly will have their turn again, and perhaps are as wise. To act with common sense according to the moment, is the best wisdom I know; and the best philosophy, to do one's duties, take the world as it comes, submit respectfully to one's lot, bless the goodness that has given so much happiness with it, whatever it is, and despise affectation, which only makes our weakness more contemptible, by showing we know we are not what we wish to appear. Adieu!

To the Hon. Henry Seymour Conway, 30 June 1776

Strawberry Hill, June 30, 1776.

I was very glad to receive your letter, not only because always most glad to hear of you, but because I wished to write to you, and had absolutely nothing to say till I had something to answer. I have lain but two nights in town since I saw you; have been, else, constantly here, very much employed, though doing, hearing, knowing exactly nothing. I have had a Gothic architect from Cambridge to design me a gallery, which will end in a mouse, that is, in an hexagon closet of seven feet diameter. I have been making a beauty room, which was effected by buying two dozen of small copies of Sir Peter Lely, and hanging them up; and I have been making hay, which is not made, because I put it off for three days, as I chose it should adorn the landscape when I was to have company, and so the rain is come, and has drowned it. However, as I can even turn calculator when it is to comfort me for not minding my interest, I have discovered that it is five to one better for me that my hay should be spoiled than not; for, as the cows will eat it if it is damaged, which horses will not, and as I have five cows and but one horse, is not it plain that the worse my hay is, the better? Do not you with your refining head go, and, out of excessive friendship, find out something to destroy my system. I had rather be a philosopher than a rich man; and yet have so little philosophy, that I had much rather be content than be in the right.

Mr. Beauclerk and Lady Di have been here four or five days—so I had both content and exercise for my philosophy. I wish Lady Ailesbury was as fortunate! The Pembrokes, Churchills, Le Texier, as you will have heard, and the Garricks have been with us. Perhaps, if alone, I might have come to you; but you are all too healthy and harmonious. I can neither walk nor sing; nor, indeed, am fit for anything but to amuse myself in a sedentary trifling way. What I have most certainly not been doing, is writing anything: a truth I say to you, but do not desire you to repeat. I deign to satisfy scarce anybody else. Whoever reported that I was writing anything, must have been so totally unfounded, that they either blundered by guessing without reason, or knew they lied—and that could not be with any kind intention; though saying I am going to do what I am not going to do is wretched enough. Whatever is said of me without truth, anybody is welcome to believe that pleases.

In fact, though I have scarce a settled purpose about anything, I think I shall never write any more. I have written a great deal too much, unless I had written better, and I know I should now only write still worse. One's talent, whatever it is, does not improve at near sixty—yet, if I liked it, I dare to say a good reason would not stop my inclination;—but I am grown most indolent in that respect, and most absolutely indifferent to every purpose of vanity. Yet without vanity I am become still prouder and more contemptuous. I have a contempt for my countrymen that makes me despise their approbation. The applause of slaves and of the foolish mad is below ambition. Mine is the haughtiness of an ancient Briton, that cannot write what would please this age, and would not, if he could.

Whatever happens in America, this country is undone. I desire to be reckoned of the last age, and to be thought to have lived to be superannuated, preserving my senses only for myself and for the few I value. I cannot aspire to be traduced like Algernon Sydney, and content myself with sacrificing to him amongst my lares. Unalterable in my principles, careless about most things below essentials, indulging myself in trifles by system, annihilating myself by choice, but dreading folly at an unseemly age, I contrive to pass my time agreeably enough, yet see its termination approach without anxiety. This is a true picture of my mind; and it must be true, because drawn for you, whom I would not deceive, and could not, if I would. Your question on my being writing drew it forth, though with more seriousness that the report deserved—yet talking to one's dearest friend is neither wrong nor out of season. Nay, you are my best apology. I have always contented myself with your being perfect, or, if your modesty demands a mitigated term, I will say, unexceptionable. It is comical, to be sure, to have always been more solicitous about the virtue of one's friends than about one's own; yet, I repeat it, you are my apology—though I never was so unreasonable as to make you answerable for my faults in return; I take them wholly to myself. But enough of this. When I know my own mind, for hitherto I have settled no plan for my summer, I will come to you. Adieu!

To Viscount Nuneham, 7 July 1777

Strawberry Hill, July 7, 1777.

As I know your Lordship and Lady Nuneham are so good as to interest yourselves about the Duke and Duchess of Gloucester, I cannot deny myself the satisfaction of telling you, that, though the express on Saturday was as bad as possible, yet another letter yesterday from the Duke's surgeon, dated three days later, brought a more favourable account. His Royal Highness had been taken out of bed and put into a post-chaise, as it was thought nothing but change of air and motion could save him. He bore the travelling for two days very well, and got eight hours of sleep. The third day he was less well from fatigue, but the surgeon did not think him otherwise worse. I hope in God this alarm will pass off like the former!—but nothing, except her own words, could paint the agonies of the Duchess. She is alarmed too for the little Prince. They are coming to England, but not to stay, as Italian winters agree with the Duke, though the summers are so prejudicial.

Now I have taken this liberty, my dear Lord, I must take a little more; you know my old admiration and envy are your garden. I do not grudge Pomona or Sir James Cockburn their hothouses, nor intend to ruin myself by raising sugar and water in tanner's bark and peach skins. The Flora Nunehamica is the height of my ambition, and if your Linnaeus should have any disciple that would condescend to look after my little flower-garden, it would be the delight of my eyes and nose, provided the cataracts of heaven are ever shut again! Not one proviso do I make, but that the pupil be not a Scot. We had peace and warm weather before the inundation of that northern people, and therefore I beg to have no Attila for my gardener.

Apropos, don't your Lordship think that another set of legislators, the Maccaronis and Maccaronesses, are very wise? People abuse them for turning days, nights, hours, and seasons topsy-turvy; but surely it was upon mature reflection. We had a set of customs and ideas borrowed from the continent that by no means suited our climate. Reformers bring back things to their natural course. Notwithstanding what I said in spite in the paragraph above, we are in truth but Greenlanders and ought to conform to our climate. We should lay in store of provisions and candles and masquerades and coloured lamps for ten months in the year, and shut out our twilight and enjoy ourselves. In September and October we may venture out of our ark and make our hay and gather in our corn, and go to horse-races, and kill pheasants and partridges for stock for our winter's supper. I sailed in a skiff and pair this morning to Lady Cecilia Johnston, and found her, like a good housewife, sitting over her fire, with her cats and dogs and birds and children. She brought out a dram to warm me and my servants, and we were very merry and comfortable. As Lady Nuneham has neither so many two-footed or four-footed cares upon her hands, I hope her hands have been better employed.

I wish I could peep over her shoulder one of these wet mornings!

Adieu, my dear Lord; forgive all my babble. Yesterday's letter raised my spirits, and I love to impart my satisfaction to those I love, which, with all due respect, I must take leave to say I feel for you, and am most sincerely, etc.

To Lady Ossory, 11 December 1777

Thursday night, Dec. 11, 1777.

I do not write, Madam, to tell you politics; you will hear them better from Lord Ossory—nor indeed have I words to paint the abject impudent poltroonery of the ministers, or the blockish stupidity of the Parliament. Lord North yesterday declared he should during the recess prepare to lay before the Parliament proposals of peace to be offered to the Americans! *I trust we have force enough to bring forwards an accommodation.* They were his very words —Was ever proud insolent nation sunk so low? Burke and Charles Fox told him the administration thought of nothing but keeping their places—and so they will—and the Members their pensions, and the nation its infamy—Were I Franklin, I would order the Cabinet Council to come to me at Paris with ropes about their necks, and then kick them back to St James's—Well, Madam, as I told Lord Ossory t'other day, I am satisfied; Old England is safe, that is, America, whither the true English retired under Charles I—This is Nova Scotia, and I care not what becomes of it.

I have just been at *Percy.*[1] The four first acts are much better than I expected, and very animated. There are good situations, and several pretty passages; but not much nature; there is a fine speech of the heroine to her father, and a strange sermon against Crusades, that ends with a description of Jesus Christ who died for our sins. The last act is very ill-conducted and unnatural and obscure. Earl Douglas is a savage ruffian. Earl Percy is converted by the virtue of his mistress, and she is *love and virtue* in the supreme degree. There is prologue and epilogue about fine ladies and fine gentlemen and feathers and buckles, and I don't doubt every word of both, Mr Garrick's, for they are commonplace and written for the upper gallery. It was very moderately performed, but one passage against *the odious Scot* Douglas was loudly applauded, and showed that the mob have no pensions.

Our brave administration have turned out Lord Jersey and Mr Hopkins, which will certainly convince all America and all Europe that they are *not* afraid; though I saw one of their tools today who assured me they are—'Nay', he said (and *he* is somebody), 'that if the Congress insists on the ministry being changed, it must be'—I do not believe the Congress will do them so much honour —but I answered, 'Sir, if the Congress should make that condition, it will not be from caring about it, but to make the pacification impossible. I do not believe they care much more for the Opposition, than for the administration; but they must know, that the Opposition could not, would not, grant terms, that this administration should refuse.'

Adieu! Madam, I am at last not sorry you have no son, and your daughters, I hope, will be married to Americans, and not in this dirty despicable island!

To Sir Horace Mann, 18 February 1778

Arlington Street, Feb. 18, 1778.

I do not know how to word the following letter; how to gain credit

1. By Hannah More.

with you. How shall I intimate to you that you must lower your topsails, waive your imperial dignity, and strike to the colours of the Thirteen United Provinces of America?— Do not tremble, and imagine that Washington has defeated General Howe, and driven him out of Philadelphia; or that Gates has taken another army; or that Portsmouth is invested by an American fleet. No: no military *new* event has occasioned this revolution. The sacrifice has been made on the altar of peace— Stop again— Peace is not made—it is only implored—and I fear only on this side of the Atlantic. In short, yesterday, *February 17th*—a most memorable era, Lord North opened his conciliatory plan—no partial, no collusive one. In as few words as I can use, it solicits peace with the states of America; it haggles on no terms, it acknowledges the Congress, or anybody that pleases to treat; it confesses errors, misinformation, ill success, and impossibility of conquest; it disclaims taxation, desires commerce, hopes for assistance, allows the independence of America, not verbally, yet virtually, and suspends hostilities till June 1779— It does a little more—not *verbally,* but *virtually,* it confesses that the Opposition have been in the right from the beginning to the end.

The warmest American cannot deny but these gracious condescensions are ample enough to content that whole continent—and yet, my friend, such accommodating facility had one defect—it came too late. The treaty between the high and mighty states and France is signed—and instead of peace we must expect war with the High Allies. The French army is come to the coast, and their officers here are recalled.

The House of Commons embraced the plan, and voted it *nemine contradicente.* It is to pass both Houses with a rapidity that will do everything, but overtake time past. All the world is in astonishment— As my letter will not set out till the day after tomorrow I shall have time to tell you better what is thought of this amazing step.

Feb. 20.

In sooth I cannot tell you what is thought. Nobody knows what to think. To leap at once from an obstinacy of four years, to a total concession of everything; to stoop so low, without hopes of being forgiven; who can understand such a transformation?— I must leave you in all your wonderment, for the cloud is not dispersed. When it shall be, I doubt it will discover no serene prospect!

All that remains certain is, that America is not only lost, but given up. We must no longer give ourselves continental airs! I fear, even our trident will find it has lost a considerable prong.

I have lived long, but never saw such a day as last Tuesday! From the first, I augured ill of this American war—yet do not suppose that I boast of my penetration. Far was I from expecting such a conclusion!—Conclusion!—*y sommes-nous?* Acts of Parliament have made a war, but cannot repeal one. They have provoked, not terrified; and Washington and Gates have respected the Speaker's mace no more than Oliver Cromwell did.

You shall hear as events arise. I disclaim all sagacity, and pretend to no foresight. It is not an Englishman's talent. Even the second sight of the Scots has proved a little purblind.

Have you heard that Voltaire is actually at Paris?—perhaps soon, you will learn French news earlier than I can.

What scenes my letters to you have touched on for eight and thirty years! I arrived here at the eve of the termination of my father's happy reign. The rebellion, as he foresaw, followed; and much disgrace. Another war ensued, with new disgraces. And then broke forth Lord Chatham's sun; and all was glory and extensive empire. Nor tranquillity nor triumph are our lot now! The womb of time is not with child of a mouse—but, adieu! I shall probably write again before you have digested half the meditations this letter will have conjured up.

To the Rev. William Mason, 12 May 1778

May 12, 1778.

I now and then write a letter for, rather than to you: that is, when they will bear delay and be equally fresh, and when they contain anecdotes that I do not care to send by the post if they are too personal, and I have not a prospect of sudden conveyance. The following will have all these ingredients, and will rather be an epitome of the manners of the time, than a letter. The characteristics of the age are frenzy, folly, extravagance and insensibility; no wonder when such stars are predominant, that Ruin both stalks on, and is not felt or apprehended.

About ten days ago I wanted a housemaid and one presented herself very well recommended; I said, 'But young woman, why do you leave your present place?' She said she could not support the hours she kept, that her lady never went to bed till three or four in the morning. 'Bless me child,' said I, 'why you tell me you live with a bishop's wife, I never heard that Mrs North gamed or raked so late.' 'No, Sir,' said she, 'but she is three hours undressing.' Upon my word, the edifice that takes three hours to demolish, must at least be double the time in fabricating! would not you for once sit up till morning to see the destruction of the pyramid and distribution of the materials? Do not mention this, for I did not take the girl and she still assists at the daily and nightly revolutions of Babel.

On Tuesday I supped after the opera at Mrs Meynel's with a set of the most fashionable company, which take notice I very seldom do now, as I certainly am not of the age to mix often with young people. Lady Melbourne was standing before the fire, and adjusting her feathers in the glass, says she, 'Lord! they say the stocks will blow up: that will be very comical.'

These would be features for comedy, if they would not be thought caricatures, but today I am possessed of a genuine paper that I believe I shall leave to the Museum,[1] and which though its object will I suppose tomorrow become record, cannot be believed authentic an hundred years hence. It would in such a national satire as *Gulliver* be deemed too exaggerated; in short Lord Foley and his brother have petitioned the House of Lords to set aside their father's will, as it seems he intended to have raised an hundred thousand pounds to pay their debts, but died before he could

1. The British Museum, of which HW was an original trustee.

execute his intention. All the ladies, Melbournes, and all the bishops' wives that kill their servants by vigils are going about the town lamenting these poor orphans, and soliciting the peers to redress their grievances; but no words, no ridicule can attain to the ridiculous pathetic of the printed case itself, which now lies before me, and of which the four first lines are these—upon my honour they are exactly these:

'The present Lord Foley and his brother Mr Edward Foley having contracted large bond debts to the amount of about ———£ and encumbered themselves by granting annuities for their lives to the amount of about seventeen thousand four hundred and fifty pounds a *year,* explained their situation to their father the late Lord ———'

Poor unfortunate children; before thirty, the eldest had spent an estate (to the possession of which he was not arrived) of twenty thousand a year—at least, forfeited his father's affections, who left him but six thousand a year and a palace; and the youngest brother had been dipped in the same extravagance with him, and the legislature is desired to set aside so just a punishment, and if it does will deserve that every lad in England should waste his father's estate before his face,—tell it not in Gath, where all the shekels that ever were in the country would give no idea of the debt, though Jews are the creditors. Burn your sermon instead of printing it; do you think you can preach up to the enormities of the times? Hyperbole is baffled, and if the fine ladies of Jerusalem were so gallant that the prophets were obliged to pass all bounds of decency in censuring Duchess Aholah and Countess Aholibah, where would they have found figures even in Eastern rhetoric to paint the enormity of two sons *explaining to their father* that they paid seventeen thousand pounds a year to usurers for money they had borrowed to pay gaming debts; and what tropes, what metaphors drawn from asses would describe a sanhedrim that suffered such a petition to be laid before it?

These have been my collections in a single fortnight in the flagrancy of a civil war. History shall not revert to Athens for decrees against diverting the revenues of the theatre to the service of the state. London shall be the storehouse hereafter, whence declamations shall be drawn on the infatuation of falling empires; nay, so potent is the intoxication that in two companies this evening I have been thought singular for seeing *this petition* in the light I do; at York perhaps I may not be held so antediluvian in my opinions. With such obsolete prejudices I certainly am not very proper at modern suppers, yet with such *entremets* one would not wholly miss them. Nations at the acme of their splendour, or at the eve of their destruction, are worth observing. When they grovel in obscurity afterwards, they furnish neither events nor reflections; strangers visit the vestiges of the Acropolis, or may come to dig for capitals among the ruins of St Paul's; but nobody studies the manners of the pedlars and banditti, that dwell in mud huts within the precincts of a demolished temple. Curio and Clodius are memorable as they paved the way to the throne of Cæsar, but equal scoundrels are not entitled to infamy after a constitution is overturned; what we shall retain, I do not conjecture. The constitution might recover, the nation cannot: but though its enemies have miscarried in their attacks on the former, is there sense or virtue enough left to restore it, though the assailants have betrayed such wretched despicable incapacity? unless sudden inspiration should seize the whole island and make it with one voice invite Dr Franklin to come over and new-model the government, it will crumble away in the hands that still hold it; they feel, they own their insufficiency. Everybody is sensible of it, and everybody seems to think like Lady Melbourne, that if we are blown up it will be very comical.

To Lady Ossory, 11 August 1778

Strawberry Hill, Aug. 11, 1778.

I had neither room nor time, Madam, to tell you in my last how much I am ashamed to hear the kind things you are so good as to say to me. Very moderate friendship and good-nature would incline one to try to amuse such reasonable grief as yours, especially if letters could effect it, and letters from one that is so accustomed to write them, that they cost but the mere half hour. The remnant of an useless life is dedicated to my friends; I have no other employment; and the long and invariable favour your Ladyship has shown me, entitles you to every suit and service I can perform. You cannot lessen yourself in my eyes by disparaging yourself—nay, though I dislike it, it exalts you; it adds to my esteem. Vanity is to me the most ridiculous of all human faults. Humility, if not a virtue, is a love of virtue, and a respect for truth. The Pharisee and the Magdalen is the most beautiful story in the New Testament. Your last has realized what Rousseau's presumption thought nobody but himself could dare to achieve. I have got his preface to his memoirs: it is the superlative of arrogant eloquence; it would be the sublime of madness, were the madness real. As it is not, it is the affectation of singularity pushed to distraction. Not content to be unlike all mankind, he hopes at the Day of Judgment to be sent to Bedlam—it is even shocking! He aims at extorting a confession—it is not right to say how far his vanity goes—that he was the most extraordinary mortal ever created. To glory in confessing our crimes, and to brave mankind to imitate him, has more of Diogenes, than of the penitent Magdalen. I will send you this frantic piece of meditated extravagance, but beg you not to give a copy. It will get about, but I should not like to be the disperser.

I told you, Madam, that I had some history of myself for you; consequently very insignificant to anybody; but it will amuse you for a moment. In the first place I have been printing for Lady Craven a translation of her *Somnambule*, and that you shall have too. It is not ill done; but if it were, she is so pretty and good-humoured, that I am pleased to please her.

The next chapter is not so agreeable to me. Contrary to my determination, I have been writing again for the public. I have a horror for the stage of authors, which they call their *senilia*, and which therefore they ought not to write, for what can age produce that is worth showing? My present case is not of choice, but necessity. Somebody has published the poems of Chatterton the Bristol boy, and in the preface intimates that I was the cause of his despair and poisoning himself, and a little more openly is of opinion that I ought to be stoned. This most groundless accusation has driven me to write the whole story—and yet now I have done it in a pamphlet of near thirty pages of larger paper than this, I think I shall not bring myself to publish it.[1] My story is as clear as daylight, I am as innocent as of the death of Julius Cæsar, I never saw the lad with my eyes, and he was the victim of his own extravagance two years after all correspondence had ceased between him and me—and yet I hate to be the talk of the town, and am more inclined to bear this aspersion, than to come again upon the stage. I intend to consult every friend I have before I resolve, and of course, Lord Ossory and your Ladyship. It is impossible to have a moment's doubt on the case. The whole foundation of the accusation is reduced to this—If I had been imposed upon, my countenance might have saved the poor lad from poisoning himself for want, which he brought on himself by his excesses. Those few words are a full acquittal, and would indeed be sufficient—but the story in itself is so marvellous, that I could not help going into the whole account of such a prodigy as Chatterton was. You will pity him, as I do; it was a deep tragedy, but interests one chiefly from his extreme youth, for it was his youth that made his talents and achievements so miraculous. I doubt, neither his genius nor his heart would have interested one, had he lived twenty years more. You will be amazed at what he was capable of before eighteen, the period of his existence—yet I had rather anybody else were employed to tell the story.

As I have taken such an aversion to the character of author, I have fallen into a taste that I never had in my life, that of music. The swan, you know, Madam, is drawing towards its end, when it thinks of warbling, but as I have not begun to sing myself, I trust it is but distantly symptomatic. In short, I have only lived with musicians lately and liked them. Mr Jerningham is here at Twickenham, and sings in charming taste to his harp. My niece Miss Churchill has been here with her harp, and plays ten times

1. HW printed it at the Strawberry Hill Press in 1779.

better and sings worse—but I am quite enchanted with Mr Gammon, the Duke of Grafton's brother-in-law. It is the most melodious voice I ever heard; like Mr Meynell's, but more perfect. As I pass a great deal of time at Hampton Court, in a way very much like the remnant of the Court of St Germain's (—and I assure you, where there are some that I believe were of that Court), I was strolling in the gardens in the evening with my nieces, who joined Lady Schaub and Lady Fitzroy, and the former asked Mr Gammon to sing. His taste is equal to his voice, and his deep notes, the part I prefer, are calculated for the solemnity of Purcel's music, and for what I love particularly, his mad songs and the songs of sailors. It was moonlight and late, and very hot, and the lofty façade of the palace, and the trimmed yews and canal, made me fancy myself of a party in Grammont's time—so you don't wonder that by the help of imagination I never passed an evening more deliciously. When by the aid of some historic vision and local circumstance I can romance myself into pleasure, I know nothing transports me so much. Pray, steal from your soldiery, and try this secret at Bevis Mount and Nettley Abbey. There are Lord and Lady Peterborough and Pope to people the former scene, and who you please at Nettley—I sometimes dream, that one day or other somebody will stroll about poor Strawberry and talk of Lady Ossory—but alas! I am no poet, and my castle is of paper, and my castle and my attachment and I, shall soon vanish and be forgotten together!

To Lady Ossory, 27 September 1778

Strawberry Hill, Sept. 27, 1778.

On my return from Nuneham I find your Ladyship's too partial letter, in which you repeat the prejudices that I perceive you have instilled into Lord Ossory. But even if they were well founded, I should beg you never would let me know them. I have long been aware, Madam, that you keep my letters; to continue to write them under that impression is a tacit conviction of vanity. I have no excuse, but that having vowed myself your gazetteer, I was too far dipped to retreat; and might plead that I trusted to the numerosity of my letters for their overwhelming themselves; and as they are stuffed with private history and allusions, I am sure great part of them must be unintelligible to most readers. But I will speak very honestly, and give your Ladyship a substantial reason for never commending me. I do try to be both as humble and as natural as I can. I cannot be the first, if *you* flatter me; and it is impossible to be quite easy and simple, while one thinks one's letters will be read more deliberately than they are written. Nay, one contracts a visionary dignity, and grows so proud and conceited of the imaginary rank of worship one expects to hold in the republic of *epistles,* that, for fear of forfeiting it, one suppresses a thousand trifles and nonsenses that make the delights of correspondence. I trust I have not been very guilty in that respect—and yet I am naturally so foolish and careless, that I am persuaded my letters would have entertained you better, if you had never commended them. Can I say everything, that comes into my head, to Lady Ossory, if Posterity stands behind my chair and peeps over my shoulder? Depend upon it, I shall be very affected, if you make all Futurity your confidants—However, Madam, I think by this time your Ladyship must be possessed of such a stock of my invaluable MSS, that the devil will be in any printer that has courage to undertake them; and as the English language will be obsolete before he can get to the year 1778, I shall write with less apprehension for the future, for whatever wants a commentary is sure of being admired.

Thus much for me and my letters. If you commend me any more, Madam, it will be tautology. Let me go on in my own way, and do not make me screw myself into a writer of fine letters. Men are but too apt to be above trifles; and I think I shall be a prodigy, if I resist all your spoiling.

I have passed four most agreeable days at Nuneham. Mr Mason, Miss Fauquier, and Sir Joshua Reynolds with his two nieces were there, besides accidents. I visited my passion, Oxford, one morning. Mr Wyat has built a handsome gateway to Christ

Church, taken, I think, from Claudius's arch; and is building an observatory, of which I have some doubts. As I had never seen General Guise's collection, I did expect something, but so execrable an assemblage my eyes never beheld. There are three or four vast chambers covered from head to foot. Not six I believe ever were originals—at present the whole collection, whether Raphael's, Rubens's, or Carlo Maratt's, are of the selfsame colours, Bonus's son having been retained at 15*s.* a day to new-paint the whole legacy. I behaved sadly in the Hall, where there is so exact a resemblance of Welbore Ellis, that it gave me a fit of laughter, that scandalized all the Society—he is in the attitude of saying, 'Oui, Sire.'

You have spelt *Matson* rightly, Madam, though you would not, if you had remembered Dick Edgcumbe's *MadSon,* and *Damn'd Son.* I doubt George deserves to inherit the former manor, as I am sure he did not the latter. Madame du Deffand gives me just the same accounts of his letters that your Ladyship does. However, I shall rejoice to see him again.

I ought not to have answered your letter so paragraphically, Madam, but to have commenced with your honours at the least of all little courts. I am glad of them, and of your compaign, as I flatter myself they will together have dispelled your recluseness. It is time to inure yourself to a world where your daughters will want you. The Duchess of Cumberland I should think is a sensible woman. I am sure she has given a sample by seeking your Ladyship.

In military lore I am totally unread. Every profession has its own idiom. Common sense, with the aid of political conjecture, would make me conclude that *the Colonel* was *not* excepted—but perhaps the order was meant to be oracular, that our Lord might be blamed in whichever sense he should interpret it. Were I in his place I would do whichever I thought became my duty and me best, and not trouble myself about comments.

Your Ladyship's account of Lady Holland is so dreadful, that, as on our political situation, I know not what I wish—nor would I remind you of it. This will arrive when you are in the midst of Io

Pæans and loyal effusions, and all those endearments that must pass between a great Prince and his people, when both are so worthy of each other! Far be it from me to intrude; my ltttle epistle cannot expect an audience before next morning, when the fumes of loyalty are a little evaporated. I have been so long out of hearing even of the echo of politics, that I do not know whether the Court is in weepers for the capture of Mr Stuart, or not. I returned but to dinner, and shall not sally into my neighbourhood till tomorrow, as I have letters and newspapers of a whole week to read and answer; so I have yet seen no soul but Mr Raftor, who told me an excellent story of his old sister Mrs Mestivyer. She is both a great politician and natural philosopher. Mrs Clive happened to say she never saw the Thames so low—'And don't you know why it is so?' said Mrs M.—'It is occasioned by the vast quantities of beer that have been brewed for the camps.'

I forgot to mention what taste has penetrated to Oxford. At St John's College they have demolished a comely old square garden of about an acre, and bestowed upon it three yards of serpentine shrubs, five loose trees that are hopping about between four walls; and I suppose will have an irregular lake of a hogshead of water—when the brewing season is over!

Your Ladyship's most etc.,

H. W.

To the Rev. William Mason, 11 October 1778

Strawberry Hill, Oct. 11, 1778.

A thousand thanks for the trouble you have given yourself, and the information you have sent me; it fully satisfies me, at least till my next visit to Nuneham. I own there is an idea in the play you describe, which had it come into my hand, I should certainly have adopted:—the mother's intention of meeting her own husband and not her son. However as you have, by a *coup de baguette,* obviated the shocking part, I trouble myself no farther. I never had any difficulty of adopting your corrections, but because my original view was to paint the height of repentance for real guilt; whereas any palliative admits a degree of weakness in the Countess, and makes her rather superstitious or delicate, than penitent upon reason; but however as I am tired of the subject I will not tire you upon it. If ever the play is acted, it must be with your improvements, which I will print with it. So I will whether it is acted or not:[1] for such marks of your genius should not be lost, though you want not other proofs; and it will please me to have furnished you with the materials. I grow tired to death of my own things, and hate to talk of them.

Lady Laura, who carries this, will tell you how many accidents prevent my obeying Lord and Lady Harcourt, and accompanying her. I have lost near £700 by a clerk, and I am on Tuesday to sign a family compact with my nephew, by which, some time or other, I shall get the fortune my father left me, which I never expected, so the balance of events is in my favour, and then the deuce is in it if I am to be pitied.

Lady Laura will describe to you a most brilliant fête that I gave her and her sisters and cousins last Thursday. People may say what they will, but splendid as it was, I am not of opinion that this *festival of nieces* was absolutely the most charming show that ever was seen. I believe the entertainment given by the Queen of the Amazons to the King of Mauritania in the Castle of Ice, and the ball made for the Princess of Persia by the Duke of Sparta in the Saloon of Roses were both of them more delightful, especially as the contrast of the sable Africans with the shining whiteness of the Thracian heroines, and the opposition between the nudity of the Lacedemonian generals and the innumerable folds of linen in the drapery of the Persian ladies, must have been more singular than all the marvels in the Castle of Strawberry last Thursday. To be sure the illumination of the Gallery surpassed the Palace of the Sun; and when its fretted ceiling, which you know is richer than the roof of paradise, opened for the descent of Mrs Clive in the full

1. HW did not adopt Mason's "improvements" of *The Mysterious Mother.*

moon, nothing could be more striking. The circular drawing-room was worthy of the presence of Queen Bess, as many of the old ladies, who remember her, affirmed, and the high altar in the Tribune was fitter for a Protestant king's hearing mass than the chapel at Lord Petre's. The tapestry bed in the great chamber looked gorgeous (though it had not an escutcheon of pretence like the Duchess of Chandos's while her father and brother are living) and was ready strewed with roses for a hymeneal; but alas! there was the misfortune of the solemnity! Though my nieces looked as well as the houris, notwithstanding I was disappointed of the house of North to set them off, and though I had sent out one hundred and thirty cards, in this region there are no swains who are under my own almost climacteric. I had three Jews of Abraham's standing, and seven Sarahs who still talk of the second temple. The rest of the company were dowagers and maidens, with silver beards down to their girdles; Henry and Frances, whose doves have long done laying; the curate of the parish; Briscoe, the secondhand silversmith; Mr Raftor; and Lady Greenwich in a riding-dress, for she came on her own broom. You may perhaps think that some of the company were not quite of dignity adequate to such a high festival, but they were just the persons made the most happy by being invited; and as the haughtiest peers stoop to be civil to shopkeepers before an election, I did not see why I should not do, out of good nature, what the proudest so often do out of interest. I do not mention two ancient Generals, because they have not been beaten out of America into red ribbands, nor a Judge [Perryn], who had solicited me to invite his daughters, and brought them on my sending a very civil card, and yet did not so much as write an answer or thank me—but I really believe it was from mere stupidity. If I could grudge your staying at Nuneham, I should regret your not being here in such noble weather. Come however as soon as you can and stay as long.

By the rise of the stocks, and the wonderful hide-and-seek of the fleets I suspect some treaty is brewing; it cannot be so scandalous but it will go down: and therefore it cannot be worse than the nation deserves. If anything prevents it, it will be the declaration of the Spanish ambassador, that King Carlos will never acknowledge the independence of America till King George does, which I suppose the latter will not do, if even the King of Monomatapa or the King of Mechlemberg will encourage him to go on—besides it is a heavenly sight to see soldiers, and not see an enemy! and a more heavenly sight to see a puppet-show, and to lock up one's son, who is of an age to enjoy one!—and yet what command of one's passions to put off a review for a christening!—what pity gazettes-extraordinary were not in fashion, when two shillings were issued out of the exchequer to Jack of Reading, for getting on the table and making the King sport. This was in the reign of Edward II, and is only recorded in a *computus* still extant. Adieu.

To the Rev. William Cole, 13 March 1780

Strawberry Hill, March 13, 1780.

You compliment me, my good friend, on a sagacity that is surely very common. How frequently do we see portraits that have catched the features, and missed the countenance or character, which is far more difficult to hit. Nor is it unfrequent to hear that remark made.

I have confessed to you that I am fond of local histories. It is the general execution of them that I condemn, and that I call *the worst kind of reading*. I cannot comprehend but they might be performed with taste. I did mention this winter the new edition of Atkyns's *Gloucestershire,* as having additional descriptions of situations, that I thought had merit. I have just got another, *A View of Northumberland* in two volumes quarto, with cuts; but I do not devour it fast, for the author's predilection is to Roman antiquities, which, such as are found in this island, are very indifferent, and inspire me with little curiosity. A barbarous country, so remote from the seat of empire, and occupied by a few legions, that very rarely decided any great events, is not very interesting, though one's own country—nor do I care a straw for the stone that preserves the name of a standard-bearer of a cohort, or of a colonel's daughter. Then I have no patience to read the tiresome disputes of antiquaries to settle forgotten names of vanished towns, and to prove that such a village was called something else in Antoninus's *Itinerary.* I do not say that the Gothic antiquities that I like are of more importance; but at least they exist. The site of a Roman camp, of which nothing remains but a bank, gives me not the smallest pleasure. One knows they had square camps—has one a clearer idea from the spot, which is barely distinguishable? How often does it happen that the lumps of earth are so imperfect, that it is never clear, whether they are Roman, Druidic, Danish or Saxon fragments—the moment it is uncertain, it is plain they furnish no specific idea of art or history, and then I neither desire to see or read of them.

I have been diverted too to another work, in which I am personally a little concerned. Yesterday was published an octavo pretending to contain the correspondence of Hackman and Miss Wray, that he murdered. I doubt whether the letters are genuine, and yet if fictitious, they are executed well, and enter into his character—hers appear less natural; and yet the editors were certainly more likely to be in possession of hers than of his. It is not probable that Lord Sandwich should have sent what he found in her apartment, to the press. No account is pretended to be given of how they came to light.

You will wonder how *I* should be concerned in this correspondence, who never saw either of the lovers in my days. In fact, my being dragged in, is a reason for my doubting the authenticity; nor can I believe that the long letter in which I am frequently mentioned, could be written by the wretched lunatic. It pretends that Miss Wray desired him to give her a particular account of Chatterton. He does give a most ample one—but is there a glimpse of probability that a being so frantic should have gone to Bristol and sifted Chatterton's sister and others with as much cool curiosity as Mr Lort could do? and at such a moment? Besides he murdered Miss Wray, I think, in March; my printed defence was not at all dispersed before the preceding January or February, nor do I conceive that Hackman could ever see it. There are notes indeed by the editor, who has certainly seen it—but I rather imagine that the editor, whoever he is, composed the whole volume. I am acquitted of being accessory to the lad's death, which is gracious; but much blamed for speaking of his bad character, and for being too hard on his forgeries, though I took so much pains to specify the innocence of them; and for his character, I only quoted the very words of his own editor and panegyrist. I did not repeat what Dr Goldsmith told me at the Royal Academy, where I first heard of his death, that he went by the appellation of *the young villain*—but it is not new to me, as you know, to be blamed by two opposite parties. The editor has in one place confounded me and my uncle, who, he says, as is true, checked Lord Chatham for being too forward a young man in 1740. In that year I was not even come into Parliament; and must have been absurd indeed if I had taunted Lord Chatham with youth, who was at least six or seven years younger than he was—and how could he reply by reproaching me with old age, who was then not twenty-three? I shall make no answer to these absurdities, nor to any part of the work. Blunder I see people will, and talk of what they do not understand; and what care I? There is another trifling mistake of still less consequence. The editor supposes that it was Macpherson who communicated Ossian to me. It was Sir David Dalrymple who sent me the first specimens. Macpherson did once come to me—but my credulity was then a little shaken.

Lady Ailesbury has promised me guinea eggs for you, but they have not yet begun to lay.

I am well acquainted with Lady Craven's little tale dedicated to me. It is careless and incorrect, but there are very pretty things in it.

I will stop, for I fear I have written to you too much lately. One you did not mention; I think it was of the 28th of last month.

Yours entirely,

H. Walpole

To the Rev. William Mason, 19 May 1780

. . . You know, I suppose, that the Royal Academy at Somerset House is opened. It is quite a Roman palace, and finished in perfect taste as well as boundless expense. It would have been a glorious apparition at the conclusion of the great war; now it is an insult on our poverty and degradation. There is a sign-post by West of his Majesty holding the memorial of his late campaign, lest we should forget that he was at Coxheath when the French fleet was in Plymouth Sound. By what lethargy of loyalty it happened I do not know, but *there* is also a picture of Mrs Wright modelling the head of Charles I, and their Majesties contemplating it. Gainsborough has five landscapes there, of which one especially is worthy of any collection, and of any painter that ever existed.

There is come out a life of Garrick, in two volumes, by Davies the bookseller, formerly a player. It is written naturally, simply, without pretensions, nay and without partiality (though under the auspices of Dr Johnson) unless, as it seems, the prompter reserved all the flattery to himself, and according to an epigram on the late Queen and the Hermitage:

> ——whispered let the incense all be mine.

In consequence the author calls the pedant the greatest man of the age, and compares his trumpery tragedy of *Irene* to *Cato*. However the work is entertaining and deserves immortality for preserving that *sublime* saying of Quin (which, by the way, he profanes by calling it a *bon mot*) who disputing on the execution of Charles I, and being asked by his antagonist by what law he was put to death, replied, *by all the laws he had left them.* I wish you would translate it into Greek, and write it in your Longinus; it has ten times more grandeur, force and meaning than anything he cites.

Apropos to the theatre, I have *read* the *School for Scandal*: it is rapid and lively, but is far from containing the wit I expected from seeing it acted.

May I leap from the stage to the bench? Sir Thomas Rumbold,

one of our Indian mushrooms, asked his father-in-law, the Bishop of Carlisle, to answer for a child that he had left in a parsley-bed of diamonds at Bengal. The good man consented; a man-child was born. The other godfather was the Nabob of Arcot,—and the new Christian's name is—Mahomet! What pity that Dr Law was the godfather and not [the] Bishop of Hagedorn or your metropolitan!

Mr Jones, the orientalist, is candidate for Oxford. On Tuesday was sennight Mrs Vesey presented him to me. The next day he sent me an absurd and pedantic letter, desiring I would make interest for him. I answered it directly, and told him I had no more connection with Oxford than with the antipodes, nor desired to have. I doubt I went a little farther, and laughed at Dr Blackstone, whom he quoted as an advocate for the rights of learning, and at some other passages in his letter. However, before I sent it, I inquired a little more about Mr Jones, and on finding it was a circular letter sent to several, I did not think it necessary to answer it at all; and now I am glad I did not, for the man it seems is a staunch Whig, but very wrongheaded. He was tutor to Lord Althorpe, and quarrelled with Lord Spencer, who he insisted should not interfere at all in the education of his own son.

There are just appeared three new *Epistles on History*, addressed to Mr Gibbon by Mr Hayley. They are good poems, I believe, weight and measure, but except some handsome new similes, have little poetry and less spirit. In short, they are written by Judgment, who has set up for herself, forgetting that her business is to correct verses, and not to write them. Mr Gibbon I doubt will not be quite pleased, for as the *Epistles* have certainly cost the author some pains, they were probably commenced before the historian's conversion to the Court, and are a little too fond of liberty to charm the ear of a convert, which too the author wants to make him in another sense, and that will not please, unless he has swallowed his Majesty's professions as well as his pay.

In another new publication, called *Antiquities and Scenery in the North of Scotland*, I have found two remarkable passages, which intimate doubts of the antiquity of Ossian, though the author is a minister in Bamff. The first, in p. 77, says, *'If only like a morning dream the visions of Ossian came in later days.'* The other humbly begs to know, p. 81, how Fingal became possessed of burnished armour, when the times knew not the use of steel and iron.

My quondam friend, George Montagu, has left your friend Frederic five hundred pounds a year. I am very glad of it.

I have heard what I should not repeat, as I do not know that it is true, but today I see it in the papers. In short they say that the unfortunate Knight of the Polar Star has disappeared. The reason given is that a demand of £300,000 more for finishing the sumptuous edifice where Somerset House stood, having been made to the House of Commons, Mr Brett, a member, begged to see an account of what had been already expended, and the next day all the telescopes in town could not descry the Swedish planet. I am sorry, considering that the constellation of the Adelphi was not *rayée* from the celestial globe after their bubble lottery. I suppose Ossian will keep his ground, and would, if Macpherson should please to maintain that he lived before Tubal.

Berkeley Square, May 19, 1780.

Most part of this letter has been written many days, I waited for a proper conveyance. Now it comes to you in what Wedgwood calls a *Druid's mug:* you must drink out of it *Ruin seize thee ruthless King.*[1] Mr Stonhewer gave me the direction but I find it will not set out before Tuesday; however, I shall not be able to add to this volume, as I go to Strawberry tomorrow and must leave it for the wagon. Sir Charles Hardy is dead suddenly. Lord Bathurst I suppose, will have the command of the fleet, as the senior *old woman on the staff.*

I shall settle at Strawberry on Tuesday sevennight, so if you have a mind to hear from me you must write, for I shall know no more there than you in Yorkshire, and I cannot talk if nobody answers me; somebody knocks, which is a very good conclusion when one has no more to say, oh it is Mr Palgrave: well he tells

1. The opening line of Gray's "The Bard."

me that Sir William Chambers is not gone away, so I retract all, but that the Adams ought to be gone. Adieu.

To Lady Ossory, 3 June 1780

Berkeley Square, June 3, 1780.

I know that a governor or a gazetteer ought not to desert their posts, if a town is besieged, or a town is full of news—and therefore, Madam, I resume my office—I smile today—but I trembled last night[1]—For an hour or more I never felt more anxiety—I knew the bravest of my friends were barricaded into the House of Commons, and every avenue to it impossible. Till I heard the Horse and Foot Guards were gone to their rescue, I expected nothing but some dire misfortune—and the first thing I heard this morning was that part of the town had had a fortunate escape from being burnt after ten last night—you must not expect order, Madam; I must recollect circumstances as they occur—and the best idea I can give your Ladyship of the tumult, will be to relate it as I heard it.

I had come to town in the morning on a private occasion, and found it so much as I left it, that though I saw a few blue cockades here and there, I only took them for new recruits. Nobody came in; between seven and eight I saw a hack and another coach arrive at Lord Shelburne's, and thence concluded that Lord George Gordon's trumpet had brayed to no purpose. At eight I went to Gloucester House; the Duchess told me there had been a riot, and that Lord Mansfield's glasses had been broken, and a bishop's, but that most of the populace were dispersed. About nine his R[oyal] Highness and Colonel Heywood arrived—and then we heard a much more alarming account. The concourse had been incredible, and had by no means obeyed the injunctions of their apostle, or rather had interpreted the spirit instead of the letter. The Duke had reached the House with the utmost difficulty, and found it sunk from the temple of dignity to an asylum of lament-

1. When the Gordon Riots began.

able objects. There were the Lords Hilsborough, Stormont, Townshend, without their bags, and with their hair dishevelled about their ears, and Lord Willoughby without his periwig, and Lord Mansfield, whose glasses had been broken, quivering on the woolsack like an aspen. Lord Ashburnham had been torn out of his chariot, the Bishop of Lincoln ill-treated, the Duke of Northumberland had lost his watch in the holy hurly-burly, and Mr Mackinsy his snuff-box and spectacles. Alarm came that the mob had thrown down Lord Boston and were trampling him to death—which they almost did. They had diswigged Lord Bathurst on his answering them stoutly, and told him he was the Pope and an old woman—thus splitting Pope Joan into two. Lord Hilsborough, on being taxed with negligence, affirmed that the Cabinet had the day before empowered Lord North to take precautions, but two justices that were called, denied having received any orders. Col. Heywood, a very stout man and luckily a very cool one, told me he had thrice been collared, as he went by the Duke's order to inquire what was doing in the other House; but though he was not suffered to pass, he reasoned the mob into releasing him—yet, he said, he never saw so serious an appearance and such determined countenances. About eight the Lords adjourned, and were suffered to go home; though the rioters declared that if the other House did not repeal the bill, there would at night be terrible mischief. Mr Burke's name had been given out as the object of resentment. General Conway I knew would be intrepid and not give way—nor did he, but inspired the other House with his own resolution. Lord George Gordon was running backwards and forwards, and from the windows of the Speaker's Chamber denouncing all that spoke against him to the mob in the lobby. Mr Conway tasked him severely both in the House and aside, and Col. Murray told him he was a disgrace to his family. Still the members were besieged and locked up for four hours, nor could divide, as the lobby was crammed. Mr Conway and Lord Fred. Cavendish, with whom I supped afterwards, told me there was a moment, when they thought they must have opened the doors and fought their way out sword in hand. Lord North was very firm, and at last they got the Guards and cleared the pass.

Blue banners had been waved from tops of houses at Whitehall as signals to the people, while the coaches passed, whom they should applaud or abuse. Sir Geo. Saville's and Ch. Turner's coaches were demolished. Ellis, whom they took for a popish gentleman, they carried prisoner to the Guildhall in Westminster, and he escaped by a ladder out of a window. Lord Mahon harangued the people from the balcony of a coffee-house and begged them to retire—but at past ten a new scene opened. The mob forced the Sardinian minister's chapel in Lincoln's Inn Fields, and gutted it. He saved nothing but two chalices; lost the silver lamps, etc., and the benches being tossed into the street, were food for a bonfire, with the blazing brands of which they set fire to the inside of the chapel, nor, till the Guards arrived, would suffer the engines to play. My cousin T. Walpole fetched poor Madam Cordon, who was ill, and guarded her in his house till three in the morning, when all was quiet.

Old Haslang's chapel has undergone the same fate, all except the ordeal. They found stores of mass-books and run tea.

This is a slight and hasty sketch, Madam. On Tuesday the House of Commons is to consider the Popish laws—I forgot to tell you that the Bishops not daring to appear, the Winchester Bill, which had passed the Commons, was thrown out.

No saint was ever more diabolic than Lord Geo. Gordon. Eleven wretches are in prison for the outrage at Cordon's, and will be hanged instead of their arch-incendiary. One person seized is a Russian officer who had the impudence to claim acquaintance with the Sardinian minister and desire to be released. Cordon replied, 'Oui Monsieur, je vous connaissais, mais je ne vous connais plus.' I do not know whether he is an associate of Thalestris, who seems to have snuffed a revolution in the wind.

I hear there are hopes of some temperament in Ireland. Somebody, I forget who, has observed that the English government pretends not to *quarter* soldiers in Ireland, and therefore must be glad of a bill—It is time some of our wounds should close!—or I believe, I shall soon have too much employment, instead of wanting materials for letters.

To Lady Ossory, 27 September 1780

Strawberry Hill, Sept. 27, 1780.

I rejoice in your triumph, Madam, though I cannot partake of your fireworks. Not only had I ordered my books[1] to be advertised, but have a more melancholy cause that detains me. The letters that I have received today from Paris bid me be prepared to receive an account of my dear old friend's death. I knew she had been very ill, but till these two last posts, I had been flattered that she was recovering. Today her own secretary, and Mr T. Walpole pronounce that there are no hopes. I had sent James's powder,[2] and had begged my cousin if possible to obtain her trying it—but alas! I knew France too well, and physicians too, and *their* physicians still more, to have much hope of its being given—but it is too shocking to be told that the physician has laid aside all medicines, and yet would not suffer her to take it! When is it best to try it, but in despair? and when, if not at eighty-four? He said, it would vomit her, and kill her—is not he killing her himself by trying nothing! and by not trying the powder in that case? This is a horrible thought, though she could not be immortal; and the terror I have been under for some time of her becoming deaf, added to blindness, had made me more reconciled to her great age, and to the probability of losing her—She retains, that is, did retain her senses, did not suffer, knew her situation, and was perfectly tranquil, and spoke little—but by the whole description she appears to me to have been almost worn out—I tremble for the next letter—though it is just as if I had already received it—Another friend gone! I scarce have one left of above my own age. It is these memorandums, that at the same time reconcile one to one's own departure—what can one expect but to survive one's friends

1. *Anecdotes of Painting*, Vol. IV.
2. A quack medicine that HW regarded as a panacea.

if one lives long?—in this unhappy mood, Madam, I should be bad company. Can I care about elections? If an opponent's death could set Mr Burke to moralizing on the hustings at Bristol, how must the loss of so dear a friend affect me! The savage physician exasperates me—what transport should I have felt, if I could have saved her, though but for six months! Perhaps I could not—I will not be unjust; it is probable that I should not—but oh! not to let me try! It augments my abhorrence of physicians and professions. Long ago I said that the Devil's three names, Satan, Lucifer and Belzebub, were given to him in his three capacities of President of Priests, Lawyers and Physicians. I repeat it now with rancour: Belzebub and Bouvard are synonymous terms in my lexicon. Five years ago I loved the wretch, for he saved her, as I thought, in my presence—Did that give him a right over her life? Has not he cancelled my gratitude? Can one love and hate at once? I would if I could—yes, I do thank him for prolonging her life for five years—but oh! professions, professions! how *l'esprit du corps* absorbs all feelings!—and how prejudice becomes principle! Dear old woman! she is now, I fear, no more!—I can write no more, Madam, for I can write on no other subject, and have no right to torment you with my concern. You shall hear no more of it. Nature takes care that hopeless griefs should not be permanent; and I have seen so much affectation of lamentation where little was felt, and I know so well that I have often felt most where I have discovered least, that I will profane my affection to my lost friend with no ostentation—much less to those who never knew her. I live enough in solitude to indulge all my sensations, without troubling others.

PS. Since I wrote my letter, I have had another shock; General Conway has broken his arm! Lady Ailesbury assures me there is as little bad as there can be in such an accident, and that I shall hear again tomorrow—Still I shall go to him on Friday.

To Lady Ossory, 4 January 1781

Jan. 4, 1781.

I return the quipos,[1] Madam, because if I retained them till I understand them, I fear you would never have them again. I should as soon be able to hold a dialogue with a rainbow by the help of its grammar a prism, for I have not yet discovered which is the first or last verse of four lines that hang like ropes of onions. Yet it is not for want of study, or want of respect for the Peruvian manner of writing. I perceive it is a very soft language, and though at first I tangled the poem and spoiled the rhymes, yet I can conceive that a harlequin's jacket, artfully arranged by a princess of the blood of Mango Capac,[2] may contain a deep tragedy, and that a tawdry trimming may be a version of Solomon's Song. Nay, I can already say my alphabet of six colours, and know that each stands indiscriminately *but* for four letters, which gives the Peruvian a great advantage over the Hebrew tongue, in which the total want of vowels left every word at the mercy of the reader; and though our salvation depended upon it, we did not know precisely what any word signified, till the invention of points, that were not used till the language had been obsolete for some thousands of years. A little uncertainty, as where one has but one letter instead of four, may give rise to many beauties. Puns must be greatly assisted by that ambiguity, and the delicacies of the language may depend on an almost imperceptible variation in the shades; as the perfection of the Chinese consists in possessing but very few syllables, each of which admits ten thousand accents, and thence pronunciation is the most difficult part of their literature.

At first sight the resemblance of blue and green by candle-light seems to be an objection to the Peruvian; but any learned mercer might obviate that by opposing indigo to grass-green, and ultramarine to *verd de pomme.* The more expert one were at nuances, the more poetic one should be or the more eloquent. A vermilion *A*

1. Quipu, a device of the ancient Peruvians for recording events, etc., consisting of cords or threads of various colors, knotted in various ways.

2. Legendary founder of the Inca Empire.

must denote a weaker accent, or even passion than one of carmine and crimson, and a straw-colour *U* be much more tender than one approaching to orange.

I have heard of a French perfumer who wrote an essay on the harmony of essences. Why should not that idea be extended? The Peruvian quipos adapted a language to the eyes, rather than to the ears. Why should not there be one for the nose? The more the senses can be used indifferently for each other, the more our understandings would be enlarged. A rose, jessamine, a pink, a jonquil and a honeysuckle might signify the vowels; the consonants to be represented by other flowers. The Cape jessamine, which has two smells, was born a diphthong. How charming it would be to smell an ode from a nosegay, and to scent one's handkerchief with a favourite song! Indeed, many improvements might be made on the quipos themselves, especially as they might be worn as well as perused. A trimming set on a new lutestring would be equivalent to a second edition with corrections. I am only surprised that in a country like Peru, where gold and silver thread were so cheap, there was no *clinquant* introduced into their poetry. In short, Madam, I am so pleased with the idea of knotting verses, which is vastly preferable to anagrams and acrostics, that if I were to begin life again, I would use a shuttle instead of a pen, and write verses by the yard. As it is, I have not been idle; nay, like any heaven-born genius, I have begun to write before I can read; and though I have not yet learn[ed] to decipher, I can at least cypher like Atahualpa himself. As a proof of my proficience, pray, Madam, construe the following colours,

Brown, blue, white, yellow green yellow yellow white,
red brown brown blue white.

As I was writing this last line, I receive your Ladyship's interpretation of the verses. Whoever made them they are excellent, and it would have been cruel to have deprived me of them, till I could have unravelled them. Pray tell me who made them, for they are really good and sterling. I am sorry I expressed myself so awkwardly, that you thought I disapproved of the quipos. On the contrary you see how much they have amused me. In good truth I was glad of anything that would occupy me and turn my attention from all the horrors one hears or apprehends. I am sorry I have read the devastation of Barbadoes and Jamaica etc., etc., etc., etc.,—when one can do no good, can neither prevent nor redress, nor has any personal share by one's self or one's friends, is not it excusable to steep one's attention in anything?—I fear, Madam, you and Lord Ossory have a suffering friend! poor Mr James, I hear, is totally ruined—his whole property swept away! —There is another dreadful history less known—The expedition sent against the Spanish settlements is cut off by the climate, and not a single being is left alive. The Duchess of Bedford told me last night that the poor soldiers were so averse, that they were driven to the march by the point of the bayonet, and that besides the men, twenty-five officers have perished.

Lord Cornwallis and his tiny army are scarce in a more prosperous way. On this dismal canvas a fourth war is embroidered; and what I think, threatens still more, the French administration is changed, and likely to be composed of more active men, and much more hostile to England. Our ruin seems to me inevitable. Nay, I know those who smile in the Drawing-Room, that groan by their fireside—They own we have no more men to send to America, and think our credit almost as nearly exhausted. Can you wonder then, Madam, if I am glad to play with quipos—Oh no! nor can I be sorry to be on the verge—does one wish to live to weep over the ruins of Carthage?

To the Rev. William Mason, 5 February 1781

Monday noon, Feb. 5, 1781.

Perhaps you think, by my letters riding on the back of one another, that I am going to tell you of my Lord George Gordon; no, poor soul! he is at this minute in Westminster Hall, and I know nothing about him. Somehow or other I dare to say the constitution will be brought in guilty, for Lord Mansfield is the judge. But

I have otherguess things to say to you: I have got your Fresnoy; it is a new proof of what I have long thought, that there is nothing you cannot do if you please. This is the best translation I ever saw; there have been disputes between literal and paraphrastic translations, and no wonder, for a third sort, the true, was not known; yours preserves the sense and substance of every sentence, but you make a new arrangement, and state and express the author's thought better than he could; Horace would have excused you if you had been simply familiar in a didactic poem, but you would not be so excused, nor allow yourself negligence in your poetry. You have exchanged the poverty of Fresnoy's Latin for Pope's rich English, and every epithet contributes its quota to every precept and develops it. This is in the style of none of your other works, and though more difficult, as masterly as any: in short, I have examined it with admiration, and only wonder how, with such powers and knowledge of the subject, you could confine yourself to the *matter* of the original. The shackles of translation have neither cramped your style nor rendered it obscure; you have enriched your author without deviating, and improved his matter without adding to it, which is an achievement indeed:—I do not flatter you—nay, you know I am frank enough upon most occasions, and were I porter of the Temple of Fame, I would not open the door to one of your babes, if it was not like you.

I think I shall soon compass a transcript at least of Gray's life by Demogorgon[1] for you. I saw him last night at Lady Lucan's, who had assembled a *bluestocking* meeting in imitation of Mrs Vesey's Babels. It was so blue, it was quite mazarine-blue. Mrs Montague kept aloof from Johnson, like the West from the East. There were Soame Jenyns, Persian Jones, Mr Sherlocke, the new Court wit Mr Courtney, besides the out-pensioners of Parnassus; Mr Wraxhall was not, I wonder why, and so will he, for he is popping into every spot where he can make himself talked of, by talking of himself; but I hear he will come to an untimely beginning in the House of Commons.

1. Dr. Johnson.

I shall return your Fresnoy as soon as I have gone through it once more, that Sir Joshua may go to work. I have proposed a subject to him that he seems to like: *little children brought to Christ.* He will not make them all brothers, like Albano's Cupids.

Pray look into the [last] *Critical Review* but one, there you will find that David Hume in a saucy blockheadly note calls Locke, Algernon Sidney, and Bishop Hoadly, *despicable writers.* I believe that ere long the Scotch will call the English *lousy!* and that Goody Hunter will broach the assertion in an anatomic lecture. Not content with debasing and disgracing us as a nation by losing America, destroying our Empire, and making us the scorn and prey of Europe, the Scotch would annihilate our patriots, martyrs, heroes and geniuses. Algernon Sidney, Lord Russel, King William, the Duke of Marlborough, Locke, are to be traduced and levelled, and with the aid of their fellow-labourer Johnson, who spits at them while he tugs at the same oar, Milton, Addison, Prior, and Gray are to make way for the dull forgeries of Ossian, and such wights as Davy and Johnny Hume, Lord Kaims, Lord Monboddo, and Adam Smith!—Oh! if you have a drop of English ink in your veins, rouse and revenge your country! Do not let us be run down and brazened out of all our virtue, genius, sense, and taste, by Laplanders and Bœotians, who never produced one original writer in verse or prose.

Tuesday morning.

My servants tell me, for I have yet seen nobody else today, that Lord George was acquitted at five this morning—a wise manœuvre truly has been made; they punish him severely for eight months, and cannot convict him! now he will be a confessor. I must finish for I have just heard that Lady Orford is dead, and must write to my family and order mourning etc. I doubt this letter is no retaining fee to Mr Palgrave.

To Lady Ossory, 7 October 1781

Strawberry Hill, Oct. 7, 1781.

I beg your Ladyship's pardon for not returning the *History of Fotheringay*, which I now enclose.

The new Veres have been returned to England these six weeks, and I visited them at their palace (as it really was of Henry VIII) at Hanworth not long after their arrival. All their near kin have done so too, and *tout s'est passé comme si de rien n'était.* Their fellow-traveller is left behind. We live in such an awkward unfashionable nook here, that we have not yet heard Lord Vere's will, nor know whether Lord Richard Cavendish is dead or alive. *I* am so much awkwarder still; and treasure up scandal so little, that, though I heard the Brightehelmstone story, I have quite forgotten who the principal personage was—so you will not fear my repeating it. I do not design to know a circumstance about Admiral Rodney and Admiral Ferguson. We are to appearance at war with half Europe and a quarter of America, and yet our warfare is only fending and proving, and is fitter for the Quarter Sessions than for history. It costs us seventeen or eighteen millions a year to inquire whether our generals and admirals are rogues or fools, and since most of them are only one or t'other, I would not give half a crown to know which. The nation is such an oaf as to amuse itself with these foolish discussions, and does not perceive that six years and above forty millions, and half our territories have been thrown away in such idle pastime. How the grim heroes of Edward III and Henry V would stare at hearing that this is our way of making war on France!

The night I had the honour of writing to your Ladyship last, I was robbed—and as if I was a sovereign or a nation, have had a discussion ever since whether it was not a *neighbour* who robbed me—and should it come to the ears of the newspapers, it might produce as ingenious a controversy amongst our anonymous wits, as any of the noble topics I have been mentioning. *Voici le fait.* Lady Browne and I were as usual going to the Duchess of Montrose at seven o'clock. The evening was very dark. In the close lane under her park pale, and within twenty yards of the gate, a black figure on horseback pushed by between the chaise and the hedge on my side. I suspected it was a highwayman, and so I found did Lady Browne, for she was speaking and stopped. To divert her fears, I was just going to say, 'Is not that the apothecary going to the Duchess?' when I heard a voice cry, 'Stop!' and the figure came back to the chaise. I had the presence of mind, before I let down the glass, to take out my watch and stuff it within my waistcoat under my arm. He said, 'Your purses and watches!' I replied, 'I have no watch.' 'Then your purse!' I gave it to him; it had nine guineas. It was so dark, that I could not see his hand, but felt him take it. He then asked for Lady Browne's purse, and said, 'Don't be frightened, I will not hurt you.' I said, 'No, you won't frighten the lady?'—He replied, 'No, I give you my word I will do you no hurt.' Lady Browne gave him her purse, and was going to add her watch, but he said, 'I am much obliged to you, I wish you good night,' pulled off his hat and rode away. 'Well,' said I, 'Lady Browne, you will not be afraid of being robbed another time, for you see there is nothing in it.' 'Oh! but I am,' said she, 'and now I am in terrors lest he should return, for I have given him a purse with only bad money that I carry on purpose.' 'He certainly will not open it directly,' said I, 'and at worst he can only wait for us at our return; but I will send my servant back for a horse and a blunderbuss,' which I did. The next distress was not to terrify the Duchess, who is so paralytic and nervous. I therefore made Lady Browne go into the parlour and desired one of the Duchess's servants to get her a glass of water while I went into the drawing-room to break it to the Duchess. 'Well,' said I laughing to her and the rest of the company, 'you won't get much from us tonight—' 'Why,' said one of them, 'have you been robbed?' 'Yes, a little,' said I. The Duchess trembled—but it went off. Her groom of the chambers said not a word, but slipped out, and Lady Margaret and Miss Howe having servants there on horseback, he gave them pistols and dispatched them different ways. This was exceedingly clever, for he knew the Duchess would not have suffered it, as lately he had detected a man who had robbed her garden, and she would not allow him to take up the fellow. These servants spread the story, and when my footman arrived on foot, he was stopped in the street by the hostler of the George who told him the highwayman's horse was then in the stable—but this part I must reserve for the second volume, for I have made this no-story so long and so tedious, that your Ladyship will not be able to read it in a breath; and the second part is so much longer, and so much less, contains so many examinations of witnesses, so many contradictions in the depositions, which I have taken myself, and I must confess, with such abilities and shrewdness that I have found out nothing at all, that I think to defer the prosecution of my narrative, till all the other inquisitions on the anvil are liquidated, lest your Ladyship's head, strong as it is, should be confounded, and you should imagine that Rodney or Ferguson was the person who robbed us in Twickenham Lane. I would not have detailed the story at all, if you were not in a forest, where it will serve to put you to sleep, as well as a newspaper full of lies; and I am sure there is as much dignity in it, as in the combined fleet and ours popping in and out alternately like a man and woman in a weather-house.

To the Rev. William Mason, 25 June 1782

Berkeley Square, June 25, 1782.

I find there is a correspondence commenced between you and Mr Hayley by the Parnassus post. I did not know you were acquainted; I suppose you met at Calliope's: if you love incense, he has fumigated you like a flitch of bacon; however, I hope in the Lord Phœbus that you will not take his advice any more than Pope did that of such another sing-song warbler Lord Lyttelton; nor be persuaded to write an epic poem, that most senseless of all the species of poetic composition and which pedants call the *chef-d'œuvre* of the human mind; well, you may frown, as in duty bound, yet I shall say what I list. Epic poetry is the art of being as long as possible in telling an uninteresting story: and an epic poem is a mixture of history without truth and of romance without imagination. We are well off when from that *mésalliance* there spring some bastards called episodes, that are lucky enough to resemble their romantic mother, more than their solemn father. So far from epic poetry being at the head of composition, I am persuaded that the reason why so exceedingly few have succeeded, is from the absurdity of the species. When nothing has been impossible to genius in every other walk, why has everybody failed in this but the inventor Homer? You will stare, but what are the rest? Virgil with every beauty of expression and harmony that can be conceived has accomplished but an insipid imitation. His hero is a nullity, like Mellefont and the virtuous characters of every comedy, and some of his incidents as the harpies and the ships turned to nymphs, as silly as Mother Goose's tales. Milton, all imagination, and a thousand times more sublime and spirited, has produced a monster. Lucan, who often says more in half a line than Virgil in a whole book, was lost in bombast if he talked for thirty lines together. Claudian and Statius had all his fustian with none of his quintessence. Camoens had more true grandeur than they, but with grosser faults. Dante was extravagant, absurd, disgusting, in short a Methodist parson in Bedlam. Ariosto was a more agreeable *Amadis de Gaul* in a bawdy-house, and Spencer, John Bunyan in rhyme. Tasso wearies one with their insuperable crime of stanza and by a thousand puerilities that are the very opposite of that dull dignity which is demanded for epic: and Voltaire who retained his good sense in heroics, lost his spirit and fire in them. In short, epic poetry is like what it first celebrated, the heroes of a world that knew nothing better than courage and conquest. It is not suited to an improved and polished state of things. It has continued to degenerate from the founder of the family, and happily expired in the last bastard of the race, Ossian.

Still as Mr Hayley has allowed such a latitude to heroic poesy as to admit the *Lutrin*, *The Dispensary*, and *The Dunciad* as epic poems, I can forgive a man who recommends to a friend to pen a tragedy, when he will accept of *The Way of the World* as one.

For Mr Hayley himself, though he chants in good tune, and has now and then pretty lines amongst several both prosaic and obscure, he has, I think no genius, no fire and not a grain of *originality,* the first of merits (in my eyes) in these latter ages, and a more certain mark of genius than in the infancy of the world, when no ground was broken, nor even, in the sportsman's phrase, *foiled.* It is that originality that I admire in your *Heroic Epistle* and in your genuine style, which I trust you will not quit to satisfy the impartial Mr Hayley (who though a good patriot equally cherishes janizaries)

That to you *do not belong*
The beauties of envenomed song.

For writing an epic poem, it would be as wise to set about copying Noah's ark, if Mons. de Buffon should beg you to build a menagerie for a couple of every living creatures upon earth, when there is no longer any danger of a general inundation.

I doubt your new friend will write his readers and his own reputation to death; every poem has a train of prose as long as Cheapside, with a vast parade of reading that would be less dear if it had any novelty or vivacity to recommend it. I know as little new as he, except that Lord Rockingham is very ill, I believe not without danger; should he fail, there would be a new scene indeed! Adieu!

PS. I find I have said above, every living *creatures*—is not that bad English? and if it is, is not it better than *a couple of every living creature?*

To Earl Harcourt, 7 September 1782

Strawberry Hill, Sept. 7, 1782.

I am most impatient, my dear Lord, for an account of the conclusion of all the various and great works carrying on at Nuneham. I am earnest to hear that the house is finished, that the tower designed by Mr. Mason is ready to receive my painted glass, that he has written several novelties, and is coming to make me a visit as he promised, and that Lady Harcourt has settled, and had transcribed the MS that I am to print. These things, and perhaps a great many more, I conclude, have been pursued with unremitting diligence, as no soul has had a moment's time to send me a line; though Mr. Mason is so punctual a correspondent, that I know he would not have been so long silent, if he had not been so occupied by the works at Nuneham, which he knows, I prefer to my own satisfaction. However, as all must be terminated in two or three days, I beg that the first holiday after the masons, bricklayers, upholsterers, muses, and amanuenses are paid off, that somebody or other will tell me the society are well, and have not broke their necks off a scaffold, nor their bones by a fall from Pegasus.

By my little specimen in Strawberry, I guess that Nuneham is in the highest beauty. As a whole, summer has been spent on decorating autumn with verdure, leaves, and rivers. Your Lordship's Thames must be brimful. I never saw it such a Ganges at this time of year: it is none of your home-brewed rivers that people make with a drain, half a bridge, and a clump of evergreens, and then overlay with the model of a ship.

I know nothing, for I live as if I were just arrived from Syria, and were performing quarantine. Nobody dares stir out of their own house. We are robbed and murdered if we do but step over the threshold to the chandler's shop for a pennyworth of plums. Lady Margaret Mordaunt is at Petersham with Lady Cecilia, and they are to dine here next week, if Admiral Millbank is returned from the Baltic, and they can obtain a convoy. Dame Cliveden is the only heroine amongst all us old dowagers: she is so much recovered that she ventures to go out cruising on all the neighbours, and has made a miraculous draught of fishes.

My nieces[1] are gone to Hackwood, and thence are to meet their sister and Lord Chewton at Weymouth. I have heard a whisper of a little miscarriage: it must have been a very small one. The Duchess,[2] when I heard last, was at Lausanne, but going to Ge-

1. The Ladies Waldegrave of Sir Joshua's famous picture.
2. The Duchess of Gloucester, their mother.

neva, and intended a visit to Madame de Virri, who is within three hours of the former. I do not know whither bound next.

Has your Lordship seen Mr. Tyrwhitt's book in answer to Mr. Bryant and Dr. Archimage? It is as good as arguments and proofs can be after what is much better, wit and ridicule. As Mr. Mason is absorbed in Fresnoy and Associations, I conclude he does not condescend to look at such trifles as Archaelogic Epistles, and dissertations on the language of Chaucer.

Charles Fox is languishing at the feet of Mrs. Robinson[1] George Selwyn says, 'Who should *the man of the people* live with, but with *the woman of the people?*' Tonton sends his compliments to Druid, and I am the whole sacred grove's devoted

H. W.

To Lady Ossory, 5 November 1782

Nov. 5, 1782.

I beg your Ladyship's pardon, but I cannot refrain from sending you a codicil to my last. I have taken to astronomy, now the scale is enlarged enough to satisfy my taste, who love gigantic ideas—do not be afraid; I am not going to write a second part to the *Castle of Otranto*, nor another account of the Patagonians[2] who inhabit the new Brobdignag planet;[3] though I do not believe that a world 160 times bigger than ours, is inhabited by pigmies—they would do very well for our page, the moon.

I have been reading Lord Buchan's letter again. He tells me that Mr. What-d'ye-call-him at Bath says that the new planet's orbit is 80 of our years. Now if their days are in proportion to their year, as our days are to our year, a day in the new planet must contain 1920 hours—and yet I dare to say, some of the inhabitants complain of the shortness of the days. I may err in my calculations, for I am a woeful arithmetician, and never could learn my

1. Mrs. Mary Robinson, the actress, known as "Perdita."
2. HW wrote a satirical *Account of the Giants Lately Discovered* in 1766.
3. Uranus, recently discovered by Sir William Herschel.

multiplication table—but no matter: one large sum is as good as another. How one should smile to hear the Duchess of Devonshire of the new planet cry, 'Lord, you would not go to dinner yet sure! it is but fifteen hundred o'clock!' or some Miss, 'Ah! that superannuated old fright, I'll lay a wager she's a year old'—but stay—here I don't go by my own rule of proportion—I ought to suppose their lives adequate to their size. Well, any way one might build very entertaining hypotheses on this new discovery.

The planet's distance from the sun is 1,710 millions of miles—I revere a telescope's eyes that can see so far! what pity that no Newton should have thought of improving instruments for hearing too! if a glass can penetrate seventeen hundred millions of miles beyond the sun, how easy to form a trumpet like Sir Joshua Reynolds's, by which one might overhear what is said in Mercury and Venus that are within a stone's throw of us! Well, such things will be discovered—but alas! we live in such an early age of the world, that nothing is brought to any perfection! I don't doubt but there will be invented spying-glasses for seeing the thoughts—and then a new kind of stucco for concealing them—but I return to my new favourite, astronomy. Do but think, Madam, how fortunate it is for us that discoveries are not reciprocal. If our superiors of the great planets were to dabble in such minute researches as we make by microscopes, how with their infinitely greater facilities, they might destroy us for a morning's amusement! They might impale our little globe on a pin's point, as we do a flea, and take the current of the Ganges or Oroonoko for the circulation of our blood—for with all due respect for philosophy of all sorts, I humbly apprehend that where people wade beyond their sphere, they make egregious blunders—at least we do, who are not accustomed to them. I am so vulgar, that when I hear of 17 millions of miles, I fancy astronomers compute by *livres* like the French, and not by pounds sterling, I mean, not by miles sterling. Nay, as it is but two days that I have grown wise, I have another whim. I took it into my head last night that our antediluvian ancestors who are said to have lived many hundred years, were not inhabitants of this earth, but of the new planet, whence might come the account, which we believe came from heaven. Whatever came from the skies where the new planet lives, would in the apprehensions of men at that time be deemed to come from heaven. Now if a patriarch lived ten of their years, which may be the term of their existence, and which according to our computation make 800 of our years, he was pretty nearly of the age of Methusalem; for what signifies a fraction of an hundred years or so?—Yet I offer this only as a conjecture; nor will I weary your Ladyship with more, though I am not a little vain of my new speculations.

Apropos to millions, have you heard, Madam, of the Prince de Guemené's breaking for 28 millions of *livres?* Would not one think it was a debt contracted by the two Foleys? I know of another Prince de Guemené, who lived, I think, early in the reign of Louis Quatorze, and had a great deal of wit. His wife was a *savante.* One day he met coming out of her closet an old Jew (not such as the present Prince and the Foleys deal with but) quite in rags, and half stark. The Prince asked, who he was? The Princess replied scornfully, 'Mais il me montre l'hebreu'—'Eh bien,' said the Prince, 'et bientôt, il vous montrera son cul'—I hope this story, if you did not know it, will make amends for the rest of my rhapsody.

PS. I fear some planet or other out of contempt for our impertinent curiosity has emptied its jordan on our heads—why, Madam, if Tonton lifts his leg over an ant's hill, do you think the pismires don't say, 'It rains terribly'?

To the Earl of Strafford, 24 June 1783

Strawberry Hill, June 24, 1783.

Though your Lordship's partiality extends even to my letters, you must perceive that they grow as antiquated as the writer. News are the soul of letters: when we give them a body of our own invention, it is as unlike to life as a statue. I have withdrawn so much from the world, that the newspapers know everything before me, especially since they have usurped the province of telling everything, private as well as public; and consequently a great deal more than I should wish to know, or like to report. When I do hear the transactions of much younger people, they do not pass from my ears into my memory; nor does your Lordship interest yourself more about them than I do. Yet still, when one reduces one's department to such narrow limits, one's correspondence suffers by it. However, as I desire to show only my gratitude and attachment, not my wit, I shall certainly obey your Lordship as long as you are content to read my letters, after I have told you fairly how little they can entertain you.

For imports of French, I believe we shall have few more. They have not ruined us so totally by the war, much less enriched themselves so much by it, but that they who have been here, complained so piteously of the expensiveness of England, that probably they will deter others from a similar jaunt—nor, such is their fickleness, are the French constant to any thing but admiration of themselves. Their *anglomanie* I hear has mounted—or descended—from our customs to our persons. English people are in fashion at Versailles. A Mr. [Ellis], who wrote some pretty verses at Bath two or three years ago, is a favourite there. One who was so, or may be still, the *beau Dillon*, came upon a very different errand—in short, to purchase at any price a book written by Linguet, which was just coming out, called *Antoinette*. That will tell your Lordship why the *beau Dillon* was the messenger.

Monsieur de Guignes and his daughters came hither—but it was at eight o'clock at night in the height of the deluge. You may be sure I was much flattered by such a visit! I was forced to light candles to show them any thing; and must have lighted the moon to show them the views. If this is their way of seeing England, they might as well look at it with an opera glass from the shore of Calais.

Mr Mason is to come to me on Sunday, and will find me mighty busy in making my lock of hay, which is not yet cut. I don't know why, but people are always more anxious about their hay than their corn, or twenty other things that cost them more. I suppose my Lord Chesterfield, or some such dictator, made it fashionable to care about one's hay.—Nobody betrays solicitude about getting in his rents.

We have exchanged spring and summer for autumn and winter, as well as day for night. If religion or law enjoined people to love light and prospects and verdure, I should not wonder if perverseness made us hate them—no, nor if society made us prefer living always in town to solitude and beauty.—But that is not the case. The most fashionable hurry into the country at Christmas and Easter, let the weather be ever so bad—and the finest ladies, who will go no whither till eleven at night, certainly pass more tiresome hours in London alone than they would in the country. —But all this is no business of mine: they do what they like, and so do I—And I am exceedingly tolerant about people who are perfectly indifferent to me. The sun and the seasons were not gone out of fashion when I was young—and I may do what I will with them now I am old: for fashion is fortunately no law but to its devotees. Were I five-and-twenty, I dare to say, I should think every whim of my cotemporaries very wise, as I did then. In one light I am always on the side of the young; for they only silently despise those who do not conform to their ordinances; but age is very apt to be angry at the change of customs, and partial to others no better founded. It is happy when we are occupied by nothing more serious. It is happy for a nation, when mere fashions are a topic that can employ its attention; for though dissipation may lead to graver moments, it commences with ease and tranquillity; and they at least who live before the scene shifts are fortunate, considering and comparing themselves with the various regions who enjoy no parallel felicity. I confess my reflections are *couleur de rose* at present. I did not much expect to live to see peace, without far more extensive ruin than has fallen on us. I will not probe futurity in search of less agreeable conjectures. Prognosticators may see many seeds of dusky hue—but I am too old to look forwards. Without any omens, common sense tells one, that in the revolution of ages nations must have unprosperous periods.—But why should I torment myself for what may happen in twenty years after my death, more than for what may happen in two hundred?

Nor shall I be more interested in the one than in the other. This is no indifference for my country.—I wish it could always be happy —But so I do to all other countries. Yet who could ever pass a tranquil moment, if such future speculations vexed him?

Adieu, my good Lord!—I doubt this letter has more marks of senility than the one I announced at the beginning. When I had no news to send you, it was no reason for tiring you with commonplaces.—But, your Lordship's indulgence spoils me. Does not it look as if I thought, that, because you commend my letters, you would like whatever I say? Will not Lady Strafford think that I abuse your patience?—I ask both your pardons—and am to both

A most devoted humble servant,

HOR. WALPOLE

TO THE EARL OF STRAFFORD, 1 August 1783

Strawberry Hill, August 1, 1783.

It would be great happiness indeed to me, my dear Lord, if such nothings as my letters could contribute to any part of your Lordship's; but as your own partiality bestows their chief merit on them, you see they owe more to your friendship than to the writer. It is not my interest to depreciate them, much less to undermine the foundation of their sole worth. Yet it would be dishonest not to warn your Lordship, that if my letters have had any intrinsic recommendation, they must lose of it every day. Years and frequent returns of gout have made a ruin of me. Dullness, in the form of indolence, grows upon me. I am inactive, lifeless, and so indifferent to most things, that I neither inquire after nor remember any topics that might enliven my letters. Nothing is so insipid as my way of passing my time. But I need not specify what my letters speak.—They can have no spirit left—and would be perfectly inanimate, if attachment and gratitude to your Lordship were as liable to be extinguished by old age as our more amusing qualities. I make no new connections; but cherish those that remain with all the warmth of youth and the piety of grey hairs.

The weather here has been, and is, with very few intervals, sultry to this moment. I think it has been of service to me; though by overheating myself I had a few days of lameness. The harvest is half over already all around us, and so pure, that not a poppy or cornflower is to be seen. Every field seems to have been weeded like B[risco]'s bowling-green. If Ceres, who is at least as old as many of our fashionable ladies, loves tricking herself out in flowers as they do, she must be mortified; and with more reason; for she looks well always with topknots of ultramarine and vermilion, which modern goddesses do not for half so long as they think they do. As providence showers so many blessings on us, I wish the peace may confirm them! Necessary I am sure it was—and when it cannot restore us, where should we have been, had the war continued! Of our situation and prospect I confess my opinion is melancholy—not from present politics, but from past. We flung away the most brilliant position—I doubt, for a long season! With politics I have totally done. I wish the present ministers may last; for I think better of their principles than of those of their opponents (with a few salvos on both sides), and so I do of their abilities.—But it would be folly in me to concern myself about new generations.—How little a way can I see of their progress!

I am rather surprised at the new Countess of Denbigh. How could a woman be ambitious of resembling Prometheus, to be pawed and clawed and gnawed by a vulture? I beg your Earldom's pardon; but I could not conceive that a coronet was so very tempting!

Lady Browne is quite recovered—unless she relapses from what we suffer at Twickenham Park from a Lord Northesk, an old seaman, who is come to Richmond on a visit to the Duke of Montrose. I think the poor man must be out of his senses—at least he talks us out of ours. It is the most incessant and incoherent rhapsody that ever was heard. He sits by the card-table, and pours on Mrs Noel all that ever happened in his voyages or his memory. He details the ship's allowance, and talks to her as if she was his first mate. Then in the mornings he carries his daughter to town to see St Paul's, and the Tower, and Westminster Abbey; and at night disgorges all he has seen; till we don't know the ace of spades from Queen Elizabeth's pocket-pistol in the armoury. Mercy on us!—And mercy on your Lordship too! Why should you be stunned with that alarum? Have you had your earthquake, my Lord? Many have had theirs. I assure you I have had mine. Above a week ago, when broad awake, the doors of the cabinet by my bedside rattled, without a breath of wind. I imagined somebody was walking on the leads, or had broken into the room under me. It was between four and five in the morning. I rang my bell. Before my servant could come it happened again; and was exactly like the horizontal tremor I felt from the earthquake some years ago. As I had rung once, it is plain I was awake. I rang again; but heard nothing more. I am quite persuaded there was some commotion; nor is it surprising that the dreadful eruptions of fire on the coasts of Italy and Sicily should have occasioned some alteration that has extended faintly hither, and contributed to the heats and mists that have been so extraordinary. George Montagu said of our last earthquake, that it was so tame you might have stroked it. It is comfortable to live where one can reason on them without dreading them! What satisfaction should you have in having erected such a monument of your taste, my Lord, as Wentworth Castle, if you did not know but it might be overturned in a moment and crush you? Sir William Hamilton is expected: he has been groping in all those devastations.—Of all vocations I could not be a professor of earthquakes! I prefer studies that are *couleur de rose*—nor would ever think of calamities, if I can do nothing to relieve them. Yet this is a weakness of mind that I do not defend. They are more respectable who can behold philosophically the great theatre of events—or rather this little theatre of ours! In some ampler sphere, they may look on the catastrophe of Messina as we do on kicking to pieces an ant-hill.

Bless me! what a farrago is my letter! It is like the extracts of books in a monthly magazine—I had no right to censure poor Lord Northesk's ramblings! Lady Strafford will think he has infected me. Goodnight, my dear Lord and Lady!

Your ever devoted

HOR. WALPOLE

To the Hon. Henry Seymour Conway, 15 October 1784

Strawberry Hill, Oct. 15, 1784.

As I have heard nothing from you, I flatter myself Lady Aylesbury mends, or I think you would have brought her again to the physicians: you will, I conclude, next week, as towards the end of it the ten days they named will be expired. I must be in town myself about Thursday on some little business of my own.

As I was writing this, my servants called me away to see a balloon; I suppose Blanchard's, that was to be let off from Chelsea this morning. I saw it from the common field before the window of my round tower. It appeared about a third of the size of the moon, or less, when setting, something above the tops of the trees on the level horizon. It was then descending; and, after rising and declining a little, it sunk slowly behind the trees, I should think about or beyond Sunbury, at five minutes after one. But you know I am a very inexact guesser at measures and distances, and may be mistaken in many miles; and you know how little I have attended to those *airgonauts:* only t'other night I diverted myself with a sort of meditation on future *airgonation,* supposing that it will not only be perfected, but will depose navigation. I did not finish it, because I am not skilled, like the gentleman that used to write political ship-news, in that style which I wanted to perfect my essay: but in the prelude I observed how ignorant the ancients were in supposing Icarus melted the wax of his wings by too near access to the sun, whereas he would have been frozen to death before he made the first post on that road. Next, I discovered an alliance between Bishop Wilkins's art of flying and his plan of an universal language; the latter of which he no doubt calculated to prevent the want of an interpreter when he should arrive at the moon.

But I chiefly amused myself with ideas of the change that would be made in the world by the substitution of balloons to ships. I supposed our seaports to become *deserted villages;* and Salisbury Plain, Newmarket Heath (another canvass for alteration of ideas), and all downs (but *the* Downs) arising into dockyards for aerial vessels. Such a field would be ample in furnishing new speculations. But to come to my ship-news:—

'The good balloon Daedalus, Captain Wing-ate, will fly in a few days for China; he will stop at the top of the Monument to take in passengers.

'Arrived on Brand Sands, the Vulture, Captain Nabob; the Tortoise snow, from Lapland; the Pet-en-l'air, from Versailles; the Dreadnought, from Mount Etna, Sir W. Hamilton, commander; the Tympany, Montgolfier; and the Mine-A-in-a-band-box, from the Cape of Good Hope. Foundered in a hurricane, the Bird of Paradise, from Mount Ararat. The Bubble, Sheldon, took fire, and was burnt to her gallery; and the Phoenix is to be cut down to a second-rate.'

In those days Old Sarum will again be a town and have houses in it. There will be fights in the air with wind-guns and bows and arrows; and there will be prodigious increase of land for tillage, especially in France, by breaking up all public roads as useless. But enough of my fooleries; for which I am sorry you must pay double postage.

To John Pinkerton, 26 June 1785

June 26, 1785.

I have sent your book[1] to Mr Colman, Sir; and must desire you in return to offer my grateful thanks to Mr Knight, who has done me an honour, to which I do not know how I am entitled, by the present of his poetry, which is very classic, and beautiful and tender, and of chaste simplicity.

To *your* book, Sir, I am much obliged on many accounts, particularly for having recalled my mind to subjects of delight, to which it was grown dulled by age and indolence. In consequence of your reclaiming it, I asked myself whence you feel so much disregard for certain authors whose fame is established. You have assigned

1. *Letters of Literature.*

good reasons for withholding your approbation from some, on the plea of their being imitators. It was natural, then, to ask myself again, whence they had obtained so much celebrity? I think I have discovered a cause, which I do not remember to have seen noted; and *that* cause I suspect to have been, that certain of those authors possessed *grace*—do not take me for a disciple of Lord Chesterfield, nor imagine that I mean to erect grace into a capital ingredient of writing—but I dǫ believe that it is a perfume that will preserve from putrefaction, and is distinct even from style, which regards *expression; grace,* I think, belongs to *manner.* It is from the charm of grace that I believe some authors, not in your favour, obtained part of their renown—Virgil, in particular—and yet I am far from disagreeing with you on his subject in general. There is such a dearth of invention in the *Æneid* (and when he did invent, it was often so foolishly), so little good sense, so little variety, and so little power over the passions, that I have frequently said, from contempt for his matter, and from the charm of his harmony, that I believe I should like his poem better, if I was to hear it repeated, and did not understand Latin. On the other hand, he has more than harmony: whatever he utters is said gracefully, and he ennobles his images, especially in the *Georgics,* or at least it is more sensible there from the humility of the subject. A Roman farmer might not understand his diction in agriculture—but he made a Roman courtier understand farming, the farming of that age; and could captivate a lord of Augustus's Bedchamber and tempt him to listen to themes of rusticity. On the contrary, Statius and Claudian, though talking of war, would make a soldier despise them as bullies. That graceful manner of thinking in Virgil seems to me to be more than style, if I do not refine too much; and I admire, I confess, Mr Addison's phrase, that Virgil tossed about his dung with an air of majesty. A style may be excellent without grace—for instance, Dr Swift's. Eloquence may bestow an immortal style, and one of more dignity; yet eloquence may want that ease, that genteel air that flows from or constitutes grace. Addison himself was master of that grace, even in his pieces of humour, which do not owe their merit to style; and from that combined secret he excels all men that ever lived, but Shakespeare, in humour, by never dropping into an approach towards burlesque and buffoonery, even when his humour descended to characters that in any other hands would have been vulgarly low. Is not it clear that Will Whimble was a gentleman, though he always lived at a distance from good company? Fielding had as much humour perhaps as Addison, but having no idea of grace, is perpetually disgusting. His innkeepers and parsons are the grossest of their profession, and his gentlemen are awkward when they should be at their ease.

The Grecians had grace in everything, in poetry, in oratory, in statuary, in architecture, and probably in music and painting. The Romans, it is true, were their imitators; but having grace too, imparted it to their copies, which gave them a merit, that almost raises them to the rank of originals. Horace's odes acquired their fame no doubt from the graces of his manner and purity of his style, the chief praise of Tibullus and Propertius, who certainly cannot boast of more meaning than Horace's odes.

Waller, whom you proscribe, Sir, owed his reputation to the graces of his manner, though he frequently stumbled, and even fell flat: but a few of his smaller pieces are as graceful as possible: one might say, that he excelled in painting ladies in enamel, but could not succeed in portraits in oil, large as life. Milton had such superior merit, that I will only say, that if his angels, his Satan, and his Adam, have as much dignity as the Apollo Belvedere, his Eve has all the delicacy and graces of the Venus of Medici, as his description of Eden has the colouring of Albano. Milton's tenderness imprints ideas as graceful as Guido's Madonnas; and the *Allegro, Penseroso,* and *Comus* might be denominated from the Three Graces, as the Italians gave singular titles to two or three of Petrarch's best sonnets.

Cowley, I think, would have had grace (for his mind was graceful) if he had had any ear, or if his taste had not been vitiated by the pursuit of wit, which, when it does not offer itself naturally, degenerates into tinsel or pertness. Pertness is the mistaken affectation of grace, as pedantry produces erroneous dignity: the familiarity of the one, and the clumsiness of the other, distort or prevent grace. Nature that furnishes samples of all qualities, and in the scale of gradation exhibits all possible shades, affords us types that are more apposite than words. The eagle is sublime, the lion majestic, the swan graceful, the monkey pert, the bear ridiculously awkward. I mention these as more expressive and comprehensive than I could make definitions of my meaning; but I will apply the swan only, under whose wings I will shelter an apology for Racine, whose pieces give me an idea of that bird. The colouring of the swan is pure, his attitudes are graceful, he never displeases you when sailing on his proper element. His feet may be ugly, his notes hissing not musical, his walk not natural, he can soar, but it is with difficulty. Still the impression the swan leaves is that of grace—so does Racine.

Boileau may be compared to the dog, whose sagacity is remarkable, as well as its fawning on its master and its snarling at those it dislikes. If Boileau was too austere to admit the pliability of grace, he compensates by good sense and propriety. He is like (for I will drop animals) an upright magistrate whom you respect, but whose justice and severity leave an awe that discourages familiarity. His copies of the ancients may be too servile—but if a good translator deserves praise, Boileau deserves more: he certainly does not fall below his originals; and, considering at what period he wrote, has greater merit still. By his imitations he held out to his countrymen models of taste, and banished totally the bad taste of his predecessors. For his *Lutrin,* replete with excellent poetry, wit, humour, and satire, he certainly was not obliged to the ancients. Excepting Horace, how little idea had either Greeks or Romans of wit and humour! Aristophanes and Lucian, compared with moderns, were, the one a blackguard, the other a buffoon. In my eyes, the *Lutrin,* the *Dispensary* and the *Rape of the Lock,* are standards of grace and elegance, not to be paralleled by antiquity, and eternal reproaches to Voltaire, whose indelicacy in the *Pucelle* degraded him as much when compared with the three authors I have named, as his *Henriade* leaves Virgil, and even Lucan, whom he more resembles, by far his superiors. The *Dunciad* is blemished by the offensive images of the games, but the poetry appears to me admirable; and though the fourth book has obscurities, I prefer it to the three others. It has descriptions not surpassed by any poet that ever existed; and which surely a writer merely ingenious will never equal. The lines on Italy, on Venice, on convents, have all the grace for which I contend as distinct from poetry, though united with the most beautiful; and the *Rape of the Lock*, besides the originality of great part of the invention, is a standard of graceful writing.

In general I believe that what I call *grace*, is denominated elegance; but by grace I mean something higher. I will explain myself by instances; Apollo is graceful, Mercury elegant. Petrarch perhaps owed his whole merit to the harmony of his numbers and the graces of his style. They conceal his poverty of meaning and want of variety. His complaints too may have added an interest, which had his passion been successful and had expressed itself with equal sameness, would have made the number of his sonnets insupportable. Melancholy in poetry, I am inclined to think contributes to grace, when it is not disgraced by pitiful lamentations, such as Ovid's and Cicero's in their banishments. We respect melancholy because it imparts a similar affection, pity. A gay writer, who should only express satisfaction without variety, would soon be nauseous.

Madame de Sévigné shines both in grief and gaiety. There is too much of sorrow for her daughter's absence; yet it is always expressed by new turns, new images, and often by wit, whose tenderness has a melancholy air. When she forgets her concern, and returns to her natural disposition, gaiety, every paragraph has novelty: her allusions, her applications are the happiest possible. She has the art of making you acquainted with all her acquaintance, and attaches you even to the spots she inhabited. Her language is correct, though unstudied; and, when her mind is full of any great event, she interests you with the warmth of a dramatic writer, not with the chilling impartiality of an historian. Pray read her accounts of the death of Turenne and of the arrival of

King James in France, and tell me whether you do not know their persons as if you had lived at the time. For my part, if you will allow me a word of digression (not that I have written with any method), I hate the cold impartiality recommended to historians; 'Si vis me flere, dolendum est primum ipsi tibi' [1]—but that I may not wander again, nor tire, nor contradict you any more, I will finish now, and shall be glad if you will dine at Strawberry Hill next Sunday and take a bed there, when I will tell you how many more parts of your book have pleased me, than have startled my opinions, or perhaps, prejudices. I am, Sir,

Your obedient humble servant,

HOR. WALPOLE.

PS. Be so good as to let me know by a line by the post to Str[awberry] Hill, whether I shall have the pleasure of seeing you on Sunday.

TO SIR HORACE MANN, 30 April 1786

Berkeley Square, April 30, 1786.

The almanac tells me that I ought to write to you; but then it ought to tell me what to say. I know nothing; people have been out of town for Easter, or rather for Newmarket, for our diversions mark the seasons, instead of their proclaiming themselves. We have no more spring than we had last year: I believe the milk-maids tomorrow will be forced to dress their garlands with Christmas nosegays of holly and ivy, for want of flowers.

The tragedy, or rather, I suppose, the farce, of Mr Hastings's trial, is also to commence tomorrow, when he is to make his defence before the House of Commons, where the majority of his judges are *ready* to be astonished at his eloquence and the transparency of his innocence, and the lustre of his merit. In the mean-

1. "If you would have me weep, you must first feel grief yourself" (Horace, *Ars Poetica*).

time, the charges are enormous, and make numbers who are not to be his jury, marvel how he will clear himself of half—and if he does, what he will do with the remainder. I have not yet looked into the charge, which fills a thick octavo. My opinion is formed more summarily: innocence does not pave its way with diamonds, nor has a quarry of them on its estate. All conversation turns on a trio of culprits, Hastings, Fitzgerald, and the Cardinal of Rohan. I have heard so much of all lately, that I confound them, and am not sure whether it was not the first who pretended to buy a brilliant necklace for the *Queen,* or who committed murders in Ireland, not in India; or whether it was not Fitzgerald who did not deal with Cagliostro for the secret of raising the dead, as he may have occasion for it soon—so much for tragedy. Our comic performers are Boswell and Dame Piozzi. The cock biographer has fixed a direct lie on the hen, by an advertisement, in which he affirms that he communicated his manuscript to Madam Thrale, and that she made no objection to what he says of her low opinion of Mrs Montagu's book. It is very possible that it might not be her real opinion, but was uttered in compliment to Johnson, or for fear he should spit in her face if she disagreed with him—but how will she get over her not objecting to the passage remaining? She must have known, by knowing Boswell, and by having a similar intention herself, that his anecdotes would certainly be published—in short, the ridiculous woman will be strangely disappointed. As she must have heard that the whole first impression of her book was sold the first day, no doubt she expects on her landing to be received like the Governor of Gibraltar, and to find the road strewed with branches of palm—Alack! she will discover, that though she has ridden an ass, she will be welcomed with no hosannahs. She and Boswell and their hero are the joke of the public. A Dr Woolcot, *soi-disant* Paul Pindar, has published a burlesque eclogue, in which Boswell and the Signora are the interlocutors, and all the absurdest passages in the works of both are ridiculed. The printshops teem with satiric prints on them: one, in which Boswell as a monkey is riding on Johnson the bear, has this witty inscription, 'My friend *delineavit*'—but enough of these mountebanks! . . .

May 4th.

I must send my letter to the office tonight, for I go to Strawberry tomorrow for two or three days—not that we have spring or summer yet! I believe both seasons have perceived that nobody goes out of town till July, and that therefore it is not worth while to come over so early as they used to do. The sun might save himself the same trouble, and has no occasion to rise before ten at night, for all nature ought no doubt to take the *ton* from people of fashion! unless Nature is willing to indulge them in the opportunity of contradicting her. Indeed at present our fine ladies seem to copy her, at least the ancient symbols of her; for though they do not exhibit a profusion of naked bubbies down to their shoe-buckles, yet they protrude a prominence of gauze that would cover all the dugs of alma mater—Don't however imagine that I am disposed to be a censor of modes, as most old folks are, who seem to think that they came into the world at the critical moment when everything was in perfection, and ought to suffer no farther innovation. On the contrary, I always maintain that the ordinances of the young are right. Who ought to invent fashions? Surely not the ancient. I tell my veteran cotemporaries that if they will have patience for three months, the reigning evil, whatever it is, will be cured—whereas, if they fret, till things are just as they should be, they may vex themselves to the day of doom. I carry this way of thinking still farther, and extend it to almost all reformations. Could one cure the world of being foolish, it were something—but to cure it of any one folly, is only making room for some other, which one is sure will succeed to the vacant place.

Mr Hastings used two days in his defence—which was not thought a very modest one, and rested rather on Machiavel's code, than on that of rigid moralists. The House is now hearing evidence; and as his counsel, Mr Machiavel, will not challenge many of the jury, I suppose Mr Hastings will be honourably acquitted. In fact, who but Machiavel can pretend that we have a shadow of title to a foot of land in India; unless as our law deems that what is done extra-parochially, is deemed to have happened in the parish of St Martin's in the Fields, India must in course belong to the crown of Great Britain. Alexander distrained the goods and chattels of Porus upon a similar plea; and the Popes thought all the world belonged to them as heirs at law to one who had not an acre upon earth. We condemned and attainted the Popes without trial, which was not in fashion in the reign of Henry VIII and by the law of forfeiture, confiscated all their injustice to our own use; and thus till we shall be ejected, have we a right to exercise all the tyranny and rapine that ever was practised by any of our predecessors anywhere—As it was in the beginning, is now, and ever shall be world without end.

To the Hon. Henry Seymour Conway, 18 June 1786

Sunday night, June 18, 1786.

I suppose you have been swearing at the east wind for parching your verdure, and are now weeping for the rain that drowns your hay. I have these calamities in common, and my constant and particular one,—people that come to see my house, which unfortunately is more in request than ever. Already I have had twenty-eight sets, have five more tickets given out; and yesterday, before I had dined, three German barons came. My house is a torment, not a comfort!

I was sent for again to dine at Gunnersbury[1] on Friday, and was forced to send to town for a dress-coat and a sword. There were the Prince of Wales, the Prince of Mecklenburg, the Duke of Portland, Lord Clanbrassil, Lord and Lady Clermont, Lord and Lady Southampton, Lord Pelham, and Mrs. Howe. The Prince of Mecklenburg went back to Windsor after coffee; and the Prince and Lord and Lady Clermont to town after tea, to hear some new French players at Lady William Gordon's. The Princess, Lady Barrymore, and the rest of us, played three pools at commerce till

1. The seat of the Princess Amelia, the aunt of George III.

ten. I am afraid I was tired and gaped. While we were at the dairy the Princess insisted on my making some verses on Gunnersbury. I pleaded being superannuated. She would not excuse me. I promised she should have an ode on her next birthday, which diverted the Prince; but all would not do. So, as I came home, I made the following stanzas, and sent them to her breakfast next morning:—

In deathless odes for ever green
  Augustus' laurels blow;
Nor e'er was grateful duty seen
  In warmer strains to flow.

Oh, why is Flaccus not alive,
  Your favorite scene to sing?
To Gunnersbury's charms could give
  His lyre immortal spring.

As warm as his my zeal for you,
  Great princess! could I show it:
But though you have a Horace too—
  Ah, Madam! he's no poet.

If they are but poor verses, consider I am sixty-nine, was half asleep, and made them almost extempore—and by command! However, they succeeded, and I received this gracious answer:—

I wish I had a name that could answer your pretty verses. Your yawning yesterday opened your vein for pleasing me; and I return you my thanks, my good Mr. Walpole, and remain sincerely your friend,

Amelia.

I think this is very genteel at seventy-five.

Do you know that I have bought the Jupiter Serapis as well as the Julio Clovio! [1] Mr. —— assures me he has seen six of the head, and not one of them so fine, or so well preserved. I am glad Sir Joshua Reynolds saw no more excellence in the Jupiter than

1. At the sale of the Duchess Dowager of Portland. (HW's note)

in the Clovio; or the Duke of Portland, I suppose, would have purchased it, as he has the vase, for a thousand pounds. I would not change. I told Sir William Hamilton and the late Duchess, when I never thought it would be mine, that I had rather have the head than the vase. I shall long for Mrs. Damer to make a bust to it, and then it will be still more valuable. I have deposited both the illumination and the Jupiter in Lady Di's cabinet,[1] which is worthy of them. And here my collection winds up; I will not purchase trumpery after such jewels. Besides, everything is much dearer in old age, as one has less time to enjoy. Good night!

To Lady Ossory, 6 September 1787

Strawberry Hill, Sept. 6, 1787.

I will not make a feigned excuse, Madam, nor catch at the pretence you kindly offer me of a lost letter—no, I confess honestly that I knew I owed you one—but was too conscientious to pay my just debts with the base currency of Richmond and Hampton Court—and I have no other specie. I know nothing, do nothing, but repeat the same insipid round that I have passed for so many summers, if summer this has been to be called. The dowagers of my canton pick up and dress up tales of what is done in London and at various watering places; but I hold it a prudery becoming old men (the reverse of that of old women) not to trouble myself about or censure the frolics of the young; and for my cotemporaries, so few of them are left, that unless by living to the age of Old Parr or Jenkins, we are not likely to commit anything remarkable. I have seen none of the French, Savoyard or Lorrain princes and princesses, sterling or pinchbeck; I broke off my *commercial treaty* with France, when I was robbed of half Madame du Deffand's papers, and care no more for their *bonne compagnie,* than for their convicts Monsieur de Calonne and Madame de la Motte.

Under such a negative existence, what could I write, Madam? I

1. A cabinet at Strawberry Hill, ornamented with drawings by Lady Diana Beauclerc. (HW's note)

have heard nothing for these two months worth telling you but this little story. There lives at Kingston a Mrs Barnard, a very wealthy hen-Quaker: she has a passion for beautiful black and white cows, never parts with a pretty calf, and consequently has now a hecatomb as striped and spotted as leopards and tigers. The Queen happened to see this ermined drove, and being struck with the beauty of their robes, sent a page to desire to purchase one. Mrs Barnard replied, she never sold cows, but would lend her Majesty her bull with all her heart—apropos to Court, it is not a recent story, I believe, but did you ever hear, Madam, that Mrs Herbert, the Bedchamberwoman, going in a hackney-chair, the chairmen were excessively drunk, and after tossing and jolting her for some minutes, set the chair down, and the foreman lifting up the top, said, 'Madam, you are so drunk, that if you do not sit still, it will be impossible to carry you.'

To prove how little I had to say, I will empty my bimensal memory with the only other scrap *I* have collected, and which I may send in part of payment for the four lines of *Latin* of Archbishop Tennison, which I have received from your Ladyship. Mine is an ancient Latin law, which proves that the famous bulse was a legal escheat to the Crown. In the new volume of the *Archæologia* is an essay on the state of the Jews in England in former times; and there it is said, 'Judæus verò nihil possidere potest, quia quic-quid acquirit, acquirit regi'—I suppose, nobody will dispute Mr Hastings being a Jew—or if you please, for *Judæus* you may read *Indicus*, so like are the words and the essence.

Many thanks for the advertisement which is curious indeed! I have not visited Mr Herschell's giant telescope, though so near me. In truth, the scraps I have learnt of his discoveries have confounded me: my little head will not contain the stupendous idea of an infinity of worlds—not that I at all disbelieve them or anything that is above my comprehension. Infinite space may certainly contain whatever is put into it; and there is no reason for imagining that nothing has been put into it, but what our short-sighted eyes can see! Worlds, systems of suns and worlds may be as plenty as blackberries—but what can such an incredibly small point as a human skull do with the possibility of Omnipotence's endless creation? Do but suppose that I was to unfold to a pismire in my garden an account of the vast empire of China—not that there is any degree of proportion in the comparison—proceed; suppose another pismire could form a prodigious, yet invisible, spying-glass that should give the student ant a glimpse of the continent of China—Oh! I must stop—I shall turn my own brain, which while it is launching into an ocean of universes, is still admiring pismire Herschell—That he should not have a *wise* look, does not surprise me—he may be stupefied at his own discoveries—or to make them, it might require a head constructed too simply to contain any diversity of attention to puny objects. Sir Isaac Newton, they say, was so absorbed in his pursuits, as to be something of a changeling in worldly matters—and when he descended to earth and conjecture, he was no phenomenon.

I will alight from my altitudes, and confine myself to our own anthill. Have you seen, Madam, the horrible mandate of the Emperor to General Murray? Think of that insect's threatening to sacrifice thousands of his fellow pismires to what he calls *his dignity!* the dignity of a mite, that, supposing itself as superior as an earwig, meditates preventing hosts of its own species from enjoying the happiness and the moment of existence that has been allotted to them in an innumerable succession of ages!—but while scorn, contempt, hatred, kindle against the imperial insect, admiration crowds in for the brave pismires who so pathetically deprecate their doom, yet seem resigned to it! I think I never read anything more noble, more touching, than the remonstrance of the Deputies to Prince Kaunitz.

If tyrant dignity is ready to burst on Brabant, appearances with us seem also too warlike. I shall be sorry if it arrives—I flattered myself that in our humiliated state, the consequence of *our dignity,* we should at least be tame and tranquil for the remnant of my time—but what signifies care about moments? I will return to your letter, which set me afloat on the vasty deep of speculation, to which I am very unequal and do not love. My understanding is more on a level with your ball, and meditations on the destruction of Gorhambury, which I regret. It was in a very crazy state, but deserved to be propped; the situation is by no means delightful.

I called at Sir Joshua's, while he was at Ampthill, and saw his Hercules for Russia;[1] I did not at all admire it: the principal babe put me in mind of what I read so often, but have not seen, *the monstrous craws:* Master Hercules's knees are as large as, I presume, the late Lady Guilford's. *Blind* Tiresias is *staring* with horror at the terrible spectacle. If Sir Joshua is satisfied with his own departed pictures, it is more than the possessors or posterity will be. I think he ought to be paid in annuities only for so long as his pictures last. One should not grudge him the first fruits. . . .

To Hannah More, 12 July 1788

Strawberry Hill, July 12, 1788.

Won't you repent having opened the correspondence, my dear Madam, when you find my letters come so thick upon you? In this instance, however, I am only to blame in part, for being too ready to take advice, for the sole reason for which advice ever is taken, because it fell in with my inclination.

You said in your last that you feared you took up time of mine to the prejudice of the public; implying, I imagine, that I might employ it in composing. Waiving both your compliment and my own vanity, I will speak very seriously to you on that subject, and with exact truth. My simple writings have had better fortune than they had any reason to expect; and I fairly believe, in a great degree, because gentlemen-writers, who do not write for interest, are treated with some civility if they do not write absolute nonsense. I think so, because I have not unfrequently known much better works than mine much more neglected, if the name, fortune, and situation of the authors were below mine. I wrote early, from youth, spirits and vanity, and from both the last when the first no longer existed. I now shudder when I reflect on my own boldness;

1. Ordered by the Czarina. It depicts the infant Hercules strangling the serpents, one in each hand.

and with mortification, when I compare my own writings with those of any great authors. This is so true, that I question whether it would be possible for me to sum up courage to publish anything I have written, if I could recall time past and should yet think as I think at present.— So much for what is over and out of my power. As to writing now, I have totally forsworn the profession, for two solid reasons. One I have already told you, and it is, that I know my own writings are trifling and of no depth. The other is, that, light and futile as they were, I am sensible they are better than I could compose now. I am aware of the decay of the middling parts I had, and others may be still more sensible of it. How do I know but I am superannuated? Nobody will be so coarse as to tell me so—but if I published dotage, all the world would tell me so—and who but runs that risk who is an author after seventy? What happened to the greatest author of this age, and who certainly retained a very considerable portion of his abilities for ten years after my age? Voltaire, at 84 I think, went to Paris to receive the incense, in person, of his countrymen, and to be witness of their admiration of a tragedy he had written at that Methusalem-age. Incense he did receive till it choked him; and at the exhibition of his play he was actually crowned with laurel in the box where he sat—but what became of his poor play?—It died as soon as he did—was buried with him—and no mortal, I dare to say, has ever read a line of it since, it was so bad.

As I am neither by a thousandth part so great, nor a quarter so little, I will herewith send you a fragment that an accidental rencounter set me upon writing, and which I found so flat, that I would not finish it. Don't believe that I am either begging praise by the stale artifice of hoping to be contradicted; or that I think there is any occasion to make you discover my caducity. No; but the fragment contains a curiosity—English verses written by a French Prince of the Blood, and which at first I had a mind to add to my *Royal and Noble Authors*; but as he was not a royal author of ours, and as I could not please myself with an account of him, I shall revert to my old resolution of not exposing my pen's grey hairs.

Of one passage I must take notice; it is a little indirect sneer at our crowd of authoresses. My choosing to send this to *you* is a proof that I think you an author, that is, a classic. But in truth I am nauseated by the Madams ———, etc. and the host of novel-writers in petticoats, who think they imitate what is inimitable, *Evelina* and *Cecilia.* Your candour I know will not agree with me, when I tell you I am not at all charmed with Miss [Seward] and Mr [Hayley] piping to one another; but *you* I exhort, and would encourage to write; and flatter myself you will never be royally gagged and promoted to fold muslins, as has been lately wittily said on Miss B——,[1] in the list of 500 living authors. *Your* writings promote virtues; and their increasing editions prove their worth and utility.—If you question my sincerity, can you doubt my admiring you, when you have gratified my self-love so amply in your *Bas Bleu*? Still, as much as I love your writings, I respect yet more your heart and your goodness. You are so good, that I believe you would go to heaven, even though there were no Sunday, and only six *working* days in the week. Adieu, my best Madam!

Yours most cordially,

HOR. WALPOLE

TO LADY OSSORY, 11 October 1788

Strawberry Hill, Oct. 11, 1788.

I am sorry, Madam, that *mes villageoises* have no better provender than my sillyisms to send to their correspondents; nor am I ambitious of rivalling the barber or innkeeper, and becoming the wit of five miles round. I remember how long ago I estimated local renown at its just value by a sort of little adventure, that I will tell you; and since that, there is an admirable chapter somewhere in Voltaire, which shows that more extended fame is but local on a little larger scale; it is the chapter of the Chinese who goes into an European bookseller's shop, and is amazed at finding none of the

1. Fanny Burney.

works of his most celebrated countrymen; while the bookseller finds the stranger equally ignorant of Western classics. Well, Madam, here is my tiny story: I went once with Mr Rigby to see a window of painted glass at Messing in Essex, and dined at a better sort of ale-house. The landlady waited on us, and was notably loquacious, and entertained us with the *bons mots,* and funny exploits of Mr Charles: Mr Charles, said this, Mr Charles played such an one that trick; oh! nothing was so pleasant as Mr Charles—but how astonished the poor soul was when we asked who Mr Charles was! and how much more astonished when she found we had never heard of Mr Charles Luckyn, who it seems was a relation of Lord Grimston, had lived in their village, and been the George Selywn of half a dozen cottages. If I have a grain of ambitious pride left, it is what in other respects has been the thread that has run through my life, that of being forgotten; so true, except the folly of being an author, has been what I said last year to the Prince of Wales, when he asked me if I was a Freemason? I replied, 'No, Sir; I never was anything.'

Apropos to the Prince, I am sorry you do not approve my offering to kiss the Duke of York's hand, when he came to see my house. I never had been presented to him: but moreover, as I am very secure of never being suspected of paying my court for interest, and certainly never seek royal personages, I always pique myself, when I am thrown into their way, upon showing that I know I am nobody, and know the distance between them and me. This I take to be common sense, and do not repent of my behaviour. If I were a grandee, and in place, I would not, like the late Duchess of Northumberland, tag after them, calling them, *my Master* and *my Mistress.* I think if I were their servant, I would, as little, like the same Grace, parade before the Queen with more footmen than her Majesty: *that* was impertinent.

I am sorry, for the third time of this letter, that I have no new village anecdotes to send your Ladyship, since they divert you for a moment—I have one, but some months old. Lady Charleville my neighbour told me three months ago, that having some company with her, one of them had been to see Strawberry. 'Pray,' said another, 'who is that Mr Walpole?' 'Lord,' cried a third, 'don't you know the great epicure Mr Walpole?' 'Pho!' said the first, 'great epicure! you mean the great antiquestrian'—There! Madam, surely this anecdote may take its place in the chapter of local fame.

If I have picked up no recent anecdotes on our common, I have made a much more, to me, precious acquisition. It is the acquaintance of two young ladies of the name of Berry, whom I first saw last winter, and who accidentally took a house here with their father for this season. Their story is singular enough to entertain you. The grandfather, a Scot, had a large estate in his own country; £5000 a year, it is said; and a circumstance I shall tell you, makes it probable. The eldest son married for love a woman with no fortune. The old man was enraged and would not see him. The wife died and left these two young ladies. Their grandfather wished for an heir male, and pressed the widower to remarry, but could not prevail—the son declaring he would consecrate himself to his daughters and their education. The old man did not break with him again, but much worse, totally disinherited him, and left all to his second son, who very handsomely gave up £800 a year to his elder brother. Mr Berry has since carried his daughters for two or three years to France and Italy, and they are returned the best informed and the most perfect creatures I ever saw at their age. They are exceedingly sensible, entirely natural and unaffected, frank, and being qualified to talk on any subject, nothing is so easy and agreeable as their conversation, nor more apposite than their answers and observations. The eldest, I discovered by chance, understands Latin, and is a perfect Frenchwoman in her language. The younger draws charmingly, and has copied admirably Lady Di's gypsies, which I lent her, though the first time of her attempting colours.

They are of pleasing figures; Mary, the eldest, sweet, with fine dark eyes, that are very lively when she speaks, with a symmetry of face that is the more interesting from being pale. Agnes, the younger, has an agreeable sensible countenance, hardly to be called handsome, but almost. She is less animated than Mary but seems out of deference to her sister to speak seldomer, for they dote on each other, and Mary is always praising her sister's talents. I must even tell you, Madam, that they dress *within* the bounds of fashion, though fashionably; but without the excrescences and balconies with which modern hoydens overwhelm and barricado their persons. In short, good sense, information, simplicity and ease characterize the Berrys—and this is not particularly mine, who am apt to be prejudiced, but the universal voice of all that know them. The first night I met them, I would not be acquainted with them, having heard so much in their praise, that I concluded they would be all pretensions. The second time, in a very small company, I sat next to Mary, and found her an angel, inside and out. Now, I don't know which I like best, except Mary's face, which is formed for a sentimental novel but is ten times fitter for a fifty times better thing, genteel comedy.

This delightful family comes to me almost every Sunday evening, as our region is too *proclamatory* to play at cards on the seventh day—I do not care a straw for cards, but I do disapprove of this partiality to the youngest child of the week, while the other poor six days are treated as if they had no souls to be saved.

I forgot to tell you that Mr Berry is a little merry man with a round face, and you would not suspect him of so much feeling and attachment. I make no excuse for such minute details, for if your Ladyship insists on hearing the humours of my district, you must for once indulge me in sending you two pearls that I found in my path.

To Mary and Agnes Berry, 23 June 1789

Strawberry Hill, Tuesday, June 23, 1789.

I am not a little disappointed and mortified at the post bringing me no letter from you today; you promised to write on the road. I reckon you arrived at your station on Sunday evening: if you do not write till next day, I shall have no letter till Thursday!

I am not at all consoled for my double loss: my only comfort is, that I flatter myself the journey and air will be of service to you both—the latter has been of use to me, though the part of the element of air has been chiefly acted by the element of water, as my poor haycocks feel! Tonton does not miss you so much as I do, not having so good a taste, for he is grown very fond of *me,* and I return it for your sakes, though he deserves it too, for he is perfectly good-natured and tractable—but he is not beautiful like his *god-dog,* as Mr Selwyn, who dined here on Saturday, called my poor late favourite; especially as I have had him clipped; the shearing has brought to light a nose an ell long; and as he has now *nasum rhinocerotis,* I do not doubt but he will be a better critic in poetry than Dr Johnson, who judged of harmony by the principles of an author, and fancied, or wished to make others believe, that no Jacobite could write bad verses, nor a Whig good.

I passed so many evenings of the last fortnight with you, that I almost preferred it to our two honeymoons, and consequently am the more sensible to the deprivation—and how dismal was *Sunday* evening compared to those of last autumn! If you both felt as I do, we might surpass any event in the annals of Dunmow: Oh! what a prodigy it would be if a husband and *two wives* should present themselves and demand the flitch of bacon on swearing that not one of the three in a year and a day had wished to be unmarried! For my part I know that my affection has done nothing but increase; though, were there but one of you, I should be ashamed of being so strongly attached at my age. Being in love with both, I glory in my passion, and think it a proof of my sense. Why should not two affirmatives make a negative, as well as the reverse? and then a double love will be wisdom—for what is wisdom in reality but a negative? It exists but by correcting folly; and when it has peevishly prevailed on us to abstain from something we have a mind to, it gives itself airs, and inaction pretends to be a personage, a nonentity sets up for a figure of importance. It is the case of most of those phantoms called virtues, which by smothering poor vices, claim a reward as thief-takers do. You know I have a partiality for drunkenness, though I never practised it: it is a reality—

but what is sobriety, only the absence of drunkenness!—however, *mes chères femmes,* I make a difference between women and men, and do not extend my doctrine to your sex. Everything is excusable in us, and nothing in you—and pray remember, that I will not lose my flitch of bacon—*though.*

Have you shed a tear over the Opera House? or do you agree with me, that there is no occasion to rebuild it? The nation has long been tired of operas, and has now a good opportunity of dropping them. Dancing protracted their existence for some time—but *the room-after* was the real support of both, and was like what has been said of your sex, that they never speak their true meaning but in the postscript of their letters. Would not it be sufficient to build an *after-room* on the whole emplacement, to which people might resort from all assemblies! It should be a codicil to all the diversions of London; and the greater the concourse, the more excuse there would be for staying all night, from the impossibility of ladies getting their coaches to drive up. To be crowded to death in a waiting room at the end of an entertainment is the whole joy; for who goes to any diversion till the last minute of it? I am persuaded that instead of retrenching St Athanasius's Creed, as the Duke of Grafton proposed, in order to draw *good company* to church, it would be more efficacious, if the congregation were to be indulged with an after-room in the vestry; and instead of *two or three being gathered together,* there would be *all the world,* before prayers would be quite over.

Wednesday.

I calculated too rightly; no letter today!—yet I am not proud of my computation; I had rather have heard of you today; it would have looked like keeping your promise—it has a bad air, your forgetting me so early! Nay, and after your scoffing me for supposing you would not write till your arrival I don't know where! You see I think of *you* and write every day, though I cannot dispatch my letter, till you have sent me a direction. Much the better I am indeed for your not going to Swisserland! Yorkshire is in the glaciers for me! and you are as cold as Mr Palmer. Miss *Agnes* was coy, and was not so flippant of promising me letters—well, but I do trust *she will* write, and then, Madam, she and I will go to Dunmow without you. Apropos, as Mrs Cambridge's beauty has kept so unfaded, and Mr Cambridge's passion is so undiminished, and as they are good economists, I am astonished they have laid in no stock of bacon, when they could have it for asking!

Thursday night.

Despairing beside a clear stream
A shepherd forsaken was laid—

not very close to the stream, but within doors in sight of it, for in this damp weather a lame old Colin cannot lie and despair with any comfort on a wet bank—but I smile against the grain, and am seriously alarmed at Thursday being come and no letter! I dread one of you being ill, and then shall detest the D. of Northumberland's rapacious steward more than ever. Mr Batt and the Abbé Nichols dined with me today, and I could talk of you *en pays de connaissance.* They tried to persuade me that I have no cause to be in a fright about you; but I have such perfect faith in the kindness of both of you, as I have in your possessing every other virtue, that I cannot believe but some sinister accident must have prevented my hearing from you. I wish Friday was come! I cannot write about anything else till I have a letter.

Friday 26.

My anxiety increases daily, for still I have no letter. You cannot all three be ill, and if any one is, I should flatter myself, another would have written, or if any accident has happened. Next to your having met with some ill luck, I should be mortified at being forgotten so suddenly. Of any other vexation I have no fear. So much goodness and good sense as you both possess, would make me perfectly easy, if I were really your husband. I must then suspect some accident, and shall have no tranquillity till a letter puts me out of pain. Jealous I am not, for two young ladies cannot have run away with their father to Gretna Green. Hymen, O Hymenææ, bring me good news tomorrow, and a direction too, or you do nothing!

Saturday.

Io pæan! Io Tonton!—at last I have got a letter, and you are all well! and I am so pleased, that I forget the four uneasy days I have passed—at present I have neither time or paper to say more, for our post turns on its heel and goes out the instant it is come in. I am in some distress still, for, thoughtless creature, you have sent me no direction—Luckily Lady Cecilia told me yesterday you had bidden her direct to you to be left at the post-house at York, which was more than you told me; but I will venture. If you do receive this, I beseech you never forget, as you move about, to send me new directions.

Do not be frightened at the enormity of this—I do not mean to continue so four-paginous in every letter. Mr C. is this instant come in—and would damp me, if I were going to scribble more. Adieu, adieu! adieu! all three.

Your dutiful son-in-law and most affectionate husband,

H. W.

PS. I beg pardon, I see on the last page of your letter there is a direction.

To Mary Berry, 26 May 1791

Berkeley Square, May 26, 1791.

I am rich in letters from you: I received that by Lord Elgin's courier first, as you expected, and its elder the next day. You tell me mine entertain you; *tant mieux;* it is my wish, but my wonder, for I live so very little in the world, that I do not know the present generation by sight, for though I pass them in the streets, the hats with valances, the folds above the chin of the ladies, and the dirty shirts and shaggy hair of the young men, who have *levelled nobility* almost as much as the *mobility* in France have, have confounded all individuality. Besides, if I did go to public places and assemblies, which my going to roost earlier prevents, the bats and owls do not begin to fly abroad till far in the night, when they begin to see and be seen. However, one of the empresses of fashion, the Duchess of Gordon, uses fifteen or sixteen hours of her four and twenty. I heard her journal of last Monday—She first went to Handel's music in the Abbey; she then clambered over the benches and went to Hastings's trial in the Hall—after dinner to the play, then to Lady Lucan's assembly; after that to Ranelagh, and returned to Mrs Hobart's faro table; gave a ball herself in the evening of that morning into which she must have got a good way, and set out for Scotland the next day. Hercules could not have achieved a quarter of her labours in the same space of time. What will the Great Duke think of our Amazons, if he has letters opened, as the Emperor was wont? One of our Camillas—but in a freer style, I hear he saw (I fancy just before your arrival) and he must have wondered at the familiarity of the dame and the nincompoophood of her Prince. Sir William Hamilton is arrived—his nymph of the attitudes was too prudish to visit the rambling peeress.

Mrs Cholmeley was so very good as to call on me again yesterday; Mr French was with me, and fell in love with her understanding, and probably with her face too—but with that he did not trust me. He says we shall have Dr Darwin's stupendous poem in a fortnight, of which you saw parts. George Cholmondeley's wife after a dreadful labour is delivered of a dead child.

The rest of my letter must be literary, for we have no news. Boswell's book[1] is gossiping, but having numbers of proper names, would be more readable, at least by me, were it reduced from two volumes to one—but there are woeful *longueurs,* both about his hero, and himself, the *fidus Achates,* about whom one has not the smallest curiosity; but I wrong the original Achates; one is satisfied with his fidelity in kee[p]ing his master's secrets and weaknesses, which modern led-captains betray for their patron's glory,

1. His *Life of Johnson.*

and to hurt their own enemies, which Boswell has done shamefully, particularly against Mrs Piozzi and Mrs Montagu, and Bishop Percy. Dr Blagdon says justly, that it is a new kind of libel, by which you may abuse anybody, by saying, some dead person said so and so of somebody alive—Often indeed Johnson made the most brutal speeches to living persons, for though he was good-natured at bottom, he was very ill-natured at top. He loved to dispute to show his superiority. If his opponents were weak, he told them they were fools; if they vanquished him, he was scurrilous—to nobody more than to Boswell himself who was contemptible for flattering him so grossly, and for enduring the coarse things he was continually vomiting on Boswell's own country, Scotland. I expected amongst the excommunicated to find myself, but am very gently treated. I never would be in the least acquainted with Johnson, or as Boswell calls it, had not a just value for him, which the biographer imputes to my resentment for the Doctor's putting bad arguments (purposely out of Jacobitism) into the speeches which he wrote fifty years ago for my father in the *Gentleman's Magazine*, which I did not read then, or ever knew Johnson wrote till Johnson died, nor have looked at since. Johnson's blind Toryism and known brutality kept me aloof, nor did I ever exchange a syllable with him; nay, I do not think I ever was in a room with him six times in my days. The first time I think was at the Royal Academy. Sir Joshua said, 'Let me present Dr Goldsmith to you'; he did. 'Now I will present Dr Johnson to you.'—'No,' said I, 'Sir Joshua, for Dr Goldsmith, pass—but you shall *not* present Dr Johnson to me.'

Some time after, Boswell camc to mc, said Dr J. was writing the lives of the poets, and wished I would give him anecdotes of Mr Gray. I said very coldly, I had given what I knew to Mr Mason. B. hummed and hawed and then dropped, 'I suppose you know Dr J. does not admire Mr Gray'—Putting as much contempt as I could into my look and tone, I said, 'Dr Johnson don't!—humph!'—and with that monosyllable ended our interview—After the Doctor's death, Burke, Sir Joshua Reynolds and Boswell sent an ambling circular letter to me begging subscriptions for a monument for him—the two last, I think impertinently, as they could not but know my opinion, and could not suppose I would contribute to a monument for one who had endeavoured, poor soul! to degrade my friend's superlative poetry—I would not deign to write an answer, but sent down word by my footman, as I would have done to parish officers with a brief, that I would not subscribe. In the two new volumes, Johnson says—and very probably did, or is made to say, that Gray's poetry is *dull*, and that he was a *dull* man! The same oracle dislikes Prior, Swift and Fielding. If an elephant could write a book, perhaps one that had read a great deal would say that an Arabian horse is a very clumsy ungraceful animal—pass to a better chapter—

Burke has published another pamphlet against the French Revolution, in which he attacks it still more grievously. The beginning is very good, but it is not equal, nor quite so injudicious as parts of its predecessor; is far less brilliant, as well as much shorter; but were it ever so long, his mind overflows with such a torrent of images, that he cannot be tedious. His invective against Rousseau is admirable, just and new. Voltaire he passes almost contemptuously. I wish he had dissected Mirabeau too: and I grieve that he has omitted the violation of the consciences of the clergy; nor stigmatized those universal plunderers, the National Assembly, who gorge themselves with eighteen *livres* a day, which to many of them would three years ago have been astonishing opulence.

When you return, I shall lend you three volumes in quarto of another work with which you will be delighted. They are state letters in the reigns of Henry VIII, Mary, Elizabeth and James, being the correspondence of the Talbot and Howard families, given by a Duke of Norfolk to the Herald's Office, where they have lain for a century neglected, buried under dust and unknown, till discovered by a Mr Lodge, a genealogist, who to gratify his passion procured to be made a Pursuivant. Oh! how curious they are! Henry seizes an alderman who refused to contribute to a benevolence, sends him to the army on the borders, orders him to be exposed in the front line, and if that does not do, to be treated with the utmost rigour of military discipline. His daughter Bess is not less a Tudor. The mean unworthy treatment of the Queen of Scots is striking; and you will find how Elizabeth's jealousy of her crown and her avarice were at war, and how the more ignoble passion predominated. But the most amusing passage is one in a private letter, as it paints the awe of children for their parents a *little* differently from modern habitudes. Mr Talbot second son of the Earl of Shrewsbury, was a member of the House of Commons and was married. He writes to the Earl his father, and tells him that a young woman of a very good character has been recommended to him for chambermaid to his wife, and if his Lordship does not disapprove of it, he will hire her. There are many letters of news that are very entertaining too—but it is nine o'clock and I must go to Lady Cecilia's.

Friday.

The Conways, Mrs Damer, the Farrens, and Lord Mt Edgcumbe supped at the Johnstones. Lord Mount Edgcumbe said excellently, that *Mlle D'Eon is her own widow.*

I wish I had seen you both in your court-*plis* at your presentation—but that is only one wish amongst a thousand.

East winds and blights have succeeded our April spring, as you guessed, but though I have been at Strawberry every week, I have caught no cold, I kindly thank you. Adieu!

To Mary Berry, 14 June 1791

Strawberry Hill, June 14, 1791.

I pity you! what a dozen or fifteen unentertaining letters are you going to receive! for here I am, unlikely to have anything to tell you worth reading: You had better come back incontinently—but pray do not prophesy any more; you have been the death of our summer, and we are in close mourning for it in coals and ashes. It froze hard last night: I went out for a moment to look at my haymakers and was starved—the contents of an English June are, hay and ice, orange-flowers and rheumatisms! I am now cowering over the fire. Mrs Hobart had announced a rural breakfast at Sans Souci last Saturday, nothing being so pastoral as a fat grandmother in a row of houses on Ham Common. It rained early in the morning; she dispatched post-boys—for want of cupids and zephyrs, to stop the nymphs and shepherds who tend their flocks in Pall Mall and St James's Street, but half of them missed the couriers and arrived. Mrs Montagu was more splendid yesterday morning and breakfasted seven hundred persons on opening her great room, and the room with the hangings of feathers. The King and Queen had been with her last week—I should like to have heard the orations she had prepared on the occasion. I was neither city mouse nor country mouse. I did dine at Fulham on Saturday with the Bishop of London; Mrs Boscawen, Mrs Garrick and Hannah More were there and Dr Beattie, whom I had never seen: he is quiet, simple and cheerful, and pleased me—There ends my tale, this instant Tuesday! How shall I fill a couple of pages more by Friday morning? Oh! ye ladies on the Common, and ye uncommon ladies in London, have pity on a poor gazetteer, and supply me with eclogues or royal panegyrics! Moreover—or rather moreunder, I have had no letter from you these ten days, though the east wind has been as constant as Lord Derby. I say not this in reproach as you are so kindly punctual, but as it stints me from having a single paragraph to answer. I do not admire specific responses to every article—but they are great resources on a dearth.

Madame de Boufflers is ill of a fever, and the Duchesse de Biron goes next week to Swisserland—*mais qu'est que cela vous fait?* I must eke out this with a few passages that I think will divert you from the heaviest of all books, Mr Malone's Shakespeare in ten thick octavos with notes that are an extract of all the opium that is spread through the works of all the bad playwrights of that age—mercy on the poor gentleman's patience! Amongst his other indefatigable researches, he has discovered some lists of effects in the custody of the property-man to the Lord Admiral's company of players in 1598. Of those effects he has given eight pages—you shall be off for a few items; viz; 'My Lord Caffe's (Caiaphas) gercken (jerkin) and his hoose (hose): one rocke, one tombe, one Hellemought (Hellmouth), two stepelles, and one chyme of belles: one chaine of dragons, two coffenes, one bulles head, one vylter, one goste's crown, and one frame for the heading in black Jone: one payer of stayers for Fayeton; and bought a robe for to goo invisabell.' The pair of stairs for Phaeton reminds one of Hogarth's strollers dressing in a barn, where Cupid on a ladder is reaching Apollo's stockings that are hanging to dry on the clouds; as the steeples do of a story in *L'Histoire du Théâtre Français*: Jodelet, who not only wrote plays, but invented the decorations, was to exhibit of both before Henry III. One scene was to represent a view of the sea, and Jodelet had bespoken two *rochers*—but not having time to rehearse, what did he behold enter on either side of the stage instead of two *rochers,* but two *clochers!*—Who knows but my Lord Admiral bought *them?*

Thursday, 16, Berkeley Square.

I am come to town for one night, having promised to be at Mrs Buller's this evening with Mrs Damer, and I believe your friend Mrs Chomley, whom I have seen two or three times lately and like much. Three persons have called on me since I came, but have not contributed a tittle of news to my journal. If I hear nothing tonight, this must depart, empty as it is, tomorrow morning, as I shall to Strawberry—I hope without finding a new mortification, as I did last time. Two companies had been to see my house last week, and one of the parties, as vulgar people always see with the ends of their fingers, had broken off the end of my invaluable eagle's bill, and to conceal their mischief, had pocketed the piece. It is true it had been restored at Rome; and my comfort is, that Mrs Damer can repair the damage—but did the fools know that? It almost provokes me to shut up my house, when obliging begets injury!

Friday noon.

We supped at Mrs Buller's with only the four Edgcumbes and Jerningham; and this moment I receive your 35th to which I have nothing to answer, but that I believe Fox and Burke are not very cordial, though I do not know whether there has been any formal reconciliation or not. The Parliament is prorogued, and we shall hear no more of them, I suppose, for some months; nor have I learnt anything new, and am returning to Strawberry, and must finish.

To John Pinkerton, 26 December 1791

Berkeley Square, Dec. 26, 1791.

Dear Sir,

As I am sure of the sincerity of your congratulations,[1] I feel much obliged by them, though what has happened, destroys my tranquillity, and if what the world reckons advantages could compensate the loss of peace and ease, would ill indemnify me even by them. A small estate loaded with debt, and of which I do not understand the management, and am too old to learn, a source of lawsuits amongst my near relations, though not affecting me, endless conversations with lawyers, and packets of letters every day to read and answer, all this weight of new business is too much for the rag of life that yet hangs about me, and was preceded by three weeks of anxiety about my unfortunate nephew and a daily correspondence with physicians and mad-doctors, falling upon me when I had been out of order ever since July; such a mass of troubles made me very seriously ill for some days, and has left me and still keeps me so weak and dispirited, that if I shall not soon be able to get some repose, my poor head or body will not be able to resist. For the empty title I trust you do not suppose it is anything but an encumbrance by larding my busy mornings with idle visits of interruption, and which when I am able to go out, I shall be forced to return—surely no man of 74, unless superannuated, can have the smallest pleasure in sitting at home in his own room, as I almost always do, and being called by a new name.

It will seem personal and ungrateful too, to have said so much

1. On his succeeding his nephew as 4th Earl of Orford.

Horace Walpole, Earl of Orford, by George Dance, 1793

about my own trist situation, and not to have yet thanked you, Sir, for your kind and flattering offer of letting me read what you have finished of your history; but it was necessary to expose my position to you, before I could venture to accept your proposal, when I am so utterly incapable of giving a quarter of an hour at a time to what I know by my acquaintance with your works will demand all my attention, if I wish to reap the pleasure they are formed to give me. It is most true that for these seven weeks I have not read seven pages, but letters, states of accounts, cases to be laid before lawyers, accounts of farms, etc., etc.—and those subject to mortgages. Thus are my mornings occupied—in an evening my relations and a very few friends come to me, and when they are gone, I have about an hour to midnight to write answers to letters for the next day's post, which I had not time to do in the morning. This is actually my case now—I happened to be quitted at ten o'clock, and I would not lose the opportunity of thanking you, not knowing when I could command another hour.

I by no means would be understood to decline your obliging offer, Sir. On the contrary I accept it joyfully, if you can trust me with your manuscript for a little time, should I have leisure to read it but by small snatches, which would be wronging [you] and would break all connection in my head. Criticism you are too great a writer to want—and to read critically is far beyond my present power. Can a scrivener, or a scrivener's hearer be a judge of composition, style, profound reasoning, and new lights and discoveries, etc?—but my weary hand and breast must finish. May I ask the favour of your calling on me any morning when you shall happen to come to town—you will find the new-old Lord exactly the same admirer of yours and

Your obedient humble servant,

HOR. WALPOLE

To Lady Ossory, 27 June 1792

Strawberry Hill, June 27, 1792.

The wet and cold weather has so retarded my recovery, Madam, that if Strawberry had had a dry thread to its back, and I had not been so unwell ever since I came hither, I should have proposed to your Ladyship and Lord Ossory to honour me with a visit—yet though that eternal weeper the month of June has certainly done me no good, I need not look beyond myself to account for my weakness. Almost half a century of gout, with the addition of a quarter of one, would undermine a stronger frame than mine; and if I live to have another fit, it will probably for the remnant confine me to my own house. As I can but just creep about, I have less reason than most people now to complain of the climate; and as I love to find out consolations, I have discovered that Nature as a compensation has given us verdure and coal-mines in lieu of summer, and as I can afford to keep a good fire and have a beautiful view from my window, why should I complain? I do not wish to amble to Ham Common and be disappointed of a pastoral at Mrs Hobart's—poor lady! She has already miscarried of two fêtes of which she was big, and yet next minute she was pregnant of another. Those *fausses couches* and Mrs Jordan's epistle to her, and daily as well as nightly robberies, have occasioned as much cackling in this district, as if a thousand hen-roosts had been disturbed at once. Three coaches coming in society, with a horseman besides, from the play at Richmond, were robbed last week by a squadron of seven footpads close to Mr Cambridge's. If some check is not put to the hosts of banditti Mr T. Paine will soon be able to raise as well-disciplined an army as he could wish—but how can I talk even of the outrages that one foresees in speculation, when one reads the recent accounts of those at the Thuilleries! What barbarity in the monsters of Paris not at once to massacre the King and Queen, who have suffered a thousand deaths for three years together, trembling for themselves, for their children, and for each other. I almost hate the Kings of Hungary and Prussia as much as the detestable Jacobins do, for not being already at the gates of Paris—aye, and while they suffer those wretches to exist, for conniving at the Tisiphone of the North! [1] They tolerate a diabolic anarchy, and countenance the destruction of the most amiable and most noble of all revolutions that ever took place—how can one make an option between monarchs and mobs?

Well! with all my lofty airs, so little is my mind, Madam, that I can turn from horror at mighty convulsions to indignation at puny spite and vulgar malice; how contemptible is the National Assembly! not content with annihilating, vilifying, plundering and driving away their nobility, they have wreaked their paltry spleen on the title-deeds and genealogies of the old families, and deprived the exiles of the miserable satisfaction of knowing who were their ancestors. Yet it will not surprise, if, as after burning the Bastile they have crammed Orléans with state-prisoners, they should turn the galleys into a Herald's Office, and like Cromwell, create Hewson the cobbler and such heroes, Ducs and peers!

Thursday.

I was interrupted yesterday, Madam, and am now going to London, not as you kindly advise, because Berkeley Square is wholesomer than the country, for *today* the weather is brave and shining and what for want of sterling summer, one may call—almost—hot, but to receive money—which I have not done yet, from my estate, or rather for selling one—Out of the wreck of my nephew's fortune, some lands that he had bought in the Fens, to *adorn* the parsonage-hovel that he inhabited at Eriswell, escaped and fell to me—by not being entailed or pocketed or remembered, and I have sold them for two thousand guineas—which will not enrich me, but will pay a fine for Church-lands that I must renew, in addition to the incumbrances charged on me for repayment of my own fortune and my brother's, the latter of which I certainly did not receive, nor either of us either, till precisely forty years after they had been bequeathed!—how little did I think of ever

1. The Czarina.

being master of fenlands and Church-lands, the latter of which I always abominated, and did not covet the former! I betray my ignorance in figures and calculations on every transaction—but thank my stars can laugh at myself as much as I suppose my lawyers and agents do at me—especially when I tell them I care not how little I receive, provided my new wealth does not draw my private fortune into debt, which I have destined to those who will want it, and therefore I still crawl about with my pair of horses, and will not add a postilion till at the end of the year I shall know whether I really am to receive anything or not. This is the sum of my worldly prudence, Madam, and I am as indifferent about the balance of the estate as I was about the title of (though not of being your Ladyship's ever-devoted servant)

ORFORD

To the Rev. Robert Nares, 12 September 1792

Strawberry Hill, Sept. 12, 1792.

Oh, Sir, what horrible tragedies since I had the pleasure of seeing you! I would write in red ink, as only suitable to such deeds, would it not look like using a Parisian dagger—a second and a third St Bartélemi in the same town!—and the same town to have plunged into such an ocean of blood after wading through three years of gore! Every day refines on the barbarity of the former. On the 4th of August seven thousand persons at least were murdered—the tigers could not rest a full month: on the third of this they butchered four thousand defenceless prisoners of both sexes, all untried, and all confined by jealousy and suspicion—amongst these were 120 conscientious priests, whose sole crime was to have preferred beggary to perjury—too familiar to the perpetrators, who enforce new oaths to every new-fangled system, and consequently are every time perjured. Amongst the victims was the good old Cardinal de la Rochefoucault, past fourscore, and the Archbishop of Arles, guilty of the same virtues.

The ferocity that assassinated the Princesse de Lamballe is

unexampled. In her terror she lost her senses—the monsters paused till she came to herself, that she might feel the whole of her sufferings! The epilogue to her martyrdom was scarce less horrible. They forced the King and Queen to stand at the window and behold the trunkless head on a pike!—and this, in that delicate Paris, that has always reproached our theatre with being too sanguinary—oh no, to be sure they required that our actors and actresses should commit actual murders on the stage. Perhaps you suppose that barbarity's invention has been exhausted—by no means—at least in the newest edition of the Jacobin Code, it is said, 'When thou committest murder, add the luxury of making the nearest relations of the sufferer witnesses to his sufferings'—accordingly, the Duc de la Rochefoucault, one of the most zealous patriarchs of the Revolution, growing shocked at the increasing enormities, quitted the party last July, and was retired with his family to the seat of his mother the Duchesse d'Anville, who had also been a staunch republican. Jacobin vengeance and Jacobin emissaries pursued him thither, and butchered him and his nephew, a youth—but previously compelled the Duke's mother and wife, this to behold her husband, the other her son and grandson, murdered before their eyes.

My pen is weary of recounting such hellish enormities—many of which you probably knew before—but I repeat them to whet your indignation—you promised me to renew your honest labours—but your pen you must dip in gall. Before, you wrote with temper and moderation, and the dulled public had no taste left for excellent sense and judgment. You must strike to make them feel, and lenitives will not work on the populace, who swallow poisons every day from Jacobin agents both French and domestic. It is the duty of every honest man to impress a sense of these horrors as much as he can, especially before servants at table, that they may have arguments to combat the enemy. Retail my facts, but do not let my letter be seen out of your own hands, nor would I by any means have you own what you write—Jacobins have long pikes as well as stilettos, and I will indubitably not counsel you to do what I would not do myself, who am with most sincere esteem and admiration, dear Sir,

Your obedient humble servant,

ORFORD

To LADY OSSORY, 7 December 1792

Strawberry Hill, Dec. 7, 1792.

Your Ladyship has made me smile beyond my Lord Chesterfield's allowed simper, by sending me to take my seat in the House of Lords out of tenderness for my character—if serious, I should not doubt your sincerity—but as you can look grave and soften your voice, when you have a mind to banter your friends, I rather think you was willing to try whether I have the lurking vanity of supposing myself of any importance—indeed I have not—on the contrary, I know that having determined never to take that unwelcome seat, I should only make myself ridiculous, by fancying it could *signify* a straw whether I take it or not. If I have anything of character, it must dangle on my being consistent. I quitted and abjured Parliament near thirty years ago; I never repented—and I will not contradict myself now. It is not in the House of Lords that I will *rise* again—I will keep my dry bones for the general review-day—a good lady last year was delighted at my becoming a peer, and said, 'I hope you will get an act of Parliament for putting down faro'—as if *I* could make Acts of Parliament!—and could I, it would be very consistent too in me, who for some years played more at faro than anybody.

A wholesome spirit is arisen, and no wonder. The French have given warnings enough to property to put it on its guard. I have been too precipitate in my predictions, and therefore am cautious of conjecturing; yet if my reasoning was too quick, it was not ill-founded; and as famine is striding over France, delusion's holiday will stop short, and give place to bitter scenes at its native home, which may save Europe from returning to primitive desolation.

Abominable as the government of France was, it is plain that speculative philosophers were the most unfit of all men to produce a salutary reformation. The French by antecedent as well as by recent proofs have never been fit to be *unchained at once,* so innate is their savage barbarity. What ignorance of human nature to proclaim to 24 millions of people that all laws are impositions! and what medium have those mad dictators been able to find between laws and the violence of force?—They will experience the reign of the latter—and perhaps go through all the revolutions of military despotism that have afflicted Egypt for so many ages—if my memory does not fail me, the *shepherd* kings of that country, who I suppose were *philosophers,* were the first tyrants deposed. Accustomed to cut the throats of their sheep, and versed in nothing but star-gazing, and hoisted from poverty to power, I do not wonder they applied their butchering knife to their subjects, and massacred away, that the rest of their people and flocks might have a fairer equality of pasture—Condorcet is just such a shepherd.

The City of London does not seem at all disposed to be reformed by the Académies de Sciences et de Belles Lettres. I always thought those tribunals most impertinent; but did not just conceive that they would spawn legions of Huns and Vandals—but extremes meet, and incense and assassination have sprung out of the same dunghill! The servility and gross adulation of that nation persuaded their kings that they were all-wise and omnipotent; and their kings being but men, and French men, no wonder they were intoxicated and arrogant. Is not Dumourier already a sketch of Louis Quatorze? and is not every brawler in the National Assembly as vain and insolent as Marshal Villars, who though having witnessed all the victories and modesty of the Duke of Marlborough, plumed himself more on one very inferior combat, gained after Marlborough was withdrawn, than our hero did after years of success?

Knowing a little of human nature, as I have lived to do, and how unfit one man or all are to be trusted with unlimited power (and consequently I remain neither a royalist nor a republican) I must admire our own constitution, that invented, or rather has formed, three powers, which battling one another with opinions, not with force, are more likely to keep the balance fluctuating, than to make one scale preponderate by flinging the sword, like Brennus the Gaul, into the one that he chose should be the heaviest.

I wish there were any other topic of discourse than politics; but as one can hear, one can talk nor think on anything else. It has pervaded all ranks and ages—a Miss not fourteen asked Miss Agnes Berry lately whether she was *aristocrate* or *démocrate?* and a waiter at the Toy at Hampton Court said of a scraper at the last ball, that he had a fine finger on the organization of a violin. It is provoking that we should catch even their fashionable and absurd pedantry! Adieu! Madam!

To Mary Berry, 29 October 1793

Strawberry Hill, Tuesday, Oct. 29, 1793.

I have just received yours of the 26th and begin to answer it directly, though not knowing when I shall dispatch it, as I cannot satisfy you nor myself in half we want to know about the most interesting of all events—and my greatest astonishment consists in the execrable monsters having let enough be known to consecrate Marie Antoinette to immortal glory, and to devote Paris and all its fiends to the horror and detestation of posterity.

You bid me go to the Princesse d'Hennin and learn what I can —no, indeed—I must be well convinced of the purity of the sentiments of any French man or woman, before I would go to them—I would rather fly their sight!—yet mine is not grief *now.* No, it is all admiration, and enthusiasm! The last days of that unparalleled Princess were so superior to any death ever exhibited or recorded, that for the sake of her glory, I think, unless I could restore her to happiness, to her children, to her untainted friends, and could see her triumph over the murderous mobs that have massacred her, I would not revive her, if I could. When did there ever exist such august simplicity! What mind was ever—I will not say, so firm, but so perfectly mistress of its own thoughts and intentions; that could be attentive to every circumstance, and distracted by none? Think of all that was comprehended in that question to the monsters called her counsellors, but certainly allotted to her as defamatory spies, 'Had she assumed too much dignity, as she passed to her trial, for she had noticed one of the furies, who said, "How proud she is"?' It proved her unaltered presence of mind, and that she was ready to condescend, if it would better become her. What hero, philosopher, or martyr had equal possession of himself in similar moments? None, none, not one! and then recollect the length of her sufferings, her education, exaltation to happiness and supreme power, her sudden fall, the disappointments she had met, the ingratitude and treachery she had experienced, the mortifications and insults heaped on her, and studiously, maliciously aggravated for five years together, the murder of her husband, the miseries of and terrors for her children; the total deprivation of all decent comforts, and perhaps the greatest cruelty of all, not to have had one friend—but a thousand times worse, to have been at every moment in the hands of the most unfeeling jailors, sum up all this mass of woes, and perhaps thousands more of which we never heard, and then see this phoenix rise superior to hosts of torturing spiteful fiends, and hear her pronounce the most sublime word that ever passed through human lips—when *they* (I have no adequate epithet for them) had declared sentence, and asked her, what she had to say, she said, *Rien.* Too calm, too sensible, too collected, and unshaken, she was above fear, indignation, and solicitation, and accountable only to herself, she showed that such a host of miscreants was not worthy of knowing a syllable of what passed in perhaps the greatest mind that ever existed. Her invincible patience was all that appeared, and that was a negative, but as unvaried as all her illustrious virtues, and great qualities, on which rancour and persecution have not been able to fix a speck of stain—Let history or legend produce a similar model!

These are the effusions of my heart—not dictated by the impulse of the moment, but the result of my cool reflections of three days. I trust them in perfect confidence to your honour, and exact from the fidelity of your friendship that you will not communicate nor read them to any mortal but your father and sister, nor let this paper pass out of your own hands, nor suffer a tittle of it be transcribed. I like that you two should know my sentiments on all important topics, but I extend this confidence not a jot farther. I firmly believe every word I have asserted, because all the facts come from the barbarians themselves—but as I cannot be positively sure they are true, I will not place my veracity on a possibility of having been misinformed—and therefore I depend on your not committing me by showing my letter—I repeat it earnestly, *to nobody but your father and sister,* and beg you will assure me that you have not. I do not mind your reading trifles out of my dispatches, though certainly calculated for nobody but you two—but this letter I do most seriously restrain from all other eyes.

Tuesday midnight.

Mrs Damer came to me at dinner today, and goes to London tomorrow. I was engaged to Lady Betty MacKinsy, and she went thither with me in the most deplorable of all nights—as bad as that when the Conways and I were detained so late at Cliveden and I stepped over my shoes into the water. We heard nothing quite new: Nieuport is reckoned safe and Ostend safer, both which were reported taken. Mr Batt, whom I met last night at Cambridge's, is as confident of the safety of Toulon—He—not Lord Hood, inquired much after you. Lord Mount Edgcumbe is recovered. The Charming Man, has actually a tragedy just coming forth at Covent Garden.

I like your account of yourselves—but hope your grandam will not *sit too close,* but let you both have air and exercise enough. *In everything else* I quite agree with her.

Lady Waldegrave and her daughter come to me today from the Pavilions, where they have been this week, and will stay till next morning. Good night.

PS. I fear you have lost your poor friend Mr Sept. West.

To Lady Ossory, 15 January 1797

Jan. 15, 1797.

My dear madam,

You distress me infinitely by showing my idle notes, which I cannot conceive can amuse anybody. My old-fashioned breeding impels me every now and then to reply to the letters you honour me with writing, but in truth very unwillingly, for I seldom can have anything particular to say; I scarce go out of my own house, and then only to two or three very private places, where I see nobody that really knows anything, and what I learn comes from newspapers, that collect intelligence from coffee-houses; consequently what I neither believe nor report. At home I see only a few charitable elders, except about fourscore nephews and nieces of various ages, who are each brought to me about once a year, to stare at me as the Methusalem of the family, and they can only speak of their own cotemporaries, which interest me no more than if they talked of their dolls, or bats and balls. Must not the result of all this, Madam, make me a very entertaining correspondent? And can such letters be worth showing? or can I have any spirit when so old and reduced to dictate? Oh, my good Madam, dispense with me from such a task, and think how it must add to it to apprehend such letters being shown. Pray send me no more such laurels, which I desire no more than their leaves when decked with a scrap of tinsel, and stuck on Twelfth-cakes that lie on the shop-boards of pastry-cooks at Christmas: I shall be quite content with a sprig of rosemary thrown after me, when the parson of the parish commits my dust to dust. Till then, pray, Madam, accept the resignation of

Your ancient servant,

O.[1]

1. Horace Walpole, Earl of Orford, died six weeks later.

Index